# LOGO DESIGN

**ED. JULIUS WIEDEMANN**

# LOGO DESIGN

**TASCHEN**

HONG KONG KÖLN LONDON LOS ANGELES MADRID PARIS TOKYO

# INTRO/
# CASE STUDIES

# LOGO CHAPTERS

# SIGNS, IMAGE, IDENTITY, AND LOGO DESIGN

In the beginning there was the sign. The first humans had no language at all, but they certainly had signs. They were able to use mimic and gesticulation by which other humans could recognise their feelings; contentment, discontentment, anger, joy, irritation, fear or aggression. Communication began with these kinds of signs.

*In the beginning there was the image. Long before humans had strung words into sentences they were already thinking in images.*

They saw a head, two eyes, two ears, a nose, a mouth and recognised a person: their mother, father, or a member of their own tribe, a friend or an enemy. They used coal to draw buffalo on walls, mammoth, deer or a man with a spear and everyone who saw it understood it was about the hunt. Culture began with these kinds of images. Signs are images. They allow humans to immediately express their thoughts and feelings and to

Au début, il y avait le signe. Les premiers humains n'avaient aucun langage, mais ils avaient les signes. Ils pouvaient utiliser les mimiques et les gestes pour que les autres humains identifient leurs sentiments : satisfaction, insatisfaction, colère, joie, irritation, peur ou agression. La communication a commencé par ce genre de signes.

*Au début, il y avait l'image. Bien avant de former des phrases avec des mots, les humains pensaient déjà en termes d'images.*

Ils voyaient une tête, deux yeux, deux oreilles, un nez, une bouche, et ils reconnaissaient une personne : leur mère, leur père, ou un membre de leur tribu, un ami ou un ennemi. Avec du charbon, ils dessinaient sur les murs un mammouth, un cerf ou un homme avec une lance et tous ceux qui voyaient le dessin comprenaient qu'il s'agissait d'une scène de chasse. La culture a commencé par ce genre d'images. Les signes sont des images. Ils permettent aux humains d'expri-

Am Anfang war das Zeichen. Die ersten Menschen hatten noch gar keine Sprache, aber sie hatten mit Sicherheit schon Zeichen. Sie verfügten über Mimik und Gestik, an denen andere Menschen ihre Gefühle erkennen konnten: Behagen, Missbehagen, Wut, Freude, Ärger, Angst oder Aggression. Mit solchen Zeichen begann die Kommunikation.

*Am Anfang war das Bild. Lange bevor die Menschen Wörter zu Sätzen aneinanderreihten, dachten sie bereits in Bildern.*

Sie sahen einen Kopf, zwei Augen, zwei Ohren, eine Nase, einen Mund und erkannten eine Person: die Mutter, den Vater, ein Mitglied der eigenen Horde, Freund oder Feind. Sie nahmen ein Stück Kohle und zeichneten einen Büffel an die Wand, das Mammut, den Hirsch, einen Mann mit Speer, und alle, die es sahen, wussten: Die Rede ist jetzt von der Jagd. Mit solchen Bildern begann die Kultur. Zeichen sind Bilder. Sie erlauben den Menschen, ihre Gefühle und

# BY **JÖRG ZINTZMEYER**

generalise and to share these with others. From signs grew written language, but the images remain; they could not be replaced. The image of a single buffalo came to stand for all other buffalo; for food, clothing, abundance and well-being; for adventure and for survival in a hostile environment.

*Where humans lived almost exclusively on buffalo, the image even came to stand for God; even today, humans need simplifying images when they want to express complicated ideas.*

Images and signs have played a part in shaping us. More and more new images were found in order to represent, distinguish and define human culture, to integrate others into one's own culture, to persuade or subjugate them; there have been the cross, the crescent moon and the Star of David. People painted their own bodies or shields in order to differentiate themselves from their enemies in battle. People used emblems and stan-

mer immédiatement leurs pensées et leurs sentiments, de les généraliser et de les partager avec les autres. Le langage écrit s'est développé à partir des signes, mais les images restent. Elles sont irremplaçables. L'image d'un seul buffle peut représenter tous les autres buffles. Elle peut aussi représenter la nourriture, les vêtements, l'abondance et le bien-être, ou bien l'aventure et la survie dans un environnement hostile.

*Lorsque les humains vivaient presque exclusivement du buffle, son image en est arrivée à représenter Dieu. Même aujourd'hui, les humains ont besoin des images pour exprimer simplement des idées complexes.*

Les images et les signes ont joué un rôle dans notre évolution. On a trouvé de plus en plus de nouvelles images pour représenter, distinguer et définir la culture humaine, pour intégrer les autres dans notre propre culture, pour les persuader ou pour les soumettre. Il y a eu la

Gedanken unmittelbar auszudrücken, sie zu verallgemeinern und mit anderen zu teilen. Aus Zeichen wurden Schriften, aber die Bilder sind geblieben. Sie waren durch nichts zu ersetzen. Das Bild des einzelnen Büffels stand für alle anderen Büffel: für Nahrung, Kleidung, Sättigung und Wohlbefinden, für das Abenteuer und für das Überleben in einer feindlichen Natur.

*Dort, wo man hauptsächlich von Büffeln lebte, stand das Bild sogar für Gott: Bis heute brauchen die Menschen vereinfachende Bilder, wenn sie etwas Kompliziertes mitteilen wollen.*

Bilder und Zeichen haben uns geprägt. Immer neue Bilder wurden gefunden, um die menschliche Kultur darzustellen, sie zu profilieren, sie abzugrenzen, um andere Menschen in die eigene Kultur zu integrieren, sie zu überzeugen oder sie ihr zu unterwerfen: Es gab das Kreuz, den Halbmond, den Davidstern. Man bemalte den Körper oder den Schild, um

dards so that everyone knew where they were marching. Out of primeval tribal signs came symbols of power. Feudal signs became national symbols. There were banners and flags, national emblems and national colours. Somebody sketched the Stars and Stripes. Somebody designed the Tricolour and the French Marianne, the Union Jack, the German Eagle or the Swiss cross. These were lasting processes which are still effective today, since upon seeing the appropriate symbol we are immediately reminded of that which we associate with a particular nation, religion or culture. Symbols have the power to stimulate the imagination and recall images, experiences and feelings in our minds from out of our memory and into the present.

*Images and signs characterise the economy. With globalisation and worldwide integration over the past decades, old traditional signs, fundamental orders and identities have disappeared or been devalued. However, people do not want to live without some kind of ideational connection.*

People constantly need values and images through which they can recognise themselves and see themselves represented, thanks either to a feeling of association or of disassociation with others. Today, it is increasingly brands which offer these kinds of values and ideas. In the place of old symbols, modern logos now stand. Whoever wears a logo, whoever identifies his or herself with a brand places his or her interests, his or her yearnings, his or her individual worldview into a larger context. In economic and social terms, brands have therefore tremendous potential.

Brands are images and ideas in the mind. The moment we are shown a logo, an internal film begins to play. We see a star in a particular form and we imagine a particular car. The star reminds us of other images, experiences we have had, of dreams, of a lifestyle, of luxury or perhaps of a remarkable driving experi-

croix, le croissant et l'étoile de David. Les gens ont peint leurs corps ou leurs boucliers pour se différencier de leurs ennemis sur le champ de bataille. Les gens ont utilisé des emblèmes et des étendards afin que chacun sache où ils allaient. Les signes tribaux primitifs sont devenus des symboles de pouvoir. Les signes féodaux sont devenus des symboles nationaux. Il y a eu les bannières et les drapeaux, les emblèmes nationaux et les couleurs de la nation. Quelqu'un a dessiné le Stars and Stripes (le drapeau des États-Unis). Quelqu'un a conçu le drapeau tricolore et la Marianne en France, l'Union Jack au Royaume-Uni, l'aigle allemand ou la croix suisse. Il s'agit de processus durables, qui sont toujours efficaces aujourd'hui : en voyant le symbole approprié, nous pensons immédiatement à ce que nous associons à une certaine nation, religion ou culture. Les symboles ont le pouvoir de stimuler l'imagination et d'évoquer dans nos esprits des images, des expériences et des sentiments, qui sont transposés de la mémoire au présent.

*Les images et les signes caractérisent l'économie. Avec la mondialisation et l'intégration mondiale des dernières décennies, les vieux signes traditionnels, les ordres et les identités fondamentaux ont disparu ou ont perdu de leur valeur. Mais les gens ne veulent pas vivre sans une certaine connexion idéationnelle.*

Les gens ont toujours besoin de valeurs et d'images au travers desquelles ils peuvent se reconnaître et se voir représentés, grâce à un sentiment d'association ou de différenciation par rapport aux autres. Aujourd'hui, et de plus en plus, ce sont les marques qui proposent ce genre de valeurs et d'idées. À la place des vieux symboles, nous avons maintenant les logos modernes. Quiconque arbore un logo, quiconque s'identifie à une marque place ses intérêts, ses aspirations ou sa vision du monde dans un contexte plus vaste. En termes économiques ou sociaux, les marques ont donc un potentiel énorme.

sich in der Schlacht vom Gegner zu unterscheiden. Man benutzte Wappen und Standarten, damit alle wussten, wo sie marschierten. Aus urzeitlichen Stammeszeichen wurden feudale Herrschaftsattribute. Aus feudalen Signeten wurden nationale Symbole. Es gab Fahnen und Flaggen, Hoheitszeichen und Landesfarben. Jemand skizzierte die Stars and Stripes. Jemand entwarf die Trikolore und die französische Marianne, den Union Jack, den deutschen Adler oder das Schweizer Kreuz. Das waren nachhaltige Prozesse, sie wirken bis heute. Denn was immer wir mit einer Nation, einer Religion oder einer Kultur verbinden: Sobald wir die passenden Symbole sehen, fällt es uns sofort ein. Symbole haben die Kraft, bestimmte Vorstellungen und Bilder, Erfahrungen und Gefühle in unseren Köpfen zu wecken, sie aus der Erinnerung zu holen und gegenwärtig zu machen.

*Bilder und Zeichen prägen die Wirtschaft. Mit der Globalisierung und weltweiten Vernetzung der vergangenen Jahrzehnte sind althergebrachte Zeichen, elementare Zuordnungen und Identifikationsmöglichkeiten überall aufgelöst und entwertet worden. Aber die Menschen wollen nicht ohne ideelle Bezüge leben.*

Menschen brauchen zu jeder Zeit Werte und Vorstellungen, durch die sie sich erkannt und repräsentiert sehen, dank derer sie sich anderen zugehörig fühlen oder sich von ihnen differenzieren können. Immer mehr sind es heute die Marken, die solche Werte und Vorstellungswelten anbieten. An die Stelle alter Symbole sind moderne Logos getreten. Wer ein Logo trägt, wer sich mit einer Marke identifiziert, stellt seine Interessen, seine Sehnsüchte, seine individuelle Weltsicht in einen größeren Zusammenhang. In Wirtschaft und Gesellschaft erhalten Marken damit ein ungeheures Potenzial.

Marken sind Bilder, Vorstellungen im Kopf. Man zeigt uns ein Logo, und so-

ence. The star evokes within us the imagery of the brand: images of a product, its performance, its environment, its communication and its prestige. These kinds of images are stored in our mind. They are created on a daily basis, through the way in which the brand presents itself and how it is communicated to us. The images are forms of identification and they are controlled. They are offered us, and we accept them.

*The logo is a promise. The logo is not the brand itself. It is a form of expression of the brand or its most condensed image. We see an M of a particular shape and colour, and suddenly we feel hungry. In our minds we have the image of a restaurant chain. The M promises us meat, salad, the smell of fresh French fries and hopefully some good times.*

The logo itself doesn't contain these images; it is a simple form. If we had to draw this logo by hand, however, we would find it difficult; it would probably just turn out an ordinary M. But when we see it we recognise immediately what's so special about it. The appropriate images form in our minds. The logo recalls them for us. The logo is the medium of the brand and it is a brilliant medium; it is the projector which plays us the film and is also the screen on which we see the images. It is a vessel for the imagination.

*No Logo? Logos are powerful because the images which they recall promise us something. Brands are powerful because we trust them and because they stand for particular values. The more clearly the brand is positioned, the more clearly defined are its values.*

Brands are unavoidable in our world today; they fill our surroundings in vast numbers. One can refuse brands of course, but no one can live without them: even before the bestselling book

Les marques sont des images et des idées mentales. Dès que l'on voit un logo, la projection d'un film intérieur commence. Nous voyons une étoile d'une certaine forme et nous imaginons une certaine voiture. L'étoile nous fait penser à d'autres images, à des expériences passées, à des rêves, à un style de vie, au luxe ou peut-être à une virée mémorable en voiture. L'étoile évoque en nous les images véhiculées par la marque : les images d'un produit, sa performance, son environnement, sa communication et son prestige. Ces images sont stockées dans notre esprit. Elles sont créées jour après jour, à travers la façon dont la marque se présente et dont elle nous est communiquée. Les images sont des formes d'identification, et elles sont contrôlées. Elles nous sont offertes, et nous les acceptons.

*Le logo est une promesse. Le logo n'est pas la marque elle-même. C'est une forme d'expression de la marque, ou son image la plus condensée. Nous voyons un M d'une certaine forme, d'une certaine couleur, et soudain nous avons faim. Nous avons à l'esprit l'image d'une chaîne de restaurants. Le M nous promet de la viande, de la salade, l'odeur des frites et, on l'espère, de bons moments.*

Le logo lui-même ne contient pas ces images, ce n'est qu'une simple forme. Mais si nous devions dessiner ce logo à main levée, ce serait difficile. Il ressemblerait sans doute à un M ordinaire. Pourtant, lorsque nous le voyons nous reconnaissons immédiatement ce qu'il a de si particulier. Les images appropriées se forment dans notre esprit. C'est le logo qui nous les rappelle. Le logo est l'ambassadeur de la marque, et c'est un ambassadeur fantastique. C'est le projecteur qui met le film en route, et c'est aussi l'écran sur lequel nous voyons les images. C'est un véhicule pour l'imagination.

*No Logo ? Les logos sont puissants parce que les images qu'ils évo-*

fort läuft der innere Film ab. Wir sehen einen Stern in bestimmter Gestalt und stellen uns ein bestimmtes Automobil vor. Der Stern erinnert an andere Bilder, an Erfahrungen oder Träume, an einen Lebensstil, an Luxus und vielleicht an ein außerordentliches Gefühl des Fahrens. Der Stern ruft die Bilderwelt der Marke in uns wach: Bilder eines Produktes, seiner Leistungen, seines Umfeldes, seiner Kommunikation, seines Prestiges. Solche Bilder sind in unseren Köpfen gespeichert. Sie entstehen im Alltag, aus der Art, wie die Marke auftritt und wie sie uns kommuniziert wird. Die Bilder sind Identifikationsmöglichkeiten. Sie werden gesteuert. Sie werden uns angeboten, und wir nehmen sie an.

*Das Logo ist ein Versprechen. Das Logo ist nicht die Marke selbst. Es ist eine Ausdrucksform der Marke, ihr komprimiertestes Bild. Wir sehen ein M in typischer Form und Farbe, und plötzlich fühlen wir Hunger. Im Kopf haben wir die Bilder einer Restaurantkette. Das M verspricht uns Fleisch, Salate, den Geruch frischer Pommes frites und im besten Fall glückliche Stunden.*

Das Logo selber enthält diese Bilder nicht. Das Logo ist einfach gebaut. Wenn wir dieses Logo von Hand zeichnen müssten, bekämen wir Schwierigkeiten: Es würde womöglich ein ganz normales M daraus. Aber wenn wir es sehen, erkennen wir sofort die Besonderheit. Im Kopf stellen sich die passenden Bilder ein. Das Logo ruft sie hervor. Das Logo ist das Medium der Marke. Es ist ein geniales Medium. Es ist der Projektor, der uns den Film abspielt und zugleich die Leinwand, auf der wir die Bilder sehen. Ein Gefäß für Vorstellungswelten.

*No Logo? Logos sind mächtig, weil die Bilder, die sie auslösen, uns etwas versprechen. Marken sind mächtig, weil wir ihnen vertrauen, weil sie für bestimmte*

9

criticising brands "No Logo!" appeared in 2000, there already existed a young fashion label with the name "No Logo!" Because we trust in brands they are valuable. They demand responsibility and careful looking after. A brand may be in danger of collapse when its imagery does not match up with reality; if the images recalled by the logo are in conflict with reality and with the actual behaviour of the brand. What the logo promises, the brand must deliver.

*Logos are beautiful. Or logos are ugly. A logo feels right, or it doesn't feel right at which point it becomes especially conspicuous. A logo is recognisable, but without a brand it would simply be an empty vessel and quickly forgotten; it would be a form without content, a projector without a film.*

If we change the logo of an existing brand, then we influence the values of that brand. Along with the sign we also change the message of the sign. We create a new sign and new images. We recognise a beautiful logo by its pretty design. We recognise a good logo by its success.

*quent nous promettent quelque chose. Les marques sont puissantes parce que nous avons confiance en elles et parce qu'elles représentent certaines valeurs. Plus une marque est clairement positionnée, plus ses valeurs sont clairement définies.*

Dans notre monde actuel, les marques sont inévitables. Elles sont partout autour de nous. On peut rejeter les marques, bien sûr, mais on ne peut pas vivre sans elles : avant même que ne soit publié en 2000 le succès de librairie « No Logo ! », qui pourfendait les marques, il y avait déjà une marque de mode pour les jeunes qui s'appelait « No Logo ! ». C'est parce que nous avons confiance dans les marques qu'elles ont de la valeur. Elles exigent responsabilité et soins minutieux. Une marque risque de s'effondrer si son image ne correspond pas à la réalité, si les images évoquées par le logo sont en conflit avec la réalité et avec le véritable comportement de la marque. La marque doit être à la hauteur des promesses du logo.

*Les logos sont beaux. Ou ils sont laids. Un logo peut sembler approprié, ou inapproprié, auquel cas il devient particulièrement visible. Un logo est reconnaissable, mais sans marque il ne serait qu'un véhicule vide et vite oublié. Il serait une forme sans contenu, un projecteur sans film.*

Si l'on change le logo d'une marque existante, alors on influence les valeurs de cette marque. Avec le signe, on change aussi le message du signe. On crée un nouveau signe et de nouvelles images. Un beau logo est bien dessiné. Un bon logo a du succès.

*Wertehaltungen stehen. Je deutlicher die Marke positioniert ist, desto klarer sind ihre Werte.*

Marken sind unvermeidlich in der heutigen Welt, unübersehbar bevölkern sie die zivilisierten Räume. Man kann Marken ablehnen, selbstverständlich, doch niemand kann ohne sie leben: Noch bevor im Jahr 2000 der markenkritische Bestseller mit dem Titel „No Logo!" erschien, existierte bereits eine junge Modemarke mit dem Namen „No Logo!". Weil wir Marken vertrauen, sind sie wertvoll. Sie verlangen Verantwortung und sorgfältige Pflege. Einer Marke droht Zerstörung, wenn ihre kommunikativen Welten nicht mehr mit der Wirklichkeit übereinstimmen, wenn die vom Logo abgerufenen Bilder mit der Realität und mit dem tatsächlichen Verhalten der Marke in Widerspruch stehen. Was das Logo verspricht, hat die Marke zu halten.

*Logos sind schön. Oder Logos sind hässlich. Ein Logo passt, oder es scheint nicht zu passen und fällt deshalb ganz besonders auf. Ein Logo ist wiedererkennbar, aber ohne Marke wäre es nur ein leeres Gefäß und schnell vergessen: Es wäre eine Form ohne Inhalt, ein Projektor ohne Bilder.*

Wenn wir das Logo einer bestehenden Marke verändern, dann nehmen wir Einfluss auf die Werte dieser Marke. Mit dem Zeichen verändern wir auch das, was uns das Zeichen sagen will. Wir schaffen ein neues Zeichen und neue Bilder. Ein schönes Logo erkennen wir am hübschen Design. Ein gutes Logo erkennen wir am Erfolg.

# Biography
# Jörg Zintzmeyer

Following professional placements in Milan and London, Jörg Zintzmeyer founded his corporate identity consultancy agency Zintzmeyer & Lux AG in 1976 which, through an alliance with Interbrand in 1996, later became Interbrand Zintzmeyer & lux, where he was president of the board of directors until 2006. He left the company in 2006 and has since been working as an independent consultant for companies and institutions. His areas of professionalism encompass the analysis, planning and conception of complex assignments in the field of integrated communication, especially the development of brands and corporate identity strategies and programmes. In addition to many other projects, the corporate identity programme for the BMW Group was created under his direction. Other projects include, most recently, the brand identity for the new Rolls-Royce. Jörg Zintzmeyer is among the world's most renowned corporate identity consultants.

Après avoir travaillé à Milan et à Londres, Jörg Zintzmeyer a fondé son agence de conseil en identité de marque Zintzmeyer & Lux AG en 1976. À la suite d'une alliance avec Interbrand en 1996, cette agence est devenue Interbrand Zintzmeyer & Lux, dont il a été président du conseil d'administration jusqu'en 2006. Il a quitté l'agence en 2006, et travaille depuis comme consultant indépendant pour des entreprises et des institutions. Ses domaines d'expertise comprennent l'analyse, la planification et la conception de projets complexes de communication intégrée, et tout particulièrement le développement de stratégies et de programmes d'identité de marque et d'entreprise. C'est sous sa direction que le programme d'identité d'entreprise du groupe BMW a vu le jour, entre autres nombreux projets. On peut également citer, parmi ses projets les plus récents, l'identité de marque de la nouvelle Rolls-Royce. Jörg Zintzmeyer est l'un des consultants en identité de marque les plus respectés sur la scène internationale.

Jörg Zintzmeyer gründete nach beruflichen Stationen in Mailand und London 1976 seine Corporate Identity Beratung Zintzmeyer & Lux AG und brachte sie 1996 in eine Allianz mit Interbrand zu Interbrand Zintzmeyer & Lux ein, wo er bis 2006 Präsident des Verwaltungsrates war. Er verliess das Unternehmen 2006 und arbeitet seitdem als selbstständiger Berater für Unternehmen und Institutionen. Seine Arbeitsgebiete umfassen die Analyse, Planung und Konzeption komplexer Aufgaben im Bereich der integrierten Kommunikation, besonders die Entwicklung von Marken und Corporate-Identity Strategien und -Programmen. Unter seiner Regie entstanden neben vielen anderen Projekten unter anderen die Corporate-Identity-Programme für die BMW Group, hier zuletzt die Brand Identity für den neuen Rolls-Royce. Zintzmeyer zählt zu den renommiertesten Markenstrategieberatern weltweit.

# THE NEW LOOK & FEEL **OF NBA TEAM HOUSTON ROCKETS**

For many years in the National Basketball Association, the Houston Rockets were the team that rarely enjoyed the spotlight. But in 2003 that all changed. The 7'5" rookie Yao Ming was emerging as a wildly popular superstar on the court.

*A beautiful new arena in downtown Houston drew more fans and showcased the rising fortunes of the team. And like Cinderella finally going to the ball, the Rockets were re-dressed in enviable fashion. Sleek new uniforms and a matching logo were introduced to signal the arrival of the now formidable Rockets.*

When the owners of the Rockets made the decision to commission the new uniforms and logo, they wanted a look that would be revolutionary—something that would set a new standard in professional sports design. So they searched for a designer from outside the traditional sports graphic branding houses. In the end they hired a pair: Eiko Ishioka, who

Pendant de nombreuses années, au sein de la NBA, l'équipe des Houston Rockets était rarement mise en vedette. Mais en 2003, tout change. Yao Ming, le jeune débutant de deux mètres vingt-cinq, s'impose comme une superstar du terrain.

*La construction d'un nouveau complexe sportif dans le centre de Houston attire plus de supporters et devient la vitrine de la bonne fortune de l'équipe. Comme Cendrillon qui finit par se rendre au bal, les Rockets sont relookés à la dernière mode. Un nouveau logo et des maillots assortis annoncent l'arrivée des redoutables Rockets.*

Quand les dirigeants de l'équipe décident de commander un nouveau logo et de nouveaux maillots, ils désirent quelque chose de révolutionnaire, quelque chose qui devienne une référence dans le monde du sport professionnel. Ils cherchent alors un designer extérieur à l'univers sportif

Viele Jahre lang standen die Houston Rockets im Nationalen Basketball-Verband nur selten im Rampenlicht. Das änderte sich 2003: Aus dem 2,25 m großen Neuling Yao Ming wurde ein berühmter Superstar.

*Ein neues Stadion in Houston zog mehr Fans an und präsentierte den wachsenden Erfolg des Teams der Öffentlichkeit. Wie Cinderella, die endlich zum Ball gehen darf, wurden die Rockets in einer beneidenswerten Mode neu einkleidet. Elegante neue Uniformen und ein passendes Logo signalisierten die Ankunft der erstarkten Rockets.*

Als die Eigentümer der Rockets die Entscheidung trafen, neue Uniformen und ein neues Logo in Auftrag zu geben, wollten sie einen revolutionären Look – einen Look, der im professionellen Sportdesign neue Maßstäbe setzte. Also suchten sie nach einem Designer jenseits der traditionellen Sportmarkengrafikern. Schließlich

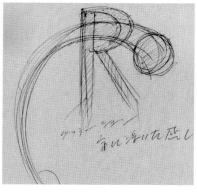

is best known in the United States as the Academy Award winner for her costume designs in Bram Stoker's *Dracula*; and Rafael Esquer, an award-winning graphic designer in New York. The Rockets project would be the third creative collaboration between Ishioka and Esquer. Together, they brought fresh perspectives and broad creative experience to the task of challenging the traditional looks that reigned in the world of professional basketball.

*Ishioka and Esquer began their design process with the simple observation that sports is entertainment. In today's culture, professional athletes are like movie stars or rock stars.*

And when it's time to go on stage, they must be "in costume." Wardrobe must transform them into the characters who will thrill the audience. In other words, to play like champions, they must look and feel like champions. So in the course of creative development, Ishioka and Esquer

traditionnel et se tournent finalement vers un tandem. Eiko Ishioka, célèbre aux États-Unis pour avoir remporté un Oscar pour les costumes du Dracula de Bram Stoker, et Rafael Esquer, un designer graphique primé à New York. Ce projet représente pour les designers leur troisième collaboration artistique. Ils vont ouvrir ensemble de nouvelles perspectives, et la variété de leur expérience créative va bouleverser les conventions esthétiques de l'univers du basket professionnel.

*Comme point de départ, Ishioka et Esquer partent de la simple observation que le sport est un spectacle. Dans la culture actuelle, les athlètes professionnels sont comme des stars du rock ou du cinéma.*

Quand l'heure est venue de monter sur scène, ils doivent être « costumés ». La garde-robe doit les changer en des personnages qui feront vibrer l'assistance. Autrement dit, pour jouer comme des champions, ils doivent avoir l'allure et

beauftragen sie ein Paar: Eiko Ishioka, in den USA als Oscargewinnerin für ihre Kostüme in Bram Stokers *Dracula* bekannt, und Rafael Esquer, ein preisgekrönter Grafikdesigner in New York. Das Rockets-Projekt sollte die dritte kreative Zusammenarbeit von Ishioka und Esquer sein. Gemeinsam brachten sie neue Perspektiven und breit gefächerte kreative Erfahrung in die Aufgabe ein, den traditionellen Look, der in der Welt des professionellen Basketballs regierte, anzufechten.

*Den Ansatzpunkt ihres Designprozesses bestand in der einfachen Beobachtung, dass Sport Unterhaltung ist. Professionelle Athleten haben in der heutigen Kultur den gleichen Status wie Film- oder Rockstars.*

Und wenn es Zeit wird, auf die Bühne zu gehen, müssen sie „kostümiert" sein. Die Kleidung muss sie in Charaktere verwandeln, die das Publikum faszinieren. Mit anderen Worten: Um wie Champions zu spielen, müssen sie wie

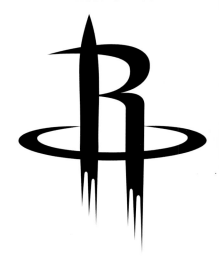

**Previous pages:** *The Chinese player Yao Ming wearing the new uniform ///* **Double page précédente:** *Le joueur chinois Yao Ming portant le nouvel uniforme ///* **Vorherige Seite:** *Der chinesische Spieler Yao Ming trägt die neue Uniform*

**Left:** *Sketches ///* **À gauche:** *Croquis ///* **Links:** *Entwürfe*

**Right:** *The final "R" decided to become the logo for the team and uniform ///* **À droite:** *Le « R » final choisi pour le logo de l'équipe et de l'uniforme ///* **Rechts:** *Das letzte "R" wurde als Logo für Team und Uniform ausgewählt*

often asked themselves questions such as: how do we want the players to look when winning a game? How do we want them to look on television? How do we want the logo and branding to look when the uniform is in movement? How can the new look make the players memorable? And how can our design enhance performance on the court, giving the team a competitive advantage?

Working tirelessly for six months, Ishioka and Esquer explored a variety of creative angles that ranged from the specific history of the team's name to the general context of the Space Age, rocket travel, and aerodynamics. They sought to graphically evoke abstract elements such as speed, precision, energy, propulsion, ascent, competitiveness, conquest, and victory. After experimenting with hundreds of graphic possibilities for the logo and uniforms, they made their initial presentation to the owners in Houston: over two dozen graphic directions and more than 50 uniform designs. From this set, five pairs of graphics and uniforms

l'attitude de champions. Au cours du processus créatif, Ishioka et Esquer essaient de répondre à plusieurs questions.

Quelle doit être l'allure des joueurs dans la victoire ? Quelle allure doivent-ils avoir à la télévision ? À quoi doit ressembler le logo de l'équipe sur le maillot en mouvement ? Comment rendre les joueurs inoubliables ? Comment améliorer les performances de l'équipe et la rendre plus compétitive grâce au design ?

Travaillant sans relâche pendant six mois, Ishioka et Esquer explorent divers axes créatifs allant de l'histoire de la marque au contexte plus général de l'aérodynamique, de l'ère spatiale et des voyages en fusée. Ils cherchent à illustrer graphiquement des éléments abstraits comme la vitesse, la précision, l'énergie, la propulsion, l'ascension, la compétitivité, la conquête et enfin la victoire. Après avoir expérimenté sur une centaine de possibilités graphiques pour le logo et les maillots, ils présentent leur sélection aux dirigeants de l'équipe, une vingtaine de

Champions aussehen und fühlen. Im Laufe des kreativen Prozesses stellten sich Ishioka und Esquer daher oft Fragen wie: Wie sollen die Spieler aussehen, wenn sie ein Spiel gewinnen? Wie sollen sie im Fernsehen aussehen? Wie sollen Logo und Marke aussehen, wenn die Uniformen in Bewegung sind? Wie kann der neue Look die Spieler unvergesslich machen? Und wie kann unser Design die sportliche Leistung auf dem Platz verbessern und dem Team einen Vorteil gegenüber den Gegnern verschaffen?

In sechs Monaten unermüdlicher Arbeit erkundeten Ishioka und Esquer zahlreiche kreative Möglichkeiten, von der besonderen Geschichte des Teamnamens bis zum generellen Kontext des Weltraumzeitalters, Raketen und Aerodynamik. Sie versuchten, abstrakte Elemente wie Geschwindigkeit, Präzision, Energie, Antrieb, Aufstieg, Wettbewerbsgeist, Eroberung und Sieg grafisch darzustellen. Nachdem sie mit Hunderten von grafischen Möglichkeiten experimentiert

15

were chosen for further development.

In the end, the winning design for the Rockets marries the energy of basketball with the legacy of the team's name. The logo is a sleek icon, capturing the thrust and thrill of a rocket's lift-off and bringing it into the context of the court. Because the futuristic uniforms and the logo were designed in tandem, the complete look is organic and fluid. Even the new typeface is custom-designed, in synch with the style of the logo.

*The letterforms and numbers on the player's jerseys and shorts were precisely drawn so that every single digit can be read well from a distance, whether by a fan in the arena or by one watching the game on television.*

While other marks in professional basketball are often cartoony and overly illustrative, the Rockets new identity succeeds in departing from these expected styles in mainstream sport graphics. It is simple, classic, energetic, and forward-thinking. Yet the logo is also extremely practical and versatile from a marketing point of view, easily adaptable for use on merchandise and billboards, in broadcast and signage, and on ticket stubs and T-shirts. In this way, Ishioka and Esquer have met the expectations of the Rockets' owners for a new standard in sports design. Their organic and collaborative design process has produced the most innovative and popular identity the NBA has seen in years.

logos et plus de cinquante dessins de maillots. De cette série, cinq paires de logos et de maillots seront retenues pour la phase de développement suivante.

Le design finalement adopté pour les Rockets marie l'énergie du basket-ball et l'héritage historique de l'équipe. Le logo est un signe épuré, évoquant la poussée d'une fusée au décollage, et transposée au contexte d'un terrain de sport. Le look futuriste du logo et des maillots, né de l'imagination du tandem, possède un côté fluide et organique. La typographie elle-même est originale, en phase avec le style du logo.

*Les lettres et les numéros sur les shorts et les maillots des joueurs ont été minutieusement étudiés pour pouvoir être lus à distance, que ce soit par un supporter dans les tribunes ou par un téléspectateur dans son fauteuil.*

Alors que d'autres marques du basket professionnel sont souvent enfantines et trop illustratives, la nouvelle image des Rockets s'éloigne de ce style conventionnel répandu dans le graphisme sportif. Il est simple, classique, dynamique, et tourné vers l'avenir. Le logo est également très pratique et polyvalent d'un point de vue commercial, et peut être facilement décliné sur les affiches et les produits dérivés, les supports multimédia, les tickets d'entrée comme les T-shirts. En ce sens, Ishioka et Esquer ont répondu aux attentes des dirigeants de l'équipe de créer une référence dans le domaine du design sportif. Leur collaboration artistique a donné naissance à l'identité populaire la plus novatrice que la NBA ait connue depuis des années.

hatten, präsentierten sie den Eigentümern in Houston ihre ersten Entwürfe: mehr als zwei Dutzend grafische Ansätze und über 50 Uniformgestaltungen. Hiervon wurden fünf Paar Grafiken und Uniformen zur Weiterentwicklung ausgewählt.

Das ausgewählte Design für die Rockets verband schließlich die Energie des Basketballs mit dem Erbe des Teamnamens. Das Logo ist ein elegantes Icon, das Stoßkraft und Nervenkitzel eines Starts einfängt und in den Kontext des Spielfeldes integriert. Da die futuristischen Uniformen gemeinsam mit dem Logo entworfen worden waren, ist der Gesamtausdruck organisch und flüssig. Sogar der neue Schrifttyp ist anwendungsspezifisch und passt zum Stil des Logos.

*Die Formen der Buchstaben und Zahlen auf den Trikots und Hosen der Spieler sind präzise gezeichnet, sodass jedes einzelne Zeichen auch aus der Distanz gut lesbar ist – ob von einem Fan im Stadion oder einem Fernsehzuschauer.*

Während andere Marken im professionellen Basketball oft extrem illustrativ sind, gelingt es dem neuen Image der Rockets, sich von dem gemeinen Stil der durchschnittlichen Sportgrafik abzusetzen. Es ist simpel, klassisch, energiegeladen und zukunftsgewandt. Vom Marketingstandpunkt aus gesehen ist das Logo extrem praktisch und vielseitig, einfach für Merchandise und Plakate, TV-Sendungen und Beschilderung, Tickets und T-Shirts adaptierbar. Damit entsprachen Ishioka und Esquer den Erwartungen der Rockets-Eigentümer an einen neuen Standard im Sportdesign. Durch ihren organischen und gemeinschaftlichen Designprozess entstand das innovativste und berühmteste Image, das der NBA seit Jahren gesehen hatte.

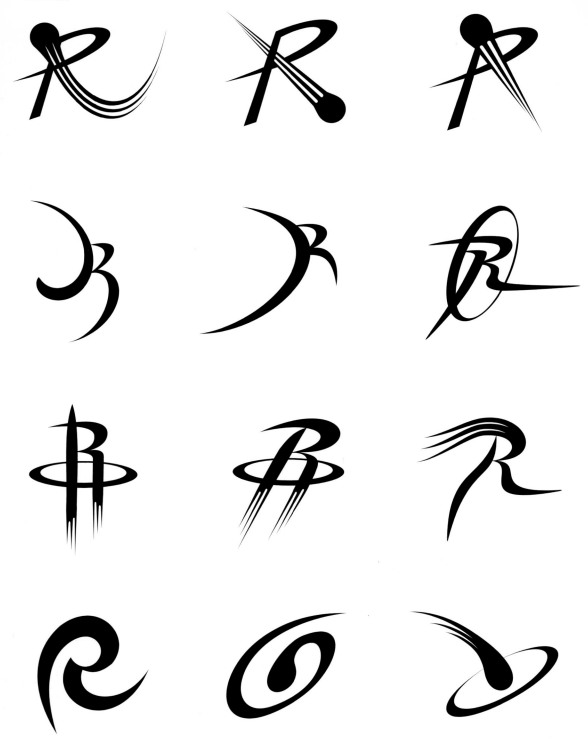

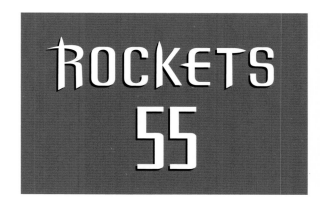

**Previous pages:** *illustration of uniforms and David Wesley using an actual one* /// **Double page précédente:** *illustrations d'uniformes, et David Wesley en portant un* /// **Vorherige Seite:** *Abbildungen von Uniformen und David Wesley in einer davon*

**Left:** *logo developments* /// **À gauche:** *différentes étapes du logo* /// **Links:** *Entwicklungsschritte für das Logo, bevor die endgültige Entscheidung getroffen wurde*

# Biography
# Rafael Esquer (Alfalfa)

www.rafaelesquer.com
Location: New York, USA
Year of foundation: 2004

Position: Founder/
Creative Director

*A native of the Sonora desert of Mexico, a student in Mexico City and Los Angeles, and has lived and worked in New York since 1996, a professional collaborator with Eiko Ishioka, Rafael is literally and figuratively a "design nomad." Widely published, Rafael's work has won numerous national and international design awards, and some of his pieces are contained in the collection of the Olympic Museum in Lausanne, Switzerland and in the poster collection of the Library of Congress in Washington, D.C. Rafael received his BFA with distinction in graphic design from Art Center College of Design. From 1997 to 2004 he worked as Art Director and then Creative Director in the design group at @radical.media. Alfalfa, Rafael's new design studio, opened its doors in New York in 2004 and is devoted to interdisciplinary projects.*

*Originaire du désert de Sonora au Mexique, il étudie à Mexico et à Los Angeles, puis s'installe à New York à partir de 1996. Collaborateur de Eiko Ishioka, Rafael Esquer est un « nomade du design » au sens propre comme au sens figuré. Objet de nombreuses publications, son travail a reçu plusieurs récompenses nationales et internationales, et on retrouve certaines de ses œuvres dans la collection du Musée Olympique de Lausanne (Suisse), ainsi que dans la collection d'affiches de la Bibliothèque du Congrès à Washington D.C. Rafael a obtenu une licence avec mention en graphisme à l'Art Center*

*College of Design. De 1997 à 2004, il a travaillé comme directeur artistique puis comme directeur de la création au sein de @radical. media. Son nouveau studio de design, Alfalfa, a ouvert ses portes en 2004 à New York et se consacre à des projets interdisciplinaires.*

*Geboren in der Sonorawüste Mexikos, Student in Mexiko City und Los Angeles, seit 1996 in New York, Mitarbeiter von Eiko Ishioka-Rafael Esquer ist ein „Design-Nomade" im wörtlichen und übertragenen Sinne. Seine Arbeiten wurden zahlreich publiziert und gewannen viele nationale sowie internationale Designpreise. Einige seiner Werke befinden sich in der Sammlung des Olympischen Museums in Lausanne, Schweiz, und in der Postersammlung der Library of Congress in Washington, DC. Rafael erhielt seinen BFA in Grafikdesign mit Auszeichnung am Art Center College of Design. Von 1997 bis 2004 arbeitete er zunächst als Art-Direktor und anschließend als Kreativchef der Designabteilung von @radical.media. Alfalfa, Rafael Esquers neues Designstudio, öffnete 2004 in New York seine Pforten und widmet sich interdisziplinären Projekten.*

# THE STORY OF DKNY: A BRAND FANTASY

Donna Karan introduced DKNY in 1989, a time when every designer had just launched, or was planning to launch, a bridge line. Anne Klein with Anne Klein II was typical of this retail strategy. Anne Klein II expressed the same aesthetic, silhouette, colors, and looks of the designer line, but produced in affordable fabrics. DKNY did not follow this model.

*Donna Karan designed her eponymous line on the belief that the aspirations of the modern working woman, starting with herself, could be represented by the lifestyle supported by the most exciting city in the world, New York City.*

The Donna Karan line consisted of clothes suitable for the female executive, appropriate for the corner office, the Power Lunch, and even the Black Tie affair. This aesthetic reflected the most telling aspects of New York City – chic, confident, flattering and sophisticated.

Donna Karan conçoit DKNY en 1989, à une époque ou tous les stylistes ont déjà lancé une ligne de prêt-à-porter, ou ont l'intention de le faire. L'exemple d'Anne Klein, avec la collection Anne Klein II, est typique de cette stratégie commerciale. Anne Klein II conservait l'esthétique, l'allure, les lignes et les couleurs de la ligne haute couture, mais déclinées dans des textiles moins coûteux. DKNY va s'écarter de ce modèle.

*Donna Karan dessine la ligne qui porte son nom selon la conviction que les aspirations de la femme active et moderne, à commencer par elle-même, trouvent leur expression dans le mode de vie encouragé par la ville la plus palpitante du monde, New York.*

La ligne de Donna Karan est une collection de vêtements destinés à la femme cadre et adaptés à la fois au bureau, aux déjeuners d'affaires, et aux dîners officiels. Ce choix esthétique reflète les aspects les plus éloquents de la ville de

Donna Karan führte DKNY 1989 ein, zu einer Zeit, in der jeder Designer eine Brückenlinie präsentierte oder dies zumindest plante. Typisch für diese Verkaufsstrategie war Anne Klein mit Anne Klein II: Ästhetik, Silhouette, Farben und Look von Anne Klein II entsprachen der Designerlinie, die Produktion erfolgte allerdings mit erschwinglichen Stoffen. DKNY folgte diesem Modell nicht.

*Donna Karan entwarf ihre namengebende Linie in der Überzeugung, dass eine moderne, berufstätige Frau – wie sie selbst eine war – vom Lifestyle der aufregendsten Stadt der Welt – New York City – repräsentiert werden könnte.*

Die Donna-Karan-Linie bestand aus Mode, die zur weiblichen Führungskraft passte, geeignet für ein Büro um die Ecke, ein Geschäftsessen, aber auch einer Abendgarderobe. Diese Ästhetik reflektierte die aufschlussreichsten Aspekte von

Essentially, Ms. Karan designed clothing for herself. Peter Arnell of Arnell Group worked closely with Karan on the branding of Donna Karan, and over the years, through his discussions with her, he noticed that she often remarked upon having nothing to wear on the weekend.

*What was missing was clothing for the off-duty, playful, casual side of her life. Neither her cocktail dress nor Power Suit was appropriate for playing with her daughter in Central Park, strolling the sidewalks of Soho with her husband, or combing the flea markets on 6th Avenue with her friends.*

During the week she was formal, powerful and high-end, dining on caviar. On the weekend, she was still stylish, but in a more accessible and casual way. She was laid-back and spontaneous, maybe stopping to grab a slice (of pizza). This side of Donna Karan needed to be dressed.

New York : élégance, assurance, beauté et raffinement. Au fond, Donna Karan dessine des vêtements pour elle-même... Peter Arnell, de Arnell Group, travaille depuis plusieurs années sur l'image de marque de Donna Karan, et en discutant avec la styliste, il réalise que celle-ci se plaint souvent de ne rien avoir à se mettre pour le week-end.

*Ce qui lui manque, c'est une garde-robe ludique et décontractée pour les jours de congé. Ni ses robes de cocktail ni ses tailleurs-pantalons n'étaient adaptés pour jouer dans Central Park avec sa fille, se promener dans Soho avec son mari, ou chiner dans le marché aux puces de la 6ème avenue avec ses amis.*

En semaine elle était très habillée, professionnelle et sophistiquée, et dînait au caviar. Le week-end, elle restait très chic, mais d'une manière plus abordable et décontractée. Elle était relax et spontanée, s'offrant même parfois une part de

New York City – schick, selbstbewusst und kultiviert. Im Wesentlichen entwarf Donna Karan Mode für sich selbst. Peter Arnell von der Arnell Group arbeitete bei der Markenbildung von Donna Karan eng mit Karan zusammen; im Laufe der Jahre bemerkte er im Zuge zahlreicher Diskussionen, dass sie sich stets darüber beschwerte, am Wochenende nichts zum Anziehen zu haben.

*Was fehlte, war Freizeitkleidung für die verspielte, lässige Seite ihres Lebens. Weder ihr Cocktailkleid noch ihr Anzug waren geeignet, um mit ihrer Tochter im Central Park zu spielen, mit ihrem Mann durch die Straßen von Soho zu bummeln oder mit ihren Freunden die Flohmärkte auf der 6th Avenue zu durchkämmen.*

In der Woche war sie formell, leistungsorientiert, erstklassig, aß Kaviar zum Abendessen. Am Wochenende war sie zwar immer noch elegant, aber auf eine zugänglichere, lässigere Art. Sie war locker und

**Left:** *display of the logo in a variety of media /// À gauche: le logo sur différents supports /// Links: Display des Logos über unterschiedliche Medien*

**Right:** *Logo on a window shop /// À droite: Le logo sur la vitrine d'une boutique /// Rechts: Logo in einem Schaufenster*

When Karan presented Arnell with the challenge of creating a second line, Arnell hit upon the idea of addressing the casual side of the Donna Karan customer. This strategy sought to widen the customer base, not by necessarily increasing the number of customers, but by increasing the amount of time the existing customers would spend in her clothing. This line would enable the Donna Karan customer to wear the clothes seven days a week instead of only five, covering her full 24/7 clock.

*The inspiration behind Donna Karan's designer line was the successful, professional woman thriving in New York City. The inspiration behind Donna Karan's second line was this woman at ease in New York City. So, to gain real insight into the brand's identity, Arnell did what everyone in New York City does: he walked.*

Arnell walked uptown and downtown, east side and west side, from Wall Street

pizza. Il fallait de quoi habiller cette facette de Donna Karan. Quand la styliste propose à Arnell de concevoir une deuxième ligne de vêtements, celui-ci a alors l'idée de cibler le côté décontracté de ses clientes. Cette stratégie visait à élargir la clientèle, non en augmentant le nombre de clients, mais en augmentant les occasions de porter les vêtements. La nouvelle ligne permettrait aux clients de Donna Karan de porter sa griffe sept jours sur sept au lieu de cinq, et ceci 24 heures sur 24.

*La collection couture de Donna Karan s'inspirait de la femme active et brillante qui s'épanouit à New York. La collection prêt-à-porter s'inspirait de la même femme, version décontractée. Afin de composer l'identité de la marque, Peter Arnell fait alors comme tout le monde à New York : il arpente les rues.*

Il sillonne Manhattan d'est en ouest et du nord au sud, de Harlem à Wall Street, et observe la ville que Karan et lui appré-

spontan, aß ein Stück Pizza im Vorbeigehen. Diese Seite von Donna Karan musste eingekleidet werden. Als Karan Arnell damit beauftragte, eine zweite Linie zu entwerfen, kam Arnell auf die Idee, die lässige Seite der Donna-Karan-Kundin anzusprechen. Diese Strategie sollte den Kundenstamm erweitern, aber nicht um die Zahl der Kunden zu erhöhen, sondern in dem Sinne, dass die Zeitspanne verlängert werden sollte, die Kunden in der Kleidung verbringen würden: Die Donna-Karan-Kundin sollte ihre Kleidung an sieben anstatt nur an fünf Tagen pro Woche tragen.

*Die Inspiration hinter Donna Karans Designerlinie war die erfolgreiche, berufstätige Frau in New York City. Die Inspiration hinter Donna Karans zweiter Linie war dieselbe Frau in New York City, aber entspannt. Um einen echten Einblick in die Markenidentität zu bekommen, tat Arnell, was jeder in New York City tut: spazieren gehen.*

WALK

WOMAN
AT WORK

# DKNY
Donna Karan New York

ABCDEF
GHIJKLM
NOPQRS
TUVWXYZ
fall 1992 kids

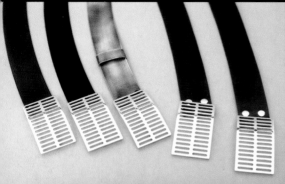
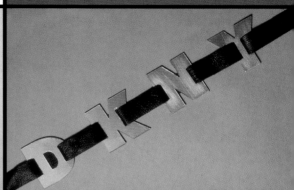

# .DKNY
### Donna Karan New York

to Harlem, observing the city that was loved by Karan, by himself, and by millions around the globe. The hum of the city, the beats and rhythms of life on its streets, the accelerating and staggered lines of its architecture and skyline, the entire city would be embedded in the brand. Along the way Arnell re-discovered that New York was a city of iconic institutions, from the façade of the Met to the local precinct house, from the New York Stock Exchange to the firehouse. The strong images of institutions such as NYPD and FDNY inspired the creation of the city's newest icon. Donna Karan New York gave birth to DKNY.

New York City became the palette of the brand. Its images and symbols became the images and symbols of DKNY. Subway tokens were re-imagined as rivets on jeans, manhole covers as buttons. Sidewalk grates inspired texture on packaging. DKNY WALK, a play on street signals, decorated shoebox covers. Photographs of the city were also layered into the logo, creating a photomontage of such icons as the Statue of Liberty, the Brooklyn Bridge, and the Empire State Building.

*In department stores, Arnell created in-store boutiques, which further illustrated the brand. This was an entirely new shopping experience. Materials and images were taken from the cityscape; lighting fixtures looked like street lamps. A customer shopping in the DKNY boutique found herself immersed in New York City. The actual city of New York itself soon became a backdrop for DKNY.*

To mark the brand's launch in the most dramatic way, Arnell Group hired a skywriter to put DKNY over the city. As it happened, the international press core was in the city to cover the President's visit to the United Nations that day. No one knew what DKNY was, and the subsequent photos and speculation on its meaning—was it a protest or a greeting or a political message of some sort—caused a media frenzy. Other novel ways

cient, comme des millions d'individus dans le monde. Le bourdonnement de la ville, les rythmes de vie propres à chaque quartier, l'architecture exaltante et les buildings vertigineux, la ville entière devait se concentrer dans la marque. En chemin, Arnell redécouvre que New York est une ville d'institutions emblématiques, de la façade du Met au petit commissariat de quartier, de la Bourse à la caserne de pompiers. Les images fortes d'institutions telles que NYPD et FDNY inspirent la conception d'une nouvelle icône de la ville. Donna Karan, New York, donne naissance à DKNY.

La ville de New York devient la palette de la marque. Ses images et ses symboles deviennent ceux de DKNY. Les jetons de métro se changent en rivets de jeans, les plaques d'égout en boutons. Les grilles de trottoir inspirent la texture des emballages. DKNY WALK, un jeu de mots rappelant les feux piétonniers, décore les boîtes à chaussures. Des photographies de la ville sont insérées dans le logo, et composent un photomontage d'icônes comme la Statue de la Liberté, le pont de Brooklyn et l'Empire State Building.

*Dans les grands magasins, Arnell installe des boutiques indépendantes qui représentent la marque. À l'époque, c'est un concept tout à fait inédit. Les matériaux et la décoration s'inspirent du paysage urbain, les luminaires ressemblent à des lampadaires. La cliente de la boutique DKNY se trouve immergée dans New York.*

La ville elle-même devient bientôt la toile de fond de DKNY. Afin de lancer la griffe de façon spectaculaire, Arnell Group recourt à de la publicité aérienne pour tracer le sigle dans le ciel au-dessus de la ville. Par un fait du hasard, la presse internationale est en ville ce jour-là pour couvrir la visite du président au siège des Nations Unies. Personne ne savait ce que signifiait DKNY, et les photos des banderoles firent la une des médias, entraînant bon nombre de conjectures. S'agissait-il d'un message de bienvenue, de protesta-

Arnell lief durch Wohn- und Geschäftsviertel, durch Eastside und Westside, von der Wall Street bis nach Harlem, und beobachtete die Stadt, die von Karan, ihm selbst und Millionen Menschen weltweit geliebt wird. Der Lärm der Großstadt, der Lebensrhythmus auf den Straßen, die beschleunigten und schwankenden Linien der Architektur und Skyline – die gesamte Stadt sollte in der Marke eingefangen werden. Auf seinen Wegen entdeckt Arnell erneut, dass New York eine Stadt ikonografischer Institutionen war, von der Fassade der U-Bahn bis zum Haus um die Ecke, vom New York Stock Exchange bis zur Feuerwache. Die starken Bilder von Institutionen wie NYPD oder FDNY inspirierten die Entstehung einer neuen Ikone. DKNY wurde geboren.

New York City war die Markenpalette: Die Bilder und Symbole der Stadt wurden zu den Bildern und Symbolen von DKNY. U-Bahn-Tickets wurden zu Nieten auf Jeans, Kanaldeckel zu Knöpfen. Gitter an Bürgersteigen inspirierten die Textur auf der Verpackung. DKNY WALK, ein Spiel mit Ampelsignalen, zierte die Deckel von Schuhschachteln. Fotos der Stadt fanden sich auf dem Logo als Fotomontage von Icons wie der Freiheitsstatue, der Brooklyn Bridge oder dem Empire State Building wieder.

*Arnell entwickelte Boutiquen innerhalb von Kaufhäusern, die die Marke noch mehr illustrierten. Dies war eine komplett neue Einkaufserfahrung. Materialien und Bilder der Stadt wurden verwendet; Lichtvorrichtungen sahen aus wie Straßenlaternen: Der Kunde einer DKNY-Boutique fand sich in New York City eingetaucht. Die Stadt New York selbst wurde zur Kulisse für DKNY.*

Zur möglichst dramatischen Markteinführung der Marke mietete die Arnell Group einen Himmelsschreiber. Durch Zufall war an jenem Tag die internationale Presse vor Ort, um über den Besuch des Präsidenten bei den Vereinten Nationen

to promote the brand included a freeway sign over the exit from the Midtown tunnel into Manhattan reading Uptown to the right, Downtown to the left, and DKNY straight ahead. Billboards of the DKNY photomontage appeared all over the city. The most notable billboard stands at Houston and Broadway, the gateway to Soho. At first, because the location was on a landmarked building, it was not available for advertisement. To acquire the site,

*Arnell collaborated with art historians and fine art restorers to create a special paint that was consistent with the surface of the building. It would reflect the building's age and condition, and make the painting look as if it had always belonged there. Through these actions, Arnell convinced city officials to allow the mural to be put up in this historic spot.*

Today, the Soho mural that Arnell Group put up seventeen years ago has become an authentic backdrop and symbol of the City, and in this way fulfills the original promise of the DKNY brand—becoming a genuine New York City icon.

---

tion, avait-il un contenu politique ? Une autre publicité originale se manifeste sous la forme d'un panneau de signalisation routière sur l'autoroute menant à Manhattan. Il indique : Manhattan Nord à droite, Manhattan Sud à gauche, DKNY tout droit.

Le photomontage de DKNY apparaît sur des panneaux d'affichage dans toute la ville. Le plus remarquable se trouve à l'angle de Houston et Broadway, à l'entrée de Soho. À l'origine, le bâtiment ne pouvait pas servir de support à de la publicité, car il s'agissait d'un immeuble classé. Pour obtenir l'autorisation d'afficher,

*Arnell collabora avec des historiens d'art et des restaurateurs spécialisés pour mettre au point une peinture spéciale qui ne nuise pas à la façade. Elle devait aussi refléter l'âge et l'état du bâtiment, et donner l'impression qu'elle avait toujours été là. Grâce à cette astuce, Arnell réussit à convaincre les autorités d'autoriser la présence de sa fresque sur un lieu historique.*

Aujourd'hui, la fresque installée par l'équipe de Peter Arnell il y a dix-sept ans est devenue à la fois un symbole et une toile de fond, réalisant ainsi la promesse de la marque DKNY : devenir une véritable icône de New York.

---

zu berichten. Niemand wusste, was DKNY war, und die nachfolgenden Fotos und Spekulationen - handelte es sich um einen Protest, eine Begrüßung oder eine politische Botschaft? - löste einen Medienrausch aus. Weitere neuartige Werbemaßnahmen für die Marke waren ein Autobahnschild über der Ausfahrt des Midtown-Tunnels nach Manhattan, auf dem rechts Uptown, links Downtown und geradeaus DKNY zu lesen war.

Plakatwände der DKNY-Fotomontage hingen in der ganzen Stadt. Die auffälligste Plakatwand steht bei Houston und Broadway, dem Tor zu Soho. Dieser Ort durfte zunächst nicht für Werbung genutzt werden, weil das Gebäude ein Wahrzeichen war.

*Arnell arbeitete mit Historikern und Kunstrestauratoren zusammen, um eine Spezialfarbe zu entwickeln, die konsistent mit der Gebäudeoberfläche war. Sie sollte Alter und Zustand des Gebäudes reflektieren, und es sollte so aussehen, als sei die Farbe immer schon da gewesen. Währenddessen überzeugte Arnell die verantwortlichen städtischen Beamten davon, das Wandgemälde an diesem historischen Ort erstellen zu dürfen.*

Heute ist die vor 17 Jahren entstandene Mauer in Soho ein authentischer Hintergrund und ein Symbol der Stadt geworden. Auf seine Art erfüllt es das ursprüngliche Versprechen der DKNY-Marke: ein authentisches New York City Icon zu werden.

**Below:** *Outdoor on the way to Manhatan, New York ///* **Ci-dessous:** *Panneau d'affichage sur la route de Manhattan, New York ///* **Unten:** *Auf dem Weg nach Manhattan, New York*

Above from left to right: *Advertising spreads for DKNY for magazines ///* **Ci-dessus de gauche à droite:** *Doubles pages de publicité pour DKNY en magazine ///* **Oben von links nach rechts:** *Werbeseiten von DKNY für Magazine*

# Biography
# Peter Arnell (Arnell Group)

www.arnellgroup.com
Location: New York, USA
Year of foundation: 1979

Position: Founder, Chairman, CEO and Chief Creative Officer

*Peter Arnell is Founder, Chairman, CEO and Chief Creative Officer of* **Arnell Group***, founded 1979, a wholly owned subsidiary of* **Omnicom***. Arnell Group is a comprehensive branding and communications consultancy incorporating a unique series of professional skill sets and disciplines in the areas of strategy, architecture, engineering, product design, corporate identity, research, channel development and enterprise architecture planning. Mr. Arnell was born in Brooklyn in 1959 of English and Russian heritage. An architect and designer by training who studied at Columbia and Princeton Universities respectively, Mr. Arnell has authored 19 books including important academic monographs on such architects as Frank Gehry, Aldo Rossi and James Stirling, for publishers including Rizzoli, Knopf and Harpers & Row.*

*Peter Arnell est le fondateur, président-directeur général et directeur de création de* **Arnell Group***, fondé en 1979, une filiale indépendante d'* **Omnicom***. Arnell Group est une agence de conseil en communication et marketing qui propose une gamme de prestations interdisciplinaires dans les domaines de la stratégie commerciale, de l'architecture, de l'ingénierie, de la conception de produit, de l'image de marque, de la recherche, du développement de réseau et de la gestion organisationnelle. Peter Arnell est né à Brooklyn en 1959, de parents d'origine russe et anglaise. Architecte et designer de forma-*

*tion, diplômé des universités de Columbia et de Princeton, il est l'auteur de 19 ouvrages dont des monographies théoriques d'architectes tels que Frank Gehry, Aldo Rossi et James Stirling, publiées chez Rizzoli, Knopf et Harpers & Row.*

*Peter Arnell ist Gründer, Vorsitzender, Hauptgeschäftsführer und Chief Creative Officer der* **Arnell Group***, 1979 gegründet und hundertprozentige Tochtergesellschaft von* **Omnicom***. Arnell Group ist eine umfassende Marken- und Kommunikationsberatung, die eine einzigartige Reihe professioneller Qualifikationen und Disziplinen auf den Gebieten der Strategie, Architektur, Ingenieurwesen, Produktdesign, Corporate Identity, Forschung, Programmentwicklung und Planung von Unternehmensarchitektur umfasst. Peter Arnell wurde 1959 in Brooklyn geboren und ist englischer und russischer Abstammung. Er ist als Architekt und Designer ausgebildet und studierte sowohl an der Columbia als auch an der Princeton Universität. Arnell ist der Autor von 19 Büchern, zum Beispiel wichtige akademische Monografien von Architekten wie Frank Gehry, Aldo Rossi oder James Stirling, für Verlage wie Rizzoli, Knopf und Harpers & Row.*

# CORPORATE DESIGN: CITY OF HANOVER

No chauffeur driven service cars, nor even any kindergartens; shortly before *EXPO2000*, the city of Hanover invested in its own image and had a new brand system developed for itself. In parallel, a radical new corporate design was also created. In a 'ranking' of German cities, Hanover comes in at eleventh place – below Bremen, but above Duisburg. Hanover has no well-known historical emblem; its architecture is unspectacular. In Hanover, a sterile, dialect-free German is spoken. Hanover is usually seen when passing by – through the window of an ICE express train, or during a trade fair visit.

The fact that the *Deutsche Messe* in Hanover is *the* German trade fair, its economic significance allows the real character of this city to show through. Hanover has no naturally immediate, directly visible self-image and is, so to speak, an outward looking city. As a result of the kingdom of Hanover's long association with England, a tradition of openness and respect towards foreign influences has

Aucun service de transport privé avec chauffeur, ni même de jardin d'enfants. Juste avant EXPO 2000, la ville d'Hanovre investit dans sa propre image et s'offre un système de gestion de marque. Une nouvelle et radicale identité visuelle est conçue en parallèle. Dans un classement des villes allemandes, Hanovre arrive en onzième place, derrière Brême mais devant Duisbourg. Hanovre ne possède aucun emblème historique célèbre, son architecture n'est pas pittoresque, et on y parle une langue stérile dénuée de patois régional. Hanovre est le genre de ville que l'on traverse lorsqu'on prend le train express ICE, ou que l'on visite à l'occasion d'une foire commerciale.

La Deutsche Messe de Hanovre est la plus grande foire commerciale allemande, et sa portée économique permet au véritable caractère de la ville de s'exprimer. Hanovre n'a pas de rayonnement naturel immédiatement visible, mais elle est pour ainsi dire ouverte sur l'extérieur. Les liens historiques du royaume de

Keine Dienstautos, nicht einmal Kindergärten: Kurz vor der EXPO2000 investiert die Stadt Hannover in das eigene Image und lässt ein neues Markensystem für sich entwickeln. Parallel dazu entsteht ein radikal neues Corporate Design. In der Liste der „Deutschen Großstädte" belegt Hannover Position 11 – hinter Bremen, vor Duisburg. Die Stadt besitzt kein altbekanntes Wahrzeichen, ihre Architektur ist unspektakulär, und es wird ein steriles dialektfreies Deutsch gesprochen. Man nimmt Hannover meistens im Vorbeifahren wahr – aus dem Fenster des ICE-Zuges oder während eines Messebesuchs.

An der Tatsache, dass die „Deutsche Messe" in Hannover von ihrer wirtschaftlichen Bedeutung die deutsche Messe schlechthin ist, lässt sich der eigentliche Charakter dieser Stadt erkennen. Hannover besitzt kein natürliches, direkt erfahrbares Eigenbild – es lebt gewissermaßen nach außen. Durch die langjährige Verbindung des Königreichs Hannover mit England hat sich bereits

# Straßen-
## verzeichnis

**97**

Hannover

developed since the 19th century. Hanover does not exclude, it focuses. Hanover does not boast, and at most it provides a setting or backdrop: "Hanover is a passe-partout" [Rainer Wagner].

How has Hanover's visual identity been formed? "…It would be absurd to represent a modern city using the image of individual objects or with a symbolic figure from mythology. … One could even say that the essence of modern urbanity eludes observation" [Fritz Seitz].

*Hanover's new emblem makes no pretence to any identity myth; it suggests no promises which the city cannot keep. It is just as the city is: clear and individual.*

Hanover's emblem is not cryptic; it can be explained more through association than through meaning. It may be seen as an open door, as a focussing point, or as two brackets turned outwards. On closer inspection, the capital letter 'H' is recognisable.

Hanovre avec l'Angleterre ont développé depuis le XIX<sup>ème</sup> siècle une tradition d'ouverture et de respect pour les influences étrangères. Hanovre n'exclut pas, elle concentre. Hanovre n'est pas arrogante, elle constitue au mieux un décor ou une toile de fond. « Hanovre est passe-partout. » (Rainer Wagner)

Comment l'identité visuelle de Hanovre a-t-elle été conçue ? « Il serait absurde de représenter une ville moderne à travers un objet particulier ou une figure symbolique de la mythologie… On peut même avancer que la nature de l'urbanité moderne échappe à l'observation. » (Fritz Seitz)

*Le nouvel emblème de Hanovre ne feint pas de se rattacher à un mythe identitaire, il ne promet rien que la ville ne puisse tenir. En fait il ressemble à la ville : limpide et personnel.*

L'emblème de Hanovre n'est pas sibyllin, il s'explique moins par le sens que par

im 19. Jahrhundert eine Tradition der Offenheit und des Respekts gegenüber Fremden entwickelt. Hannover grenzt nicht aus, es fokussiert. Hannover gibt nicht an, es gibt höchstens einen Rahmen vor: „Hannover ist ein Passe-partout." [Rainer Wagner].

Wie ist nun Hannovers visuelle Identität entstanden? „Es wäre absurd, eine moderne Stadt durch das Abbild einzelner Objekte oder durch eine symbolische Figur aus der Mythologie zu repräsentieren. … Man kann sogar sagen, dass sich das Essenzielle moderner Urbanität der Anschauung entzieht." [Fritz Seitz].

*Hannovers neues Zeichen täuscht keinen Identitätsmythos vor, es suggeriert kein Versprechen, das die Realität der Stadt nicht einlösen könnte. Es ist so wie die Stadt selbst: klar und eigen.*

Hannovers Zeichen ist nicht kryptisch, es erklärt sich nur eher durch Assoziation als durch Bedeutung. Es lässt sich

Previous spread: *brochure cover* /// **Double page précédente** : *Couverture de brochure* /// **Vorherige Seite:** *Broschüre*

**Left:** *exhibition about the new identity project* /// **À gauche** : *Exposition sur le nouveau projet d'identité* /// **Links:** *Ausstellung über das New Identity-Projekt*

**Next spread:** *corporate identity manual* /// **Double page suivante** : *Manuel d'identité d'entreprise* /// **Nächste Seite:** *Leitfaden Corporate Identity*

This emblem is open to interpretation – and open to change. It is less formal than the usual logo, but provides more. The designation and identity structure for the city council's departments can be derived from its shape. But there's more: the *Hannover* logotype can, for example, be extended to the slogan 'Hannover überrascht' (Hanover surprises) or to the campaign brand 'Standort Hannover' (Location Hanover).

The Hanover brand is functional, and it works. It is not dismissive, but invites use and interaction. The playing rules are not complicated, but precise. A city's corporate design should not be complicated and it must be precise; "Whoever has followed the process of finding and creating an identity in a simply structured company must think in terms of new dimensions for a city. There are only few companies which are as inhomogeneous as a city district" [Christoph Eichenseer].

The essential substance of Hanover's visible appearance is the typography; it

une association d'idées. On peut le voir comme une porte ouverte, comme une mire, ou comme deux parenthèses ouvertes vers l'extérieur. À y regarder de plus près, on reconnaît un H majuscule.

Cet emblème est ouvert à l'interprétation, et ouvert au changement. Il est moins formel qu'un logo classique, mais il est plus riche. La désignation et la structure identitaire des différents services municipaux peuvent être déclinées à partir de sa forme. Mais il y a plus encore : le logotype de Hanovre peut par exemple s'étendre au slogan « Hanovre surprend » ou à la campagne « Localité Hanovre ».

La marque Hanovre est fonctionnelle, et ça marche. Elle n'est pas dédaigneuse, mais invite à l'interaction. Les règles du jeu ne sont pas compliquées, mais elles sont précises. Et ces qualités doivent se retrouver dans l'identité visuelle d'une ville. « Celui qui a l'expérience de l'étude et de la conception de l'identité visuelle d'une entreprise à la structure simple doit repenser les choses à un autre

als offenes Tor betrachten, als fokussierender Punkt, als zwei nach außen gedrehte Klammern. Auf den zweiten Blick erkennt man das große „H".

Dieses Zeichen ist offen für Interpretation – und offen für Wandlung. Es ist formal weniger als ein übliches Logo, leistet aber mehr. Aus seiner Form lässt sich die Kennzeichnung und Identitätsstruktur für die Ressorts der Stadtverwaltung ableiten. Aber es geht noch weiter: Der Schriftzug „Hannover" kann sich zum Beispiel im Slogan „Hannover überrascht" oder in der Kampagnenmarke „Standort Hannover" fortsetzen.

Die Marke Hannover ist funktional, und sie funktioniert. Sie ist nicht abweisend, sondern lädt zur Nutzung, zur Interaktion ein. Die Spielregeln sind nicht kompliziert, aber präzise. Das Corporate Design einer Stadt darf gar nicht kompliziert und muss präzise sein: „Wer schon einmal den Prozess der Identitätsfindung und -bildung bei einem einfach strukturierten Unternehmen begleitet hat, der

# Das Zeichen, seine Konstruktion und seine Standardgrößen.

Zu dem neuen Erscheinungsbild von Hannover, zu seinem Corporate Design, gehört das neue Hannover-Logo.

Das neue Hannover-Logo ist kein Hoheitszeichen und kein Dienstsiegel. Es ist auch kein Wappen der Stadt. Das traditionelle Stadtwappen von Hannover wird durch das Logo weder abgelöst noch ersetzt.

Das Hannover-Logo ist zugleich mehr und weniger als ein Zeichen. Einerseits ist es kein Zeichen, das identisch ist mit der Sache, für die es steht. Das H für Hannover als Grundsymbol offenbart sich erst auf den zweiten Blick. Andererseits ist das Logo integrierbar in andere Zeichenzusammenhänge.

Die Schrift im Logo ist speziell für Hannover entwickelt. Es ist die „Hannover Millennial". Das Wort „Hannover" ist noch einmal gesondert bearbeitet. Die Schrift im Logo ist also keine reine Satzschrift.

Die Konstruktion des Zeichens basiert auf einer Ausgangsgröße von 122,5 mm Zeichenbreite, die wir hier nicht abbilden können.

Für die verkleinerte Anwendung des Logos sind die abgebildeten sechs Standardgrößen vorgesehen: 70%, 50%, 35%, 25%, 17,5% und 13,5%, von oben nach unten. Die Maßstäbe für vergrößerte Anwendungen sind frei.

Für die verkleinerte Anwendung des Logos, z.B. im Briefbogen, gilt die Standardgröße 25%, auf der Visiten karte 17,5%.

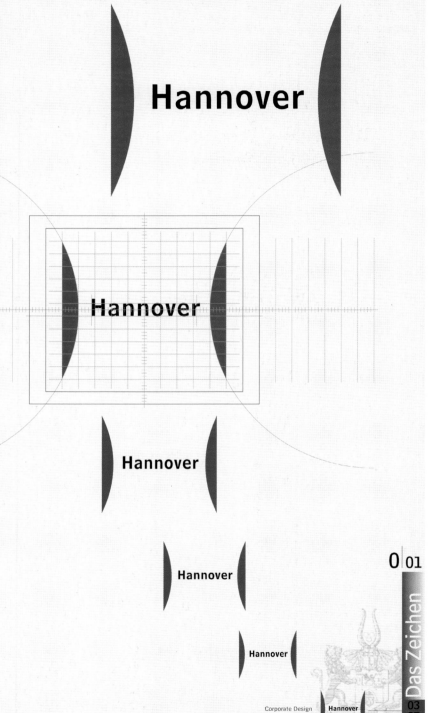

0|01

## Das Zeichen und seine Farben.

In seiner Grundform enthält das Zeichen die Farben Schwarz und Rot (1). Das Rot des Zeichens ist das Rot des Stadtwappens und der Stadtfahne von Hannover.

Dieses Rot besteht in den Definitionen HKS 15, Pantone 186, RAL 3020 und Euroskala 100% Magenta + 70% Yellow + 10% Cyan.

Einfarbig kann das Zeichen in positiv schwarz und negativ weiß verwendet werden.

Auf rotem oder schwarzem Hintergrund erscheint das Logo negativ weiß (2 und 3). Auf grauen Flächen mit einem Tonwert von 40% ist sowohl die negative, als auch die positive Version möglich. Bei einem Tonwert der Graufläche unter 40% ist nur die positive, darüber nur die negative Version möglich (4 und 5). Bei farbigen Hintergründen muß jeweils entschieden werden, welchem Tonwert die Helligkeit der Fläche entspricht.

Die Verwendung des Logos vor unruhigen Hintergründen, insbesondere Fotos empfiehlt sich nicht, da die exakte Definition der Farb- oder Grauwerte nicht gewährleistet ist.

Die Verwendung des Zeichens in anderen Farben als Schwarz und Rot kann nur in Ausnahmefällen vorkommen und bedarf der Zustimmung der Stadt Hannover.

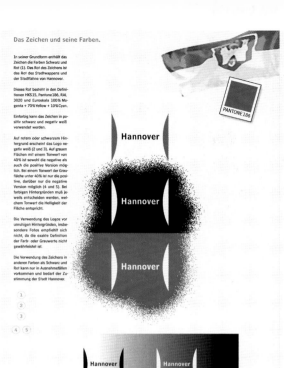

PANTONE 186

Hannover

Hannover

Hannover

Hannover Hannover

( 1 )
( 2 )
( 3 )

( 4 ) ( 5 )

## Das Zeichen und seine Anwendungsbedingun

Das Hannover-Logo bietet eine Fülle von Anwendungsmöglichkeiten und ist offen für unterschiedlichste Gestaltungszusammenhänge. Dennoch muß die Integrität des Zeichens in Form, Farbe und Schrift gewahrt werden. Verboten sind Nachbildungen und Veränderungen oder Ergänzungen innerhalb des Zeichens.

Die einfarbige Version des Zeichens ist schwarz. Eine einfarbige Version in rot ist nicht zulässig. Ebenso sind Grauwerte in den Kreissegmenten nicht zulässig (6).

Die Schrift des Zeichens darf nicht nachgesetzt, d.h. neu konstruiert werden, weder in der Hannover Millennial noch in irgend einer anderen Schrift. Unzulässig ist ebenso die Neukonstruktion der Kreissegmente (7).

Das Zeichen darf in keiner Weise verzerrt werden, weder gedehnt noch gestaucht oder komprimiert (8).

Das Zeichen ist ausschließlich horizontal verwendbar. Es darf nicht gekippt, gestürzt oder gedreht werden (9).

Das Verhältnis der Elemente des Zeichens zueinander darf nicht verändert werden (10).

Innerhalb des Zeichens sind keine Ergänzungen zulässig, weder zum Wort noch zur Form (11).

Das Wort „Hannover" im Zeichen darf durch nichts ersetzt werden (12).

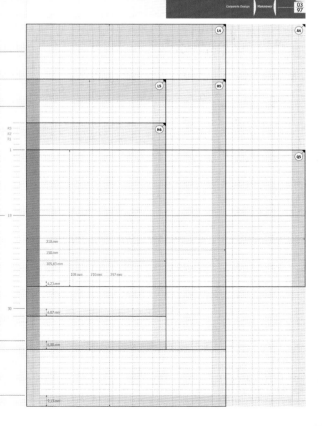

Hann

Hann

Hann

Hann

Hann

6
7
8
9
10

11
12
13

Das neue Hannover-Logo ist mit allen Nutzungsrechten Eigentum der Landeshauptstadt Hannover. Es ist in seiner Originalversion patentrechtlich geschützt.

Die Verwendung des Zeichens außerhalb der Stadtverwaltung bedarf der Zustimmung des Eigentümers und ist nur nach erfolgter Freigabe durch die Landeshauptstadt gestattet.

Die vorliegenden Anwendungshinweise sind für jeden Einsatz des Hannover-Logos verbindlich. Einzelfälle der Anwendung sind mit der Landeshauptstadt Hannover abzusprechen.

**Die Querverweise**
*Das Zeichen:*
*Verwendung außerhalb*
*des eigenen CD.*
*Die Schrift.*

Corporate Design  Hannover (

03
97

## Das Raster, die Inhalte und die Formate.

6

Für Druckschriften der Stadt Hannover sind vier Standardformate (unten rot dargestellt) und drei Ausnahmeformate für besondere Anwendungen (weiß) vorgesehen. Sie entsprechen alle exakt der DIN – mit zwei Ausnahmen:

Das Maß 148,5 mm, das sich in der DIN-Reihe beim Format A5 ergibt, ist auf 150 gerundet (B). Das erleichtert die Anwendung des Rasters und läßt sich dennoch ohne Verlust aus denselben Papierbogen herstellen wie DIN A5.

Wo das Format DIN-Lang quer (D) über mehrseitige Faltblätter verwendet wird, sollte die Seitenhöhe auf 105,83 mm erhöht werden. So läßt sich erreichen, daß sich jeder Falz mit einer Rasterlinie deckt.

Die genauen Maße der sieben möglichen Formate sind der nebenstehenden Tabelle zu entnehmen.

Der Gestaltungsraster wird so auf die Seiten gelegt, dass er am linken und rechten Seitenrand jeweils mit einem halben 10 mm-Feld beginnt, und die obere Seitenkante sich mit einer Rasterlinie deckt. Dadurch ergeben sich regelmäßige Randbereiche, die lediglich am unteren Rand krumme Maße aufweisen.

| FORMAT | BREITE | HÖHE | DIN |
|---|---|---|---|
| H6 | 105 | 150 | DIN A6 (hoch) |
| L5 | 105 | 210 | DIN A5 (modifiziert) |
| Q5 | 210 | 105,83 | DIN-Lang (quer) |
| H5 | 150 | 210 | DIN-Lang (hoch) |
| L4 | 150 | 297 | Drittel DIN A3 (quer) |
| A4 | 210 | 297 | DIN A4 (hoch) |
| A3 | 420 | 297 | DIN A3 (quer) |

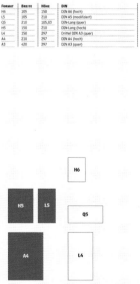

H6

H5  L5

Q5

A4  L4

A3

R3
R2
R1

L4   A4

1

R3
R2
R1

L5   H5

11   1

R3
R2
R1

H6

1

21   31

31  21  13

Q5

41   31

210 mm
150 mm
105,83 mm

105 mm  210 mm  297 mm

4,23 mm

51   31

30

6,07 mm

44

6,80 mm

61

64

9,13 mm

unites brand systems and corporate design. The font family developed especially for the city, *Hannover Millennial*[1], performs a three-part balancing act; it is contemporary, it is unobtrusive, and it is sophisticated. This balance is not self-evident; it is not easy to go against the norm without being loud. In the late nineties, it was all about getting away from the faceless and elegant omnipotence of the forms of the Frutiger, Meta and Thesis typefaces.

The name of Hanover's house font is not only an ironic play on the closing years of the previous millennium. The name conceals a further reference: *Bell Centennial* served as a prototype, which was designed by Matthew Carter for the American telephone directories. Similarly to the Bell, the Hannover is economically and outstandingly suitable for form and table use in small point sizes.

***They demonstrate surprising character in job printing applications, where, through enlargement, an ornamental aesthetic has developed out of functional elements.***

The corporate design for the City of Hanover[2] is an original creation with an awareness of tradition. Overall, it is based on functional considerations, and its aesthetic manifests itself initially through its function. Fortunately, this path does not forcibly lead to a puritanical or militant 'less is more' attitude. A series of examples (publications, exhibition graphics) demonstrate eccentric design, which neither compromises layout grids, nor sets the uniformity of the brand presentation in question.

This interaction of logic and subtle excess also has a tradition in Hanover. It was none other than Kurt Schwitters who standardised the Hanover city council's printed matter on their behalf in the late twenties in a modern and uncompromising way. This took place long before the term 'corporate design' had been invented. Schwitters' design legacy, and above all his way of thinking, could not

niveau en ce qui concerne une ville. Car très peu d'entreprises sont aussi hétérogènes qu'une communauté urbaine. » (Christoph Eichenseer)

L'élément essentiel de l'emblème de Hanovre est la typographie, elle marie identité de marque et design graphique. La police de caractère inventée tout spécialement, *Hannover Millennial*[1], joue une pièce en trois actes : elle est contemporaine, discrète et raffinée. Cet équilibre n'est pas évident en soi, car il n'est pas facile d'aller contre la norme sans être tapageur. À la fin des années 1990, tout le monde cherchait à s'écarter de l'omnipotence élégante et anonyme des polices Frutiger, Meta et Thesis.

Le nom de la fonte conçue pour Hanovre n'est pas uniquement un jeu de mots sur les dernières années du siècle passé. Il cache une référence plus profonde. C'est Bell Centennial, la fonte créée par Matthew Carter pour les annuaires téléphoniques américains, qui a servi de prototype. Comme Bell, Hannover a l'atout économique d'être remarquablement adaptée à l'utilisation dans les formulaires et les tableaux, en petit corps de caractère.

*Elle fait aussi preuve de personnalité dans les applications d'impression, où, une fois agrandie, elle démontre d'intéressantes qualités ornementales.*

L'identité visuelle de la ville de Hanovre[2] est une création originale mais consciente de la tradition. Globalement, elle se base sur des considérations fonctionnelles, et ses qualités esthétiques se manifestent avant tout à travers sa fonction. Heureusement, ce chemin ne mène pas forcément à l'attitude puritaine ou militante de certains minimalistes. Une série d'exemples (publications, visuels d'expositions) démontrent une capacité à l'excentricité, mais ne menacent ni la grille de montage ni l'uniformité de la présentation de la marque.

Cette interaction entre la logique et l'excès subtil a également une tradition à

muss bei einer Stadt in neuen Dimensionen denken. Es gibt nur wenige Unternehmen, die ähnlich inhomogen sind wie eine Kommune." [Christoph Eichenseer].

Die wesentliche Substanz der visuellen Erscheinung Hannovers ist die Typografie: Sie vereint Markensystematik und Corporate Design. Die eigens für die Stadt entwickelte Schriftenfamilie – „Hannover Millennial"[1] – gelingt der dreifache Spagat: Sie ist zeitgemäß, sie ist unaufdringlich, sie differenziert. Diese Balance ist nicht selbstverständlich: Es ist nicht einfach, sich der Norm zu widersetzen, ohne laut zu werden. In den späten 1990ern galt es, sich formal von der gesichtlos-eleganten Omnipräsenz der Frutiger, Meta und Thesis abzusetzen.

Der Name von Hannovers Hausschrift ist nicht nur eine ironische Anspielung auf die letzten Jahre vor der Jahrtausendwende. In diesem Namen verbirgt sich eine weitere Referenz: Als Prototyp diente die „Bell Centennial", die von Matthew Carter für die amerikanischen Telefonbücher geschnitten worden war. Wie die Bell ist die Hannover ökonomisch und hervorragend geeignet für Formular- und Tabellensatz in kleinen Punktgrößen.

*Ihren überraschenden Charakter zeigt sie in Akzidenzanwendungen, wo sich aus funktionalen Elementen durch die Vergrößerung eine ornamentale Ästhetik entwickelt.*

Bei aller Eigenwilligkeit ist das Corporate Design der Stadt Hannover[2] im Bewusstsein der Tradition entstanden. Im Ganzen basiert es auf funktionalen Überlegungen, und seine Ästhetik manifestiert sich erst durch seine Funktion. Erfreulicherweise führt dieser Weg nicht zwangsläufig zur puristisch-militanten „Weniger-ist-mehr"-Haltung. Eine Reihe von Beispielen (Publikationen, Ausstellungsgrafik) zeigt ein exzentrisches Design, das weder das Gestaltungsraster verletzt, noch die Einheitlichkeit des Markenauftritts in Frage stellt.

be ignored when working on Hanover's new brand image. "The most important thing is to never do it the way someone has done it before you."

*In times of visual saturation and indistinct form and textual communication, it is becoming ever more difficult to efficiently apply classic – aggressive, solid, though strong and clear-cut brand models. Hanover's visual presence is based on a reduced open brand system, which displays its effect first in function – through its changeability and connectivity.*

This is not simply a gesture in innovation of form. It is also perhaps a metaphor for the way in which the public administration should be presenting itself to the public; flexible and capable of dialogue.

Hanovre. Kurt Schwitters en personne a standardisé les imprimés de la municipalité de Hanovre à la fin des années 1920, de façon moderne et catégorique. Cela s'est passé bien avant la naissance du terme d'identité visuelle. L'héritage du design de Schwitters, et par-dessus tout sa façon de penser, ne pouvaient être ignorés dans la conception de la nouvelle image de la ville. « L'essentiel est de ne jamais faire ce que quelqu'un a fait avant vous. »

*À une époque de saturation visuelle et de communication de forme et de contenu indistincts, il est de plus en plus difficile d'imposer un modèle classique qui soit simple et accrocheur. La présence visuelle de Hanovre est basée sur un système iconique ouvert dont l'effet apparaît d'abord dans la fonction, à travers sa modularité et sa connectivité.*

Ce n'est pas seulement un geste d'innovation dans la forme. C'est peut-être aussi une métaphore de la manière dont devrait se présenter l'administration publique aux citoyens, flexible et ouverte au dialogue.

Auch diese Wechselwirkung von Logik und subtilem Exzess hat in Hannover Tradition. Kein geringerer als Kurt Schwitters hat in den späten 1920ern im Auftrag der Stadtverwaltung Hannovers ihre Drucksachen auf eine kompromisslos modernistische Art vereinheitlicht. Dies passierte lange, bevor der Begriff „Corporate Design" erfunden wurde. Schwitters gestalterisches Erbe, vor allem aber seine Denkweise, konnte man bei der Arbeit an Hannovers neuem Markenimage nicht ignorieren. „Das Wichtigste ist: Mach es niemals so, wie es jemand vor dir gemacht hat."

*In Zeiten visueller Übersättigung und unscharfer formaler und inhaltlicher Positionen wird es immer schwieriger, klassische – offensive, solide, aber starre und brüchige – Markenmodelle effizient anzuwenden. Hannovers visueller Auftritt basiert auf einer reduzierten, offenen Markensystematik, welche erst in der Funktion – durch ihre Wandelbarkeit und Verbindungsfähigkeit – ihre Wirkung entfaltet.*

Dies ist nicht nur eine Geste formaler Innovation. Vielleicht ist es auch eine Metapher für die Art, wie sich die öffentliche Verwaltung den Bürgern gegenüber darstellen sollte: flexibel und dialogfähig.

---

1. The *Hannover Millennial* typeface family was optimised in 2003 and added to; it comprises seven designs and is available at <www.die-gestalten.de>.
2. The corporate design for the City of Hanover has been developed by HardCase design on behalf of the advertising agency Odeon Zwo, Hanover, between 1996 and 1999. The design of the trademark is based on an idea from Michael Kronacher.

1. La police de caractères Hannover Millennial a été optimisée et complétée en 2003. Elle comprend 7 fontes et est disponible sur le site <www.die-gestalten.de>.
2. L'identité visuelle de la ville de Hanovre a été développée par Hardcase Design pour le compte de l'agence de publicité Odeon Zwo de Hanovre, entre 1996 et 1999. Le design de la marque vient d'une idée de Michael Kronacher.

1. Die Schriftenfamilie Hannover Millennial wurde 2003 optimiert und ergänzt: Sie umfasst sieben Schnitte und ist über <www.die-gestalten.de> erhältlich.
2. Das Corporate Design für die Stadt Hannover ist von HardCase Design 1996 bis 1999 im Auftrag der Werbeagentur Odeon Zwo, Hannover, entwickelt worden. Die Gestaltung des Markenzeichens basiert auf einer Idee von Michael Kronacher.

# Das dritte Jahr tausend beginnt in Hannover.

Standort ) Hannover

;

**Left:** *Brochure cover /// À gauche :*
*Couverture de brochure ///* **Links:** *Deckblatt*
*Broschüre*

**Right:** *official logo of the city of Hanover ///* **À**
**droite** : *le logo officiel de la Ville de Hanovre*
*///* **Rechts:** *Offizielles Logo der Stadt*
*Hannover*

# Biography
# Dmitri Lavrow (HardCase Design)

**www.hardcase.de**
Location: Berlin, Germany
Year of foundation: 1994

Position: Founder/
Creative Director

Awards: Type Directors Club
New York and Tokyo; Hong
Kong International Poster

Design Triennial; 100 Posters
of the Year. German Corporate
Design Award

*Dmitri Lavrow was born in the St. Petersburg (which at that time had a different name). He studied mathematics, and, after having graduated from the local university, started working as a photographer and designer. In the late 80s he transferred several Latin typefaces into Cyrillic. In 1991 he moved to Germany and worked for several advertising agencies. In 1994 he started HardCase Design. Lavrow has designed book covers, annual reports, CD and LP jackets, advertising campaigns, invitation cards, posters, web sites, exhibitions, logotypes, fashion catalogues, stationeries, orientation systems. HardCase Design has been involved in creating a considerable number of large scale territorial and institutional identity programmes, among others: City of Hanover, Federal Government of Germany, Federal State of Hesse, City of Rome.*

*Dimitri Lavrov est né à Saint-Pétersbourg (qui à l'époque avait un autre nom). Il étudie les mathématiques et, après avoir obtenu son diplôme universitaire, commence à travailler en tant que photographe et designer. À la fin des années 1980, il transpose plusieurs polices de caractères latins en cyrillique. En 1991, il part vivre en Allemagne et travaille pour plusieurs agences de publicité. En 1994, il fonde HardCase Design. Dimitri Lavrov a conçu des couvertures de livres, des rapports annuels, des couvertures de CD et de 33 tours, des campagnes de publicité, des cartes d'invitation, des affiches, des*

*sites Internet, des expositions, des logotypes, des catalogues de mode, des fournitures de bureau, des systèmes d'orientation. HardCase Design a participé à la création d'un nombre considérable de programmes d'identité territoriale et institutionnelle à grande échelle, entre autres : la Ville de Hanovre, le gouvernement fédéral d'Allemagne, l'État fédéral de Hesse, la Ville de Rome.*

*Dmitri Lavrow wurde in St. Petersburg geboren (das damals noch Leningrad hieß). Er studierte Mathematik und begann nach seinem Abschluss als Fotograf und Designer zu arbeiten. In den späten 1980er-Jahren übertrug er mehrere lateinische Schriftarten ins Kyrillische. 1991 zog er nach Deutschland und arbeitete für einige Werbeagenturen. 1994 gründete er HardCase Design. Lavrow hat Buchcover, Geschäftsberichte, CD- und LP-Hüllen, Werbekampagnen, Einladungskarten, Poster, Websites, Ausstellungen, Logos, Modekataloge, Schreibwaren und Ordnungssysteme entworfen. HardCase Design hat an verschiedenen großen Corporate-Design-Programmen mitgearbeitet, darunter Stadt Hannover, Deutsche Bundesregierung, Bundesland Hessen, Stadt Rom.*

# THE ARGENTINEAN NATIONAL IDENTITY

Like many Argentinians, in the midst of the 2002 crisis, we found ourselves asking ourselves «What are we going to do?» The events called for serious thought, the eyes of the world were on us and it was hard – with the din of the *cacerolazo* still echoing in the background – to face our image in the mirror. We decided to react through what we do – design. Suffering from *Argentinianism*, we set about externalising it by means of icons. And we became immersed in an argument which was not only aesthetic but also about selection, and which was, of course, ideological. «Whether the *milanesa* is more Argentinian than the *empanada* or whether Coca Sarli should be on TV as much as Monzón», were just some of the subjects that kept us going throughout that time. Thus arose *industriargentina*, a book, as yet unpublished, complemented by other printed products, and the launch, in 2005, of the *Nobrand* line of clothing. That was our response, how we discovered, almost unknown to ourselves, how to put on the t-shirt.

Comme beaucoup d'Argentins, pris dans la crise de l'année 2002, nous nous sommes demandé : « Qu'allons-nous faire ? » Les événements exigeaient une réflexion sérieuse, le monde entier nous observait et, le vacarme du *cacerolazo* (manifestation où les protestataires tapent sur des casseroles) toujours en fond sonore, il était pénible de se regarder en face. Nous avons décidé de réagir à travers notre travail : le design. Souffrant d' « argentinianisme », nous avons entrepris de l'extérioriser dans des icônes. Nous nous sommes plongés dans des discussions qui concernaient à la fois la sélection et les choix esthétiques, et qui avaient bien sûr un caractère idéologique. La *milanesa* est-elle plus argentine que l'*empanada*, Coca Sarli devrait-il être aussi médiatisé que Monzón, voici quelques-uns des sujets qui nous ont occupés à l'époque. C'est ainsi que naquit « Industriargentina », un ouvrage inédit à ce jour, suivi d'autres publications, et que la ligne de vêtements Nobrand fut lancée. C'était là notre réponse, une manière presque inconsciente de nous assumer.

Wie viele andere Argentinier auch sahen wir uns während der Krise von 2002 mit der Frage konfrontiert: „Was sollen wir machen?" Der Zeitpunkt zwang uns zur Reflexion, man beobachtete uns aus dem Ausland und es kostete uns einiges, uns dem dargebotenen Spiegelbild zu stellen, da das Protestrasseln der Kochtöpfe im Hintergrund noch nicht abgeklungen war. Wir entschieden uns dafür, die Stirn auf dem uns vertrauten Terrain des Designs zu bieten. Da die argentinische Identität litt, kam uns der Einfall, sie durch Ikonen gewissermaßen zu exterritorialisieren. Und wir stellten uns einer nicht nur ästhetischen Diskussion, sondern einer, die sich um Auswahl drehte und natürlich ideologischer Natur war. „Wenn paniertes Schnitzel argentinischer ist als gefüllte Teigtaschen oder *Sarli-Cola*, dann verdient es auch, genauso oft wie *Monzón* zu erscheinen" – das war nur eines der Themen, das uns über Monate begleitete. So entstand *Industriargentina*, ein noch unveröffentlichtes Buch, das von anderen Printmaterialien und der Lancierung der Kleidermarke „*Nobrand*"

Previous spread: *Maradona, Carlos Gardel, Juan Manuel Fangio, Evita Peron* /// **Double page précédente** : *Maradona, Carlos Gardel, Juan Manuel Fangio, Evita Peron* /// **Vorherige Seite**: *Maradona, Carlos Gardel, Juan Manuel Fangio, Evita Peron*

Left: *Che Guevera* /// **À gauche** : *Che Guevera* /// **Links**: *Che Guevera*

Above: *BKF Chair, Coffee, Charango, Bandoneon, Siku flute, Native* /// **Ci-dessus** : *fauteuil BKF, café, charango, bandonéon, flûte siku, autochtone* /// **Oben**: *BKF Stuhl, Kaffee, Charango, Bandoneon, Siku-Flöte, Indio*

**BE.**

*By Norberto Chaves*

National identity is nothing other than a list of recurrent features, tenacious and unchanging, transmitted involuntarily from generation to generation and transcending the boundaries of social class. A menu which articulates, in space and time, this «us».

*These features are slowly hatched, in silence; they then blossom and manifest themselves in distinctive and autonomous actions. Deep down, what characterises them in not so much their singularity as their autonomy. Identity does not ask permission, for it is not voluntary but rather inevitable: while one is, one doesn't notice. One is universal.*

In order to be, it is necessary to be different: we are what the other is not. If some primitive cultures thought that

**ÊTRE.**

*Par Norberto Chaves*

L'identité nationale n'est rien d'autre qu'un ensemble de caractéristiques récurrentes, invariables et tenaces, transmises involontairement de génération en génération, et qui dépassent les frontières de classes. Une carte qui articule le « nous », dans le temps et dans l'espace.

*Ces caractéristiques éclosent doucement, en silence. Puis elles s'épanouissent et se manifestent à travers des actions singulières et autonomes. Au fond, ce qui les caractérise, c'est moins leur singularité que leur autonomie. L'identité ne demande pas la permission, car elle n'est pas volontaire, mais plutôt inévitable. Je suis, mais sans m'en rendre compte. Le « un » est universel.*

Pour être, il faut se différencier. On est ce que l'autre n'est pas. Si les individus de

im Jahre 2005 ergänzt wurde. Das war unsere Antwort, die fast unbewusst entdeckte Art, uns das Nationaltrikot überzustreifen.

**SEIN.**

*Von Norberto Chaves*

Nationale Identität ist nichts anderes als eine Liste von wiederkehrenden, bleibenden, unveränderlichen Eigenschaften, die unfreiwillig von Generation zu Generation weitergegeben werden und die Grenzen sozialer Klassen überschreiten. Ein Menü das dieses „wir" in Zeit und Raum ausdrückt.

*Diese Eigenschaften entstehen still und leise; sie wachsen und manifestieren sich in unverwechselbaren und autonomen Handlungsweisen. Im Grunde werden sie eher durch ihre Autonomie als ihre Einzigartigkeit beschrieben. Identität fragt nach keiner Erlaubnis, denn sie entsteht nicht freiwillig, sondern eher unvermeidlich:*

From left to right: *Alfajor, T-bone steak, poncho, Cataratas del Iguazu* /// **De gauche à droite** : *alfajor, entrecôte, poncho, les chutes d'Iguazu* /// **Von links nach rechts:** *Alfajor, T-Bone-Steak, Poncho, Cataratas del Iguazu*

calling themselves «human beings» was enough, that was almost certainly due to the fact that they had enough in knowing themselves to be different from nature around them. They were «a» culture, only one among many; yet they did not know. They were then, humanity. The «other» was all of nature. Like in the Garden of Eden. They were «rough and ready». That is, in the beginning, for us to be aware of our singularity we had enough with a comparison with the animals. But to be a nation, other nations are needed. For collective identity to flower as consciousness, we need others. And, fundamentally, we need others to oppose us. Without rivals, nobody is anything. That's us.

The restlessness of consciousness

Those spontaneous gestures of sovereignty that made us are, sooner or later, objected to by someone, questioned: peace is a bird of another world. Thus, the legitimacy of that sovereignty is questioned: identity then emerges and be-

certaines cultures primitives se contentaient de se dénommer « êtres humains », c'est très probablement parce qu'il leur suffisait de se savoir différents de la nature qui les entourait. Ils représentaient « une » culture, seulement une parmi d'autres, mais ils l'ignoraient. Ils étaient ainsi l'humanité. L'autre était la nature. Comme dans le jardin d'Éden. C'était rudimentaire. À l'origine, pour se rendre compte de notre singularité, il nous suffisait de nous comparer aux animaux. Mais pour être une nation, il faut d'autres nations. Pour que l'identité collective devienne une prise de conscience, nous avons besoin des autres. Fondamentalement, il nous faut nous opposer aux autres. Sans rival, nous ne sommes rien. C'est notre cas.

Les remous de la conscience

Les gestes spontanés de souveraineté qui nous définissent sont tôt ou tard récusés et remis en question par les autres : la paix est un oiseau d'un autre monde. Avec la contestation de cette légitimité, l'identité émerge et devient prise de

*Während man sie lebt, bemerkt man sie nicht. Man ist universal.*

Um zu sein, ist es notwendig, anders zu sein: Wir sind, was der andere nicht ist. Einige primitive Kulturen dachten, sich selbst „Mensch" zu nennen reiche aus, und zwar deshalb, weil es genügte, sich selbst als anders als die Natur um sie herum zu erkennen. Sie waren „eine" Kultur, allerdings nur eine von vielen – ohne es zu wissen. Damals waren sie die Menschheit. Das „andere" war die Natur. Wie im Garten Eden. Das bedeutet, um uns unserer Einzigartigkeit bewusst zu sein, genügte es, uns mit den Tieren zu vergleichen. Aber um eine Nation zu sein, braucht es andere Nationen. Für die Entwicklung einer kollektiven Identität brauchen wir andere. Im Grunde genommen brauchen wir andere gegen uns. Ohne Gegner ist niemand etwas. Das sind wir.

Die Unruhe des Bewusstseins

Diese spontanen Gesten der Souveränität, die uns ausmachen, werden früher oder

comes consciousness. It becomes demands, action programmes, a search. Anthems are born. «There arises from the face of the earth a new and glorious nation». For that it was necessary to «overcome the lion».

He who overwhelms or invades, tends to do so in the name of what is universal. The overwhelmed, in contrast, demands recognition of his individuality. Nationalism is essentially reactive, and there is no harm in it. It is natural that it should be so. Nobody exists other than in opposition to someone else. Pacifists are good people who lack an historical culture.

Colonies, former colonies and neo-colonies are the laboratory of permanently rewoven identities. No imperial power spends so much time on being, taken up as they are by the enormous task of dominating. The dominator must always have an element of stupidity: his power incapacitates him. Confirmed in his hegemony, the powerful does not ever doubt. That is, he does not ever think. He merely acts. The dominated, on the other hand, does nothing but doubt: his question regarding identity arises, for this identity is endangered, all the certainties concerning his being have been thrown into crisis, other reasons also question it.

*If the question exists, it is because something has crumbled: a continuity, a unity, an all. When we ask ourselves about our identity we are bending down to pick up the shattered shards of a broken discourse.*

Yet, in this task, consciousness stumbles and hesitates. It fails. It reassembles the broken pieces in the wrong order. It seems to have been made to make mistakes. In its compulsion to capture being, it provides a caricature of its own identity and, sooner or later, betrays it. Yet identity, imperviously entrenched in the ineffable, immune to all forms of debasement, perseveres, flows, like a underground river, and reappears in involuntary reflex actions: gestures, speech, the last bastions of nationality.

conscience. Elle appelle des exigences, un programme d'action, une quête. La création d'un hymne national. « S'élève alors à la face du monde une nouvelle nation glorieuse. » Pour cela, il fallait d'abord « terrasser le lion ».

Celui qui écrase ou envahit le fait souvent au nom de quelque chose d'universel. Celui qui est envahi, à l'inverse, exige la reconnaissance de son individualité. Le nationalisme est essentiellement réactif, et il n'y a pas de mal à ça. C'est un mouvement naturel. Personne n'existe hors de l'opposition à un autre. Les pacifistes sont des gens sympathiques qui manquent de culture historique.

Les colonies, les anciennes colonies et les néo-colonies sont des laboratoires où se retissent en permanence les identités. Aucun pouvoir impérialiste ne s'interroge sur la sienne, trop occupé qu'il est par son travail de domination. Le dominateur doit toujours être un peu stupide, son pouvoir l'handicape. Confirmé dans son hégémonie, le puissant ne doute même pas. À vrai dire, il ne réfléchit pas, il se contente d'agir. Le dominé, en revanche, ne fait que douter. Il questionne son identité, car elle est menacée, et le bouleversement de ses certitudes n'est qu'une conséquence parmi d'autres.

*Si la question se pose, c'est que quelque chose s'est effondré, une continuité, une unité, un tout. S'interroger sur son identité, c'est comme se baisser pour ramasser les tessons épars d'un discours fracturé. Et ce faisant, la conscience vacille et hésite. Elle échoue.*

Elle recompose les morceaux dans le désordre. À croire qu'elle a été conçue pour se tromper. Dans sa précipitation, elle n'offre qu'une caricature de sa propre identité et la trahit tôt ou tard. Mais l'identité, retranchée hermétiquement dans l'ineffable, immunisée contre toute forme de dépréciation, persévère, coule comme une rivière souterraine et ressurgit dans d'involontaires actions réflexes. Les gestes, les paroles, derniers bastions de la nationalité.

später von anderen in Frage gestellt: *Peace is a bird of another world*. Dadurch wird die Legitimität unserer Souveränität in Frage gestellt: So entsteht Identität und wird zum Bewusstsein. Sie wird zu Forderungen, Aktionsprogrammen, einer Suche. Hymnen werden geboren. „There arises from the face of the earth a new and glorious nation". Dafür war es notwendig, to „overcome the lion".

Wer erobert oder überfällt, tendiert dazu, im Namen des Universellen zu handeln. Im Gegensatz dazu fordert der Eroberte die Anerkennung seiner Individualität. Nationalismus ist von seinem Wesen her reaktiv, und es ist auch nichts dabei; es ist nur natürlich, dass es so ist. Niemand existiert in anderer Form als im Gegensatz zu jemand anderem. Pazifisten sind gute Menschen, denen es an einer historischen Kultur fehlt.

Kolonien, ehemalige Kolonien und Neo-Kolonien sind das Versuchslabor von permanent neu miteinander verflochtenen Identitäten. Keine Imperialmacht verbringt so viel Zeit mit dem Leben an sich, da sie mit der schwierigen Aufgabe des Herrschens beschäftigt ist. Der Herrscher muss immer einen Anteil von Dummheit in sich haben: Seine Macht macht ihn unfähig. In seiner Hegemonie bestätigt, zweifelt der Mächtige nicht. Er handelt nur. Auf der anderen Seite tun die Unterdrückten nichts anderes, als zu zweifeln: Die Frage bezüglich ihrer Identität entsteht, denn die Identität ist in Gefahr, alle Sicherheiten bezüglich ihrer Existenz sind in eine Krise geraten, andere Gründe kommen hinzu.

*Die Frage existiert, weil etwas ins Wanken geraten ist: eine Kontinuität, eine Einheit, ein alles. Wenn wir uns nach unserer Identität fragen, bücken wir uns nach den verstreuten Scherben eines zerbrochenen Diskurses.*

Bei dieser Aufgabe jedoch stolpert und zögert das Bewusstsein. Es versagt. Es setzt die zerbrochenen Stücke in der falschen Reihenfolge zusammen. Es scheint zum Irren gemacht zu sein. In

## The puzzle

A collage, the arbitrary accumulation of unconnected fragments, of unknown origin and meaning, imposed as natural by force of simple reiteration, a chaotic catalogue assembled according to a random principle, identity is not an articulate discourse, rather mere enumeration: not a paragraph but a list. «La vidriera irrespetuosa de los cambalaches».[1]

*Celebrated allegory of ethical scandal, it should be reread, from time to time, as a rigorous surrealistic metaphor of identity: it is not so much a catastrophe as the genuine image of the insuperable chaos of our historical condition.*

The smell of the roast overflying the kosher gives it a certain flavour of *milonga*. The dessert milk-trained taste bud enables the ear to hear, uniquely, the voice of the voiceless. And the cheers for Maradona's goal become the background music for the Iguazú Falls. Above or from behind this *Cambalache*, we hear the regular repetition, like an automatic answering machine, of the fateful warning of our founding father: «you will be what you should be, or otherwise, you'll be nothing».

## Le puzzle

Collage, accumulation arbitraire de fragments décousus, d'origine et de sens inconnus, imposés comme naturels par la simple force de la répétition, catalogue chaotique assemblé selon le principe du hasard, l'identité n'est pas un discours articulé, mais plutôt une simple énumération, une liste et non un paragraphe. « *La vidriera irrespetuosa de los cambalaches* »[1].

*Célèbre allégorie de scandale moral, elle devrait être relue de temps en temps comme une rigoureuse métaphore surréaliste de l'identité. C'est moins une catastrophe qu'une véritable image du chaos insurmontable de notre condition historique.*

L'odeur du rôti flottant sur le repas kasher lui donne un certain goût de *milonga* (sorte de tango). La papille gustative, désorientée, permet à l'oreille d'entendre, de façon unique, la voix des sans voix. Et le but acclamé de Maradona devient la musique de fond des chutes d'Iguazú. Par-delà ce *cambalache*, on entend la répétition automatique, comme un répondeur téléphonique, de la mise en garde fatale de notre père fondateur : « Tu seras ce que tu dois être, sinon tu ne seras rien. »

seinem Zwang, das Sein zu erfassen, liefert es eine Karikatur seiner eigenen Identität und betrügt es früher oder später. Dennoch: Identität, fest verwurzelt im Unaussprechlichen, ist immun gegen alle Formen von Entwürdigung, hält durch und fließt wie ein unterirdischer Fluss und erscheint wieder in unfreiwilligen Reflexhandlungen: Gesten, Sprachen – die letzten Bastionen der Nationalität.

## Das Puzzle

Als eine Collage, die zufällige Zusammenstellung nicht miteinander verbundener Fragmente, von ungewisser Herkunft und Bedeutung, natürlich erzwungen durch die Kraft simpler Wiederholung, ein chaotischer, nach dem Zufallsprinzip zusammen gestellter Katalog, ist Identität kein artikulierter Diskurs, sondern eine bloße Aufzählung: kein Paragraf, sondern eine Liste. *„La vidriera irrespetuosa de los cambalaches"*.[1]

*Gefeierte Allegorie eines ethischen Skandals, sollte sie von Zeit zu Zeit als eine rigorose surrealistische Metapher neu interpretiert werden: Es ist weniger eine Katastrophe als das wahrhaftige Bild des unüberwindlichen Chaos unseres historischen Zustands.*

Der Geruch des Bratens, der den Kosheren streift, erzeugt einen gewissen Geschmack von *milonga*. Die sensible Geschmacksknospe verhilft dem Ohr, die Stimme des Stimmlosen zu hören. Und der Jubel über Maradonas Tor wird zum Hintergrund für die Musik der Iguassu-Wasserfälle. Über oder hinter dieser *cambalache* hören wir die regelmäßige Wiederholung der schicksalhaften Warnung wie einen automatischen Anrufbeantworter: „Du wirst sein, was du sein sollst, oder du wirst nichts sein."

---

1. Author's note: A line from the tango «Cambalache» by Enrique Santos Discépolo, which was banned under the military dictatorships. The lyrics denounce the corruption and impunity of the 1930s and are still surprisingly valid today.

1 Note de l'auteur : Vers du tango « Cambalache » (bric-à-brac, brocante), de Enrique Santos Discépolo, censuré sous les dictatures militaires. Les paroles dénoncent la corruption et l'impunité des années 1930 et restent étonnamment d'actualité.

1 Bemerkung des Autors: Ein Zitat aus dem Tango «Cambalache» von Enrique Santos Discépolo, der unter den Militärdiktaturen verboten war. Der Text prangert die Korruption und Straflosigkeit der 30er Jahre an und ist noch bemerkenswert aktuell.

**Above:** *Project launch ///* **Ci-dessus :** *Lancement du projet ///* **Oben:** *Projekteinführung*

**Below:** *Merchandising material ///* **Ci-dessous :** *Articles de merchandising ///* **Unten:** *Verkaufsmaterial*

Right: *Argentina ///* À droite : *L'Argentine ///*
Rechts: *Argentinien*

# Biography
# ImagenHB

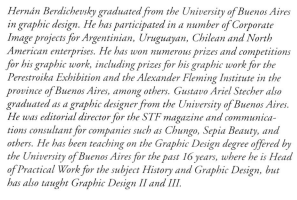

**www.imagenhb.com**          Year of foundation: 1995
Location: Buenos Aires,
Argentina

*Hernán Berdichevsky graduated from the University of Buenos Aires in graphic design. He has participated in a number of Corporate Image projects for Argentinian, Uruguayan, Chilean and North American enterprises. He has won numerous prizes and competitions for his graphic work, including prizes for his graphic work for the Perestroika Exhibition and the Alexander Fleming Institute in the province of Buenos Aires, among others. Gustavo Ariel Stecher also graduated as a graphic designer from the University of Buenos Aires. He was editorial director for the STF magazine and communications consultant for companies such as Chungo, Sepia Beauty, and others. He has been teaching on the Graphic Design degree offered by the University of Buenos Aires for the past 16 years, where he is Head of Practical Work for the subject History and Graphic Design, but has also taught Graphic Design II and III.*

*Hernán Berdichevsky est diplômé en graphisme de l'Université de Buenos Aires. Il a participé à de nombreux projets concernant l'identité visuelle d'entreprises américaines, argentines, uruguayennes et chiliennes. Il a remporté de nombreux prix et concours, entre autres pour ses travaux graphiques sur l'exposition Pérestroïka et l'Institut Alexander Fleming dans la province de Buenos Aires. Gustavo Ariel Stecher est lui aussi diplômé en graphisme de l'Université de Buenos Aires. Il a été directeur de la rédaction du magazine STF et consul-*

*tant en communication pour des sociétés comme Chungo et Sepia Beauty. Il enseigne le design graphique à l'université de Buenos Aires depuis seize ans. Il dirige les travaux pratiques de l'option Histoire et Graphisme, et a aussi donné les cours de deuxième et troisième cycle en design graphique.*

*Hernán Berdichevsky absolvierte seinen Hochschulabschluss in Grafikdesign an der Universität von Buenos Aires. Er arbeitete an vielen Corporate Identity-Projekten für Unternehmen in Argentinien, Uruguay, Chile und Nordamerika. Mit seinen grafischen Arbeiten gewann er viele Preise und Wettbewerbe, unter anderem für seine Arbeit an der Perestroika-Ausstellung und dem Alexander-Fleming-Institut in der Provinz von Buenos Aires. Gustavo Ariel Stecher schloss sein Grafikdesignstudium an der Universität von Buenos Aires ab. Er wurde leitender Redakteur des STF-Magazins und Kommunikationsberater für Firmen wie Chungo oder Sepia Beauty. Seit 16 Jahren unterrichtet er an der Universität von Buenos Aires Grafikdesign und ist dort Praxisleiter für die Fächer Geschichte und Grafikdesign; außerdem unterrichtete er Grafikdesign II und III.*

# MINI: RELAUNCH OF A CULT BRAND

Only very rarely does the opportunity of creating a new brand in the automobile industry come up; many once famous brands have disappeared from view in recent decades as a result of economic consolidation processes.

The MINI was British design engineer Sir Alec Isigonis' inspired contribution to human transport. Perhaps it was because it succeeded in getting the maximum use out of the smallest space, that this idea quickly became more than simply a means of transport. Its extraordinary driving characteristics and its unique spatial concept rapidly transformed the MINI into a cult object, which developed into an icon for alternative lifestyle and subculture. From professed Beatle fans to Enzo Ferrari, whether as a racing car or as a lifestyle symbol, the MINI has always been able to captivate people with its great individuality and attitude. Excellent prerequisites, then, for the BMW Group to orientate this brand for the future as a successful model against the rather emo-

Il est très rare d'avoir l'occasion de créer une nouvelle marque dans l'industrie automobile, et de nombreuses marques jadis célèbres ont disparu ces dernières décennies suite à des opérations de fusion économique.

La MINI, contribution inspirée aux moyens de transports humains, est l'œuvre de l'ingénieur en design britannique Sir Alec Isigonis. Réussissant à tirer le maximum d'un minimum d'espace, le résultat a dépassé le simple moyen de transport. Ses étonnantes qualités de conduite et son concept spatial unique ont vite transformé la MINI en objet culte, emblématique d'un mode de vie alternatif. Des fans de la Coccinelle à Enzo Ferrari, la MINI a toujours séduit le public par son esprit et son originalité, qu'on la voie comme une voiture de course ou comme un symbole social. Les meilleures conditions étaient donc réunies pour que le groupe BMW en fasse à l'avenir un modèle à succès dans le segment des petites voitures, où la concurrence s'attache plutôt à la fonctionnalité

Nur noch selten bietet sich in der Automobilindustrie die Gelegenheit, eine Marke neu aufzubauen, sind doch in den letzten Jahrzehnten viele einst berühmte Marken durch wirtschaftliche Konsolidierungsprozesse von der Bildfläche verschwunden.

Obwohl oder gerade weil MINI der geniale Beitrag des britischen Konstrukteurs Sir Alec Isigonis war, für die Mobilität der Menschen auf kleinstem Raum den maximalen Nutzen zu erreichen, wurde diese Idee schnell mehr als nur zu ein Fortbewegungsmittel. Seine außerordentlichen Fahreigenschaften und das einzigartige Raumkonzept machten den MINI zu einem Kultobjekt, das sich über Jahrzehnte hinweg ohne nennenswerte technische Veränderungen zur Ikone für Andersdenken und subkulturellen Lebensstil entwickelte. Bekennende Fans von den Beatles bis zu Enzo Ferrari, ob als Rennauto oder Lebenshaltung – immer konnte der MINI durch seine große Eigenwilligkeit und Haltung die Menschen in seinen Bann ziehen. Gute

50

tionless and functionally orientated competition in the small car segment; the MINI is practically the only vehicle which delivers not just useful service, but also brings emotional expression to a way of life. An outstanding starting position for the first small car in the premium segment.

*When this product was new it was already the ideal embodiment of this claim. Physiognomy and character were interpreted for the era in which it was manufactured and the attractive originality was combined with the most modern technology, of the time.*

This formula was also useful for the further development of the brand identity. The trademark was thus distilled from numerous vintage model badges. The most characteristic and finest aspects of all of them are concentrated in a new and brilliant form which promises finesse and emotion. A colour palette

et la neutralité. La MINI est quasiment le seul véhicule qui ne s'appuie pas uniquement sur l'utilité, mais qui apporte une touche émotionnelle à l'expression d'un mode de vie. C'est une position de départ remarquable pour la première petite voiture à figurer dans le créneau des véhicules haut de gamme.

*Quand le produit était encore nouveau, il incarnait déjà cette revendication. Sa physionomie et sa personnalité étaient déjà le reflet de son époque, et son originalité se conjuguait avec les technologies les plus modernes.*

La formule fut conservée pour le développement de l'identité de marque. La nouvelle série est donc un condensé des caractéristiques d'anciens modèles. On y retrouve les éléments les plus distinctifs, concentrés dans une nouvelle forme qui promet élégance et sensations. Elle est déclinée dans une palette de couleurs qui, sans être inédite, apparaît plus intense et plus fraîche. Le noir est la nou-

Voraussetzungen also für die BMW Group, diese Marke zukunftsgerichtet als Erfolgsmodell gegen die eher emotionslose, funktional bestimmte Konkurrenz im Kleinwagensegment auszurichten: Der MINI ist praktisch das einzige Fahrzeug, das nicht nur vernünftigen Nutzen erbringt, sondern emotional eine Lebenshaltung zum Ausdruck bringt. Eine hervorragende Ausgangsposition für den ersten Kleinwagen im Premiumsegment.

*Schon das neue Produkt verkörperte diesen Anspruch idealtypisch: Physiognomie und Charakter wurden zeitgemäß interpretiert, die sympathische Eigenständigkeit von einst mit modernster Technik kombiniert.*

Dieses Muster galt es auch für die Weiterentwicklung der Markenidentität zu nutzen. So wurde das Markenzeichen aus unzähligen historischen Modellplaketten destilliert. Das Typische und das Beste von allem, konzentriert auf eine neue, brillante Form,

From left to right: *website developed to support the correct use of the identity* /// **De gauche à droite :** *Le site Internet créé pour encourager une utilisation correcte de l'identité* /// **Von links nach rechts:** *Die Webseite wurde entwickelt, um die richtige Verwendung der Identity zu unterstützen*

Next spread: *identity guideline, release promotion (second page top) and promotional material (second page bottom)* /// **Double page suivante :** *Lignes directrices de l'identité, promotion de lancement (en haut de la deuxième page) et articles promotionnels (en bas de la deuxième page)* /// **Nächste Seite:** *Identity-Richtlinie, Einführungswerbung (zweite Seite oben) und Werbematerial (zweite Seite unten)*

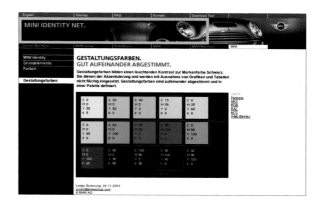

which in fact has not been newly invented, but which appears to have been completely freshly defined and intensified, complements the MINI's new dominant base colour of black, which creates a platform for the other colours and design elements.

**The MINI typeface, which developed out of the available typeface, also contributes to an original and consistent sharpening of the brand image.**

Not least, powerful and emotional imagery also contributes to the visualisation of this claim: MINI stands for modern urban lifestyle; extrovert, chic and cosmopolitan. However, a central and immediately recognisable element of the new MINI brand appearance is the so-called *frame*. This is a presentation platform for a young, dynamic market; the communicative anchor for the entire MINI experiential chain. Uniform in shape, while at the same time playfully variable, it holds the MINI communica-

velle couleur de base dominante de la MINI, et elle est le point de départ pour les autres couleurs et les autres éléments du design.

*La typographie du logo, adaptée de la typographie d'origine, contribue aussi à affiner le visuel de la marque de façon exclusive et cohérente.*

Les images puissantes et chargées d'émotion véhiculées par la publicité réaffirment les valeurs et le positionnement du constructeur. La MINI incarne un mode de vie actuel et urbain, elle est extravertie, chic et cosmopolite. Un élément central et immédiatement reconnaissable de la nouvelle apparence de la MINI est le fameux « cadre ». C'est une plate-forme de présentation pour une cible jeune et dynamique, la base de communication de toute la chaîne expérientielle de MINI. Homogène dans la forme, tout en étant modulaire et ludique, elle donne de la cohésion à la communication, attire l'attention sur le mes-

die Raffinesse und Emotion verspricht. Ergänzt durch eine Farbwelt, die nicht neu erfunden, sondern in ihrer Anwendung völlig neu gewichtet und zugespitzt erscheint: Schwarz ist die neue dominierende Grundfarbe bei MINI, die die Basis für alle weiteren Farben und Gestaltungselementen bildet.

*Die aus der vorhandenen Schrift entwickelte MINI-Type trägt zudem dazu bei, das Markenbild eigenständig und konsequent zu schärfen.*

Und nicht zuletzt begünstigt auch eine kraftvolle emotionale Bildwelt die Visualisierung dieses Anspruchs: MINI steht für modernen urbanen Lebensstil, extrovertiert, chic und kosmopolitisch. Zentrales und sofort wiedererkennbares Element des neuen MINI-Markenauftritts ist aber der sogenannte Frame geworden. Er ist die Präsentationsplattform für eine junge dynamische Marke – die kommunikative Klammer über die ge-

Wortmarke.

# MINI

Schriftschnitte.

**MINI TYPE HEADLINE**    MINI Type regular    **MINI Type bold**

Designfarben.

Bildwelt.

Frames.

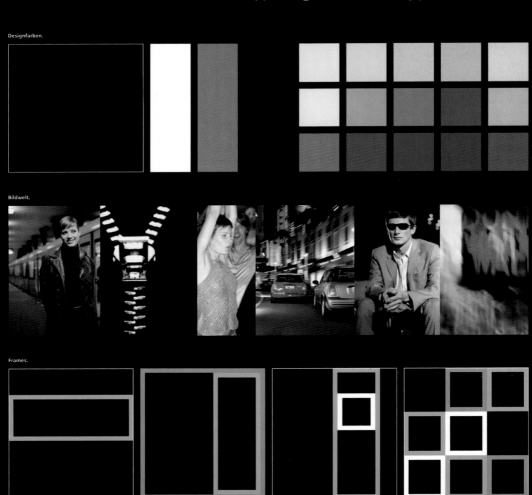

tion together, draws attention to the central messages and serves to give structure to the communication. Exciting layouts are generated, focussed product presentations, brand characteristic furnishings and trade fair appearances which "stand out from the picture frame."

*In interaction, all these elements form a very original, highly emotional brand environment, which has been catapulted into the present with a fresh and new effect, though it has been developed from its very core material outwards. A distinctive appearance which has already, once again, achieved standard status within its segment.*

Corporate Identity Net

In the place of comprehensive CI handbooks, the MINI Identity Net has been developed. The CI guidelines are no longer printed and are now communicated through the electronic media. They are available at all times via the Internet and are complemented by practical examples of application and tips. Above all, this has the advantage of being easy to bring up to date, ensuring that the most current version of the guidelines is applied worldwide. The Identity Net also makes it possible to directly download digital files of symbols, trademarks and artwork. The Identity Net especially supports a consistent MINI presence worldwide.

Show Room

The MINI world will also become experienceable in dealerships, the decisive contact point between customer and brand, by means of three dimensional frames and cubes in the characteristic colour scheme. The variable display space system fulfils all requirements: markings, interior and exterior communication, vehicle presentation, café or bar, lifestyle shop, information, checkout and vehicle delivery. The system can be changed with the minimum of effort at any time, for example, for model in-

sage et structure la promotion. Elle inspire de fascinantes mises en page, des promotions de produits personnalisées, des aménagements et des stands de salon qui « se détachent du cadre. »

*Dans leur interaction, tous ces éléments composent un environnement de marque original et émotionnel, catapulté dans le présent avec un nouvel effet pimpant, bien qu'il ait été développé à partir d'éléments d'origine. Une apparence unique qui lui a déjà donné un statut de référence dans son segment.*

Corporate Identity Net

Au lieu d'un manuel général d'application, un site Web a été développé pour l'identité visuelle. Les instructions ne sont plus sous forme imprimée, mais sont communiquées par voie électronique. Elles sont disponibles en ligne à toute heure et proposent des conseils et des exemples pratiques d'application. Avant tout, cela offre l'avantage d'être facilement mis à jour, et garantit l'application de la version la plus récente des instructions dans le monde entier. Le site Web permet aussi de télécharger des fichiers de symboles numériques, de logos et de graphismes. Le service électronique garantit la cohérence de la marque au niveau mondial.

Show Room

On pourra aussi découvrir l'univers de la MINI chez les concessionnaires, point de rencontre capital entre les consommateurs et la marque, à travers des cubes et des cadres tridimensionnels déclinés dans la palette de couleurs maison. Le système modulaire d'espace d'exposition remplit toutes les exigences : signalétique, communication interne et externe, présentation de véhicules, espace café et art de vivre, information, contrôle et livraison des véhicules. Le système peut être modifié à tout moment avec un minimum d'efforts, pour accueillir par exemple un nouveau modèle, une campagne temporaire, des événements ou des rétrospecti-

samte MINI-Erlebniskette hinweg. Formal einheitlich und doch spielerisch variabel hält er die MINI-Kommunikation zusammen, lenkt die Aufmerksamkeit auf die zentralen Botschaften und dient der Strukturierung der Kommunikation. Es entstehen spannungsreiche Layouts, fokussierte Produktpräsentationen, markentypisches Mobiliar und außergewöhnliche Messeauftritte.

*All diese Elemente formen im Zusammenspiel eine sehr eigenständige, hochemotionale Markenwelt, die in ihrer Wirkung frisch und neu, im Kern aber aus der Substanz heraus entwickelt und in die Gegenwart katapultiert wurde. Eine profilierte Erscheinung, die bereits wieder zum Maßstab in ihrem Segment geworden ist.*

Corporate Identity Net

Statt umfangreicher CI-Handbücher wurde das MINI Identity Net entwickelt. Die CI-Richtlinien werden nicht mehr gedruckt, sondern über elektronische Medien kommuniziert. Sie sind jederzeit per Internet abrufbar und werden durch praktische Anwendungsbeispiele und Tipps ergänzt. Das hat vor allem den Vorteil, dass problemlos Aktualisierungen möglich sind und so weltweit immer die aktuellste Version der Guidelines zur Anwendung kommt. Das Identity Net ermöglicht es auch, digitale Files von Bildzeichen, Wortmarken und Vorlagen direkt herunterzuladen. Das Identity Net unterstützt in besonderer Weise den weltweit konsistenten Auftritt von MINI.

Show Room

Auch im Handelsbetrieb als dem entscheidenden Kontaktpunkt zwischen Kunde und Marke wird die MINI-Welt durch dreidimensionale Frames und Kuben in der charakteristischen Farbgebung erlebbar gemacht. Das variable Schauraumsystem erfüllt alle Bedürfnisse: Kennzeichnung, Kommunikation außen und innen, Fahrzeugpräsentation, Café oder Bar, Lifestyle-Shop, Information,

troductions, seasonal campaigns, general brand themes or events. All elements can be employed flexibly, contribute to transparency in the presentation space and create a MINI-type atmosphere. Materials and technical implementation are appropriate to the brand's premium standard.

*This flexible system is suitable for operations of all sizes. Worldwide implementation is guaranteed by online guidelines in MINI Identity Net.*

Trade Fairs

Trade fairs form a central component in the perception of MINI. They are a permanent driving force behind the development of brand and identity. MINI's trade fair appearances are made under the leitmotiv 'Scenes of Urban Streetlife'. Unconventional communication media emphasise the character of the brand. Surprising and fascinating exhibits interactively draw in the visitor and make the brand's messages experienceable in a playful fashion. Thus trade fair visits become exciting and unforgettable MINI brand experiences.

MINI Architecture

It began with the MINI trade fair building at the IAA 2001: communication carried by the architecture of a black shining cuboid within an orange coloured image frame. Meanwhile, binding guidelines for MINI Architecture have been developed and first dealerships have in the meantime been completed which have been designed according to these specifications.

ves. Tous les éléments sont d'emploi flexible, contribuent à la limpidité de l'espace d'exposition et créent une ambiance dans l'esprit MINI. Les matériaux comme la mise en œuvre technique sont adaptés aux standards de qualité de la marque.

*Ce système se plie à des opérations de toutes tailles. La mise en œuvre mondiale est garantie par les instructions fournies sur le site Web d'identité de la marque.*

Salons Commerciaux

Les salons commerciaux jouent un rôle essentiel dans la perception de la MINI. Ils sont un élément moteur du développement de la marque et de son identité. Les apparitions de la MINI obéissent au concept de « scènes de la vie urbaine ». Des supports de promotion non conventionnels soulignent l'originalité de la marque. Des expositions surprenantes attirent le visiteur de façon interactive et transmettent les messages de la marque sur un mode ludique. La visite de ces salons devient ainsi une expérience amusante et inoubliable.

MINI Architecture

L'architecture commerciale fit son entrée sur le stand MINI au salon mondial de l'automobile de Francfort en 2001, sous la forme d'un cube noir brillant dans un cadre orange. Dans le même temps, des directives ont été mises en place et les premières concessions ont été réalisées selon ces spécifications.

Kasse und Fahrzeugauslieferung. Das System kann jederzeit mit minimalem Aufwand verändert werden, zum Beispiel für Modelleinführungen, saisonale Aktionen, allgemeine Markenthemen oder Events. Alle Elemente sind flexibel einsetzbar, tragen zur Übersichtlichkeit im Schauraum bei und schaffen eine MINI-typische Atmosphäre. Materialien und technische Umsetzung entsprechen dem Premiumanspruch der Marke.

*Das flexible System ist für Betriebe jeder Größe geeignet. Die weltweite Implementierung wird durch Online-Richtlinien im MINI Identity Net gewährleistet.*

Messen

Ein zentraler Bestandteil der Wahrnehmung von MINI sind Messen. Messen sind ein ständiger Motor für die Entwicklung von Marke und Identität. Die Messeauftritte von MINI stehen unter dem Leitmotiv „Scenes of Urban Streetlife". Unkonventionelle Kommunikationsmedien unterstreichen den Charakter der Marke. Überraschende und faszinierende Exponate binden den Besucher interaktiv mit ein und machen die Botschaften der Marke spielerisch erlebbar. So werden Messebesuche zu aufregenden, unvergesslichen MINI-Markenerlebnissen.

MINI-Architektur

Es begann mit dem MINI-Messegebäude auf der IAA 2001: Architektur gewordene Kommunikation aus einem schwarz glänzenden Quader innerhalb eines orangefarbenen Frames. Inzwischen wurden verbindliche Richtlinien für MINI-Architektur entwickelt, erste Händlerbetriebe sind fertiggestellt, die nach diesen Vorgaben konzipiert wurden.

All images: *Trade fairs ///* Toutes les images :
*Salons professionnels ///* Alle Abbildungen:
*Verkaufsmessen*

# Profile
# Interbrand Zintzmeyer & Lux

www.interbrand.de
Location: Worldwide
Year of foundation: 1976

Awards: Interbrand wins
several awards every year in
both national and

international level

*Brands change the world. Brands establish differentiation, orientation, identification and create values. They are therefore an important factor for success in competition. Interbrand Zintzmeyer & Lux has been advising international companies on the development of brand identities for over thirty years as a leading agency for corporate and brand identity. Among its most renowned clients are the BMW Group, including the BMW, MINI and Rolls-Royce brands, Deutsche Telekom, Unilever Bestfoods, TUI and many more. Interbrand Zintzmeyer & Lux has offices in Hamburg, Cologne, Moskow, Munich and Zurich. With offices worldwide, Interbrand is part of Omnicom, one of the largest communications groups in the world.*

*Les marques changent le monde. Les marques établissent une différenciation, une orientation, une identification et créent des valeurs. Elles sont donc un facteur de succès important dans la compétition entre les entreprises. Depuis plus de trente ans, Interbrand Zintzmeyer & Lux conseille des entreprises internationales sur la création de leurs identités de marque, et est une agence de tout premier ordre dans le domaine de l'identité de marque et d'entreprise. Parmi ses clients les plus connus, on peut citer le groupe BMW, dont les marques BMW, MINI et Rolls-Royce, Deutsche Telecom, Unilever Bestfoods, TUI et bien d'autres encore.*

*Interbrand Zintzmeyer & Lux a des bureaux à Hambourg, Cologne, Moscou, Munich et Zurich. Interbrand fait partie d'Omnicom, l'un des plus grands groupes de communication du monde.*

*Marken verändern die Welt. Marken schaffen Differenzierung, Orientierung, Identifikation und Werte. Sie sind somit ein wichtiger Erfolgsfaktor im Wettbewerb. Seit über 30 Jahren berät Interbrand Zintzmeyer & Lux internationale Unternehmen bei der Entwicklung von Markenidentitäten als Lead-Agentur für Corporate und Brand Identity. Zu den renommierten Kunden zählen unter anderem die BMW Group mit den Marken BMW, MINI und Rolls-Royce, die Deutsche Telekom, Unilever Bestfoods, TUI und viele andere. Interbrand Zintzmeyer & Lux ist mit Büros in Hamburg, Köln, Moskau, München und Zürich vertreten. Interbrand mit Büros weltweit ist Teil von Omnicom, einer der größten Kommunikationsgruppen der Welt.*

# CREATING A NEW BRAND: THE SIBERIA AIRLINES

The Siberia Airlines management team appointed Landor Associates to help it reflect its status as the market leader in domestic Russian passenger air travel. The new brand had to be radical; challenging passengers' existing perceptions that travel in Russia is a rather 'grey' experience. At the same time, the plan to introduce Western aircraft into the Russian fleet offered the opportunity to rebrand. Peter Knapp, Executive Creative Director Europe & Middle East, Landor Associates, explains the details of the project.

**T:** What a branding company does is to transform the scientific data into a creative solution, which means going from data to intuition. What is the methodology that works for Landor?
**PK:** *We have a combination of people, a combination of left and right brain thinkers. I think the trick, the art of what we do, is take an intellectual concept and translate that exactly into a creative expression. We have a process that combines words using the strategic intent paralleled with pictures in*

L'équipe de direction de Siberia Airlines a demandé à Landor Associates de les aider à exprimer leur position de leader national dans le transport aérien de passagers en Russie. La nouvelle marque devait être radicale, et changer la perception des passagers, pour qui voyager en Russie est une expérience peu réjouissante. Dans le même temps, l'introduction d'avions occidentaux dans la flotte russe donnait une occasion de revoir la stratégie de marque. Peter Knapp, le directeur de la création pour l'Europe et le Moyen-Orient chez Landor Associates, explique les détails de ce projet.

**T:** Les agences spécialisées dans la stratégie de marque transforment des données scientifiques en solution créative, c'est-à-dire qu'elles passent des données à l'intuition. Quelle est la méthodologie de Landor ?
**PK:** *Nous avons une équipe équilibrée, une combinaison de personnes rationnelles et intuitives. Je pense que le truc, l'essentiel de notre art, c'est de prendre un concept intellectuel et de le traduire fidèlement dans une*

Das Management-Team von Siberia Airlines beauftragte Landor Associates, um ihren Status als Marktführer im Bereich russischer Inlandspassagierflüge zu repräsentieren. Die neue Marke musste radikal sein und eine Herausforderung der bestehenden Meinung darstellen, dass Reisen innerhalb von Russland eine ziemlich „graue" Erfahrung darstellt. Gleichzeitig bot der Plan, Flugzeuge aus dem Westen in den russischen Flugzeugbestand einzuführen, die Gelegenheit eines Rebranding. Peter Knapp, Geschäftsführer im Bereich Europa & Naher Osten, Landor Associates, erläutert das Projekt.

**T:** Eine Branding-Firma setzt wissenschaftliche Daten in kreative Lösungen um, d.h., der Weg führt von Daten zur Intuition. Welche Methode wendet Landor an?
**PK:** *Bei uns gibt es eine Kombination von Leuten, die mit der linken bzw. mit der rechten Gehirnhälfte denken. Der Trick, die Kunst bei dem, was wir tun, besteht darin, ein intellektuelles Konzept exakt in*

order that the left and right brain are working at all times in the original brand strategy. They then help deliver that strategy into the creative world and the expression. So we have a very specific process which we think safeguards the original intellectual idea into an appropriate creative expression.

T: When you think about the rebranding, do you start from zero, from the basics, the name? Do you usually propose a new naming or is it something that the client requests?
PK: *The way that we work is that we think of a piece of commercial territory, a marketing position, for the company and decide how best to describe them relative to their competitors and relative to their ambition and then we work everything from that piece of positioning. So when Siberia Airlines wanted to be quite radically repositioned it gave us the opportunity to make sure that when the customer saw them they would reconsider Siberia in a very dramatic way. A new name is often a very good way to flag the fact that something has changed radically. The name is a component of the way of demonstrating*

*expression créative. Nous avons un processus qui combine les mots, l'intention stratégique, et les images afin que la logique et l'intuition travaillent ensemble à tout moment dans la stratégie de marque originale. Ils aident alors à traduire cette stratégie dans le monde créatif et l'expression. Alors oui, nous avons un processus très spécifique, et nous pensons qu'il protège l'idée intellectuelle d'origine lors de sa transformation en expression créative.*

T: Lorsque vous pensez à la redéfinition de la stratégie de marque, partez-vous de zéro, de l'essentiel, du nom ? Proposez-vous habituellement un nouveau nom, ou bien est-ce quelque chose que le client doit demander ?
PK: *Notre façon de travailler, c'est de penser au territoire commercial, au positionnement marketing de la société, et de chercher la meilleure manière de la décrire par rapport à ses concurrents et à ses ambitions, puis tout part de ce positionnement. Alors, quand Siberia Airlines nous a demandé un repositionnement assez radical, cela nous a donné l'occasion de nous assurer que les clients allaient voir Siberia sous un jour complètement*

*einen kreativen Ausdruck zu übersetzen. Bei diesem Prozess kombinieren wir Wörter, die die strategische Absicht verdeutlichen, mit Bildern, sodass die rechte und linke Gehirnhälfte stets gleichzeitig an der Markenstrategie arbeiten. Diese Strategie wird dann kreativ und ausdruckstaste umgesetzt. Das ist ein sehr spezifischer Prozess, der gewährleistet, dass die ursprüngliche intellektuelle Idee in einen angemessenen kreativen Ausdruck umgesetzt wird.*

T: Wenn Sie über Rebranding nachdenken, beginnen Sie bei Null, bei der Basis, dem Namen? Schlagen Sie einen neuen Namen vor, oder wird er vom Kunden verlangt?
PK: *Wir überlegen uns einen kommerziellen Bereich, eine Marketingposition für das Unternehmen und entscheiden dann, wie wir sie am besten in Relation zu ihren Konkurrenten und ihrer Ambition beschreiben. Diese Positionierung ist die Basis unserer Arbeit. Siberia Airlines wollten radikal positioniert werden, was uns die Gelegenheit gab, dafür zu sorgen, dass die Kunden Siberia auf sehr dramatische Weise in einem*

**From left to right:** *Interior design concept drawings ///* **De gauche à droite :** *Dessins conceptuels de décoration intérieure ///* **Von links nach rechts:** *Entwürfe zur Innenausstattung*

the fact that Siberia Airlines has changed a lot in what it's become and where it's going as a company.

T: For a company like Siberia, what is the type of time line you have for implementation?
PK: *Typically an airline is a very complex commercial body so the implementation can ultimately take up to several years. It really depends on the operational requirements of that company. Whether they are, for example, receiving new planes which can just arrive in the new colours or whether they are repainting planes which means that the planes have to be out of the air for longer and that has a significant commercial impact. So the implementation is always a complicated and quite difficult thing to navigate. But typically airlines will take anything up to 12 months to three years to complete the rebrand because of the operational complexity that they represent.*

T: And that usually involves training people in the company because companies are probably not just interested in

nouveau. Souvent, un nouveau nom est un très bon moyen de signaler un changement radical. Le nom sert à montrer que Siberia Airlines a considérablement modifié ses services et sa stratégie.

T: Pour une société comme Siberia, quel calendrier avez-vous pour la mise en œuvre ?
PK: *Une compagnie aérienne est une entité commerciale très complexe, alors la mise en œuvre peut arriver à prendre plusieurs années. Cela dépend vraiment des contraintes opérationnelles de la compagnie. Par exemple, les nouveaux avions incorporés à la flotte peuvent arriver déjà aux nouvelles couleurs de la compagnie, mais s'ils doivent être repeints, cela veut dire qu'ils resteront à terre plus longtemps, et cela a un impact commercial considérable. Alors la mise en œuvre est toujours compliquée et assez difficile à gérer. Mais en général, pour les compagnies aériennes il faut entre douze mois et trois ans pour la refonte de la stratégie de marque, car elles représentent une grande complexité opérationnelle.*

neuen Licht sehen würden. Ein neuer Name ist oft ein guter Weg, die Tatsache zu verdeutlichen, dass sich etwas radikal verändert hat. Der Name ist eine Komponente der Art und Weise, zu zeigen, dass sich Siberia Airlines sehr verändert hat hinsichtlich dessen, was es geworden ist und wohin es als Unternehmen geht.

T: Wie viel Zeit haben Sie bei einem Unternehmen wie Siberia für die Implementierung?
PK: *Eine Airline ist ein sehr komplexer kommerzieller Körper, sodass die Implementierung bis zu einigen Jahren dauern kann. Es hängt von den betrieblichen Anforderungen des Unternehmens ab; ob sie beispielsweise neue Flugzeuge in den neuen Farben bekommen oder ob sie Flugzeuge neu anstreichen, was bedeuten würde, dass sie länger aus dem Verkehr gezogen würden – dies hat bedeutende kommerzielle Auswirkungen. Die Implementierung ist also immer sehr kompliziert und schwierig. Meist dauert das komplette Rebranding einer Airline wegen ihrer betrieblichen Komplexität zwischen einem und drei Jahren.*

having a new logo, but having a new soul as well?

**PK:** *What we try and do is infuse the brand personality into the corporate heart of the company so the brand doesn't live by just being a new badge. It is much more about creating the flag that people feel an allegiance to. So that they feel a loyalty and a motivation so that they understand the values of the flag they follow. We strongly believe that there is no point in just creating a new badge.*

***You have to create something which people understand and feel an emotional attachment to and an obligation to act and behave in a certain way because that represents the new direction and new ambition of the company – putting the brand at the centre of the business.***

**T:** So it is pretty much about learning.

**PK:** *It is all about learning and identifying the future market position that they aspire to and trying to create a unique answer. I think our business spins entirely on the axis of creating differentiation. You try and do something, which separates a company from everyone else, that makes them look unique. Having identified that position, what you are trying to do is then create preference and loyalty in the eyes of the customer. Preference that they would pick this company before anyone else and loyalty in that once the customer has picked it they then feel trust and loyalty and obligation to stay with them. The background situation for Siberia was they looked dated and their brand image was very undifferentiated in the airport situation.*

**T:** Did it have to do with the system in a country like Russia as well?

**PK:** *There wasn't as strong a use of branding as much as there is perhaps in Western Europe, albeit Russia is increasing in its appetite for branding as a business tool, but when we started work they had, what I think it is fair to say, a very generic appearance. They had a white aircraft with a stripe down the side of it, almost identical to most other Russian airlines. We looked at everything including the on board experience and really needed to radically represent it. If you capture the strategy it is trying to get a sense of a*

---

**T:** En général, il faut aussi former le personnel de la compagnie, car les entreprises ne veulent pas seulement un nouveau logo, mais aussi une nouvelle âme, n'est-ce pas ?

**PK:** *Nous essayons d'infuser la personnalité de la marque au cœur de l'entreprise afin que la marque ne soit qu'un nouveau badge. Il s'agit plutôt de créer un drapeau autour duquel les gens peuvent se rallier, afin qu'ils ressentent une loyauté et une motivation, parce qu'ils comprennent les valeurs du drapeau qu'ils suivent. Nous croyons fermement que se contenter de créer un nouveau badge est complètement inutile.*

***Il faut créer quelque chose que les gens comprennent, auquel ils puissent s'attacher émotionnellement, et qui leur donne l'envie d'agir et de se comporter d'une certaine manière parce que cela représente la nouvelle direction et la nouvelle ambition de la compagnie. Il faut mettre la marque au centre de l'activité.***

**T:** Alors, il s'agit en fait d'apprentissage.

**PK:** *Il s'agit d'apprendre et d'identifier le positionnement auquel ils aspirent sur le marché, et d'essayer de créer une réponse sur mesure. Je pense que la création de la différenciation est au centre de notre activité. On essaie de démarquer la compagnie par rapport aux autres, de la rendre unique. Après avoir identifié ce positionnement, il faut essayer de créer des critères de préférence et de loyauté pour les clients. La préférence, cela veut dire que les clients choisissent cette compagnie avant toute autre, et la loyauté, cela veut dire qu'une fois que le client a choisi, il a un sentiment de confiance et de loyauté, une obligation à rester avec eux. Pour Siberia, la situation de départ était que la compagnie avait une image démodée, et leur image de marque se fondait avec celle des autres compagnies de l'aéroport.*

**T:** Cela avait-il aussi quelque chose à voir avec le système en place dans un pays comme la Russie ?

**PK:** *Là-bas, on n'utilisait pas autant la stratégie de marque qu'en Europe occidentale, bien que la Russie ait un appétit croissant pour la stratégie de marque comme outil com-*

---

**T:** Das bedeutet auch die Schulung der Angestellten, denn Unternehmen sind nicht nur an einem neuen Logo, sondern auch an einer neuen Seele interessiert, nicht wahr?

**PK:** *Wir versuchen, die Marke in den Kern des Unternehmens einfließen zu lassen, sodass sie nicht nur aus einem neuen Kennzeichen besteht. Es geht vielmehr darum, ein Identifikationsmodell zu erstellen, demgegenüber die Leute Loyalität empfinden, die wiederum eine Motivation erzeugt, sodass sie die Werte dieses Identifizierungssignals verstehen, dem sie folgen. Wir sind überzeugt davon, dass es keinen Sinn macht, nur ein neues Kennzeichen zu kreieren.*

***Man muss etwas schaffen, dass die Menschen verstehen, etwas, das sie emotional anspricht und dem gegenüber sie sich verpflichtet fühlen, auf eine gewisse Weise zu handeln, da es eine neue Richtung und eine neue Ambition des Unternehmens repräsentiert – die Marke wird ins Zentrum des Unternehmens gestellt.***

**T:** Es geht also ums Lernen.

**PK:** *Es geht ums Lernen und die Identifizierung der zukünftigen Marktposition, die man anstrebt, und darum, eine einzigartige Antwort zu finden. Ich denke, in unserem Business dreht sich alles darum, sich abzugrenzen. Man versucht, etwas zu tun, das ein Unternehmen von allen anderen abgrenzt, das es einzigartig macht. Hat man diese Position identifiziert, erzeugt man die Bevorzugung und Loyalität der Kunden. Bevorzugung meint, dass sie dieses Unternehmen vor allen anderen wählen; Loyalität, dass sie Vertrauen in das Unternehmen setzen und die Verpflichtung empfinden, es auch in Zukunft zu wählen. Der Hintergrund bei Siberia war, dass sie altmodisch wirkten und ihr Markenimage innerhalb der Flughafensituation sehr undifferenziert war.*

**T:** Hatte dies auch mit dem System eines Landes wie Russland zu tun?

**PK:** *Es gab keinen so starken Gebrauch von Branding, wie es vielleicht in Westeuropa der Fall ist; allerdings erhöht sich der Appetit Russlands auf Branding als Business Tool. Aber als wir mit der Arbeit begannen, hatten*

breath of fresh air in what is otherwise a very grey customer experience. Russian transportation can be quite difficult. It needs a lot of stamina to get through it so we decided to come up with a very bright colour to signify this radical difference, which is the bright green. But then inside that, almost like a present, when you unwrap it you find a very colourful, multidimensional product inside the green wrapping. So on the outside you get a radical bright new signal of a new age for S7, but when you go inside it is not just a green interior as well. There is a very fresh use of multi-coloured palettes on the inside of the plane. We have used this idea of putting silhouettes of the passengers throughout the brand to demonstrate that the passenger is the hero.

**There is a sense of obligation from S7 to respect their passengers and put them at the centre of all their activity.**

We have created a number of different ways of interpreting this concept into their lounges and into their print material. This radical repositioning is carried out through the different aspects of the brand so you feel this concept beyond just the logo. The breath of fresh air exists at any of the customer interfaces you come across. Eventually, we are hoping the S7 brand will become similar in its perception and flexibility as the Virgin brand is over here in Europe to allow them the possibility to stretch into different types of activities. It is a graphic image that represents a brand that has a lot of elasticity built into it to accommodate its future because I think these days the future of businesses is so uncertain that you need a degree of future-proofing to make sure you don't have to undo and rebuild the work that you have been doing. Hopefully the work that we have done here safeguards their activities as they move forward and they can stretch and flex into different types of business activities.

T: How is the team divided to create? How many people are working on a project like this?

PK: A project like this, which is a large project because it goes into many different interfaces and applications, is probably made up of over 20 different types of people with dif-

mercial, mais lorsque nous avons commencé à travailler ils avaient, je pense qu'on peut le dire, une apparence très générique. Ils avaient des avions blancs avec une bande sur le côté, presque identiques à ceux de la majorité des autres compagnies aériennes russes. Nous avons tout examiné, y compris le service à bord. Il fallait vraiment revoir la présentation de façon radicale. La stratégie essaie d'insuffler de l'énergie dans l'expérience que les clients ont avec la compagnie, qui sinon est assez peu réjouissante. En Russie, les transports peuvent être assez compliqués à emprunter. Il faut beaucoup d'énergie pour les utiliser, c'est pourquoi nous avons décidé d'utiliser une couleur très vive pour signifier cette différence radicale, le vert vif. Ensuite, à l'intérieur, presque comme un cadeau, on découvre un produit très coloré dans son emballage vert. À l'extérieur, on a donc le signe radical d'une nouvelle ère pour S7, mais lorsque l'on regarde à l'intérieur, il n'y a pas que du vert. Nous avons utilisé des palettes multicolores très audacieuses à l'intérieur de l'avion. Nous avons eu l'idée de mettre des silhouettes de passagers dans tous les graphismes, afin de montrer que le passager est au centre de l'attention.

**Chez S7, il y a un fort sentiment de devoir envers le passager, il est au centre de toutes leurs activités.**

Nous avons créé plusieurs façons différentes d'interpréter ce concept dans leurs salons et dans leurs documents imprimés. Ce repositionnement radical est transposé dans tous les différents aspects de la stratégie de marque, et l'on peut sentir ce concept bien au-delà du logo. Ce souffle nouveau est présent dans toutes les interfaces client que vous pouvez rencontrer. Nous espérons que la marque S7 finira par devenir similaire en termes de perception et de flexibilité à la marque Virgin ici en Europe, ce qui leur permettrait de diversifier leurs activités. C'est une image graphique qui représente une marque. Elle est très flexible afin de permettre des évolutions futures, car je pense qu'aujourd'hui l'avenir commercial est tellement incertain qu'il faut un certain degré de prévoyance afin de s'assurer que l'on ne sera pas obligé de tout défaire et de recommencer le travail qu'on a déjà fait. J'espère que le travail que nous avons fait ici pourra s'adapter à leurs

sie einen – ich denke, es ist fair, es zu sagen – sehr langweiligen Auftritt: Ein weißes Flugzeug mit einem Streifen auf der Seite, fast identisch mit den meisten anderen russischen Airlines. Wir sahen uns alles an, auch die Erfahrung an Bord, und mussten es wirklich radikal neu repräsentieren. Die Strategie war, frischen Wind in eine bislang langweilige Kundenerfahrung zu bringen. Russisches Transportwesen kann ziemlich schwierig sein. Man braucht viel Ausdauer, also entschieden wir uns für eine sehr helle Farbe, um die radikale Veränderung zu kennzeichnen: das helle Grün. Darin befindet sich, fast wie ein Geschenk, das man auspackt, ein sehr farbenfrohes, mehrdimensionales Produkt. Von außen betrachtet erhält man also ein helles, neues Signal für ein neues Zeitalter des S7, aber wenn man hineingeht, ist die Inneneinrichtung nicht nur grün, sondern besteht aus einer bunten Farbskala. Wir hatten die Idee, Silhouetten der Passagiere in die Marke zu integrieren, um zu zeigen, dass der Passagier König ist.

**S7 fühlt sich verpflichtet, ihre Passagiere zu respektieren und in das Zentrum aller Aktivitäten zu stellen.**

Wir haben dieses Konzept auf verschiedene Weisen in ihre Lounges und Druckerzeugnisse eingearbeitet. Diese radikale Umpositionierung wird durch die verschiedenen Aspekte der Marke vorgenommen, sodass das Konzept über das bloße Logo hinausgeht. Der frische Wind findet sich auf allen Kunden-Interfaces, denen man begegnet. Wir hoffen, dass die Marke S7 mit der Zeit, was Wahrnehmung und Flexibilität angeht, Virgin in Europa ähnlich wird, sodass sie sich auf verschiedene Aktivitäten ausweiten wird. Es ist ein anschauliches Bild, das eine Marke repräsentiert, die sehr viel Spannkraft für die Zukunft hat, denn ich denke, heutzutage ist die Zukunft von Unternehmen so unsicher, dass man ein gewisses Maß an Zukunftssicherung braucht, damit man die getane Arbeit nicht rückgängig machen oder erneuern muss. Ich hoffe, dass die Arbeit, die wir geleistet haben, ihre zukünftigen Aktivitäten gewährleisten wird und sie ihre Geschäftsaktivitäten auf verschiedene Gebiete ausweiten können.

*ferent types of skills. Whether it is graphic designers, 3-dimensional interior designers, consultants, account services people, behavioural specialists or brand engagement specialists, there will be a very varied collection of people who constitute an entire team all working off of the same brand platform, what we call the Brand Driver, so everyone knows what it is the brand has to do. We are all working to a common mission, to a common definition of the brand, but delivering through different strategies. Everyone interacts, everyone is very much a part of the whole team and the work is all cross-referenced against each other.*

*activités futures, et qu'ils pourront se diversifier dans plusieurs types d'activités.*

T: <u>Comment l'équipe créative est-elle divisée ? Combien de personnes travaillent sur un projet comme celui-ci ?</u>
PK: *Pour un projet comme celui-ci, colossal parce qu'il s'agit de nombreuses interfaces et applications différentes, l'équipe est composée de plus de 20 personnes, avec différents types de compétences. Qu'il s'agisse de graphistes, de décorateurs d'intérieurs en 3D, de consultants, de commerciaux, de spécialistes du comportement ou de spécialistes de la motivation des employés autour de la marque, il y aura un ensemble très varié de personnes qui constituera une équipe entière travaillant à partir de la même plateforme, ce que nous appelons le Brand Driver (le moteur de la marque), afin que chacun sache comment la marque doit fonctionner. Nous travaillons tous vers une mission commune, vers une définition commune de la marque, mais à travers différentes stratégies. Tout le monde interagit, chacun fait partie intégrante de l'équipe, et le travail de chacun se recoupe avec celui des autres.*

T: <u>Wie ist das Team aufgeteilt? Wie viele Personen arbeiten an einem Projekt wie diesem?</u>
PK: *Hier handelt es sich um ein großes Projekt, weil es um viele Interfaces und Anwendungen geht. Es arbeiten über 20 Menschen mit unterschiedlichen Fähigkeiten daran. Ob es Grafiker, dreidimensionale Innenarchitekten, Berater, Buchhalter, Verhaltensspezialisten oder Markenspezialisten sind – es handelt sich um eine sehr vielschichtige Gruppe von Leuten, aus denen ein Team zusammengesetzt ist, das auf derselben Markenplattform arbeitet, die wir Brand Driver nennen, sodass jeder weiß, was die Marke leisten muss. Wir arbeiten alle an derselben Mission, aber mit verschiedenen Strategien. Wir interagieren miteinander, jeder ist ein Teil des Ganzen, und die Arbeiten sind miteinander verknüpft.*

**All images:** *Identity applications* /// **Toutes les images :** *Applications de l'identité* /// **Alle Abbildungen:** *Anwendungen der Identity*

**Left:** *interior Design of the Siberia Airline lounge in the Moscow airport ///* **À gauche :** *Décoration du salon de Siberia Airline à l'aéroport de Moscou ///* **Links:** *Innenausstattung der Siberia Airline Lounge im Moskauer Flughafen*

# Biography
# Peter Knapp (Landor)

www.landor.com
Location: London, United Kingdom

Year of foundation: 1941
Position: Executive Creative
Director for Europe and

Middle East
Awards: Multiple

*Peter has worked with Landor for over twelve years. His tenure with the company began in 1993 in London, subsequently he moved to the Hong Kong office in 1995 where he was Creative Director and held overall responsibility for steering and directing creative solutions across projects in South East Asia. Now based at Landor London as Executive Creative Director Europe and Middle East, he oversees all creative work generated from all EMEA offices across three design platforms - corporate identity, brand experience and brand identity. Peter has responsibility for all creative output: 2D, 3D and across interactive media. Peter specialises in integrated design programmes where graphic and three-dimensional design are used together to form the total brand experience. Peter holds a First Class Bachelor of Arts Honours Degree, with commendation in Dimensional design from Middlesex University.*

*Peter a travaillé avec Landor pendant plus de douze ans. Il a pris ses fonctions avec la société en 1993 à Londres, puis il est allé au bureau de Hong Kong en 1995 en tant que directeur de la création, où il a dirigé les solutions créatives des projets dans l'Asie du Sud-Est. Il est maintenant basé à Londres et exerce la fonction de directeur de la création pour l'Europe et le Moyen-Orient. Il supervise tout le travail créatif généré par tous les bureaux EMEA sur trois plateformes de design : identité d'entreprise, expérience de marque et identité de*

*marque. Peter est responsable de toute la production en matière de création : 2D, 3D et médias interactifs. Peter est spécialisé en programmes de design intégré, où design graphique et tridimensionnel s'allient pour donner corps à la stratégie de marque globale. Peter est titulaire d'une licence de l'université du Middlesex, obtenue avec une mention très bien et une mention spéciale en design dimensionnel.*

*Peter Knapp arbeitet seit über zwölf Jahren mit Landor. Seine Anstellung im Unternehmen begann 1993 in London. 1995 zog er als Kreativdirektor in das Büro in Hongkong und war verantwortlich für die Steuerung und Leitung kreativer Lösungen von Projekten in Südwestasien. Heute arbeitet er als kreativer Geschäftsführer für Europa und den Nahen Osten und betreut die gesamte kreative Arbeit aller EMEA-Büros dreier Designplattformen: Corporate Identity, Markenerfahrung und Markenidentität. Knapp ist für den gesamten kreativen Output verantwortlich: 2D, 3D und interaktive Medien. Er ist auf integrierte Designprogramme spezialisiert, bei denen grafisches und dreidimensionales Design kombiniert verwendet werden, um die gesamte Markenerfahrung zu formen. Er hat einen First Class Bachelor of Arts Honours Degree mit Auszeichnung in Dimensional Design der Middlesex University.*

# DEVELOPMENT OF AN UMBRELLA BRAND FOR SOUTH TYROL

"The creation of a brand is a worthwhile investment in the future of our region." This is a remark made ever more frequently by representatives of regional interests. The claim is not always as simple as it may appear, however. In order that a brand pays off as an investment in the long-term, it must not only be created and transferred conscientiously and accurately into a consistent corporate design, but clear and unambiguous, practical guidelines for its daily application must also be provided. How this can be done successfully and what obstacles must be overcome in order to achieve this, is shown by the example of the development of an umbrella brand for the region of South Tyrol.

## Brand power

Our world is full of interchangeable products and services. An ever greater variety of these compete against each other for consumers' favour. Manufacturers and service providers need to help people in their decision for, or against, a particular

« La création d'une marque est un investissement utile pour l'avenir de notre région. » Cette remarque est faite de plus en plus fréquemment par les représentants d'intérêts régionaux. Mais ce n'est pas toujours aussi simple qu'il y paraît. Si l'on veut qu'une marque rapporte sur le long terme, elle doit se refléter de façon fidèle et délibérée à travers une identité visuelle cohérente. Et pour éviter toute ambiguïté, elle doit également être accompagnée d'un manuel d'instructions pratiques guidant son application quotidienne. Comment y parvenir et quels sont les obstacles à franchir, c'est ce qu'illustre l'exemple de la création d'une marque ombrelle pour le Tyrol du Sud.

## Le pouvoir de la marque

Notre monde est plein de produits et de services interchangeables. Ils sont de plus en plus nombreux à rivaliser pour gagner les faveurs des consommateurs. Les fabricants et les prestataires de service doivent aider leurs clients à se déclarer pour ou contre un produit ou un service particu-

„Der Aufbau einer Marke ist eine lohnenswerte Investition in die Zukunft unserer Region." Diese Feststellung machen Vertreter regionaler Interessen immer häufiger. Die Aussage trifft aber nicht in jedem Fall zu. Damit sich eine Marke als Investition langfristig auszahlt, gilt: Ihre Macher müssen sie nicht nur gewissenhaft herleiten und sauber in ein konsistentes Corporate Design überführen, sondern auch eindeutige und praxisnahe Regeln für ihre tägliche Anwendung vorgeben. Wie dies gelingen kann und welche Hürden es dabei zu überwinden gilt, zeigt das Beispiel der Entwicklung einer Dachmarke für das Land Südtirol.

## Die Macht der Marke

Unsere Welt ist voll von austauschbaren Produkten und Dienstleistungen. Immer mehr Angebote konkurrieren miteinander um die Gunst der Verbraucher. Ihre Anbieter müssen den Menschen Hilfestellungen bei ihrer Entscheidung für oder gegen ein Angebot an die Hand geben. Der Preis allein reicht heute längst

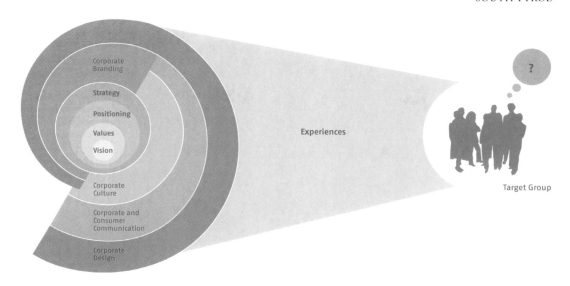

*MetaBrand model for corporate image ///*
*Modèle de MetaBrand pour l'image*
*d'entreprise /// MetaBrand Modell für die*
*Corporate Identity*

product or service. Consideration of price alone is no longer sufficient. Brands provide consumers with the necessary orientation. They are images and ideas which form in people's minds about companies and about their products and services. A large part of the product which we see actually only exists as a world of ideas within our minds. This image is decisive for sales. In addition, strong brands realise higher prices. These are frequently those brands which know how to combine the elements of reliability and high quality (trust mark) with an element more of emotion and experience (love mark).

Without a clear corporate identity, there is no clear brand. Whoever wants to win points with customers must define a clear brand strategy which builds upon the identity of the company. This transforms the corporate design into a lively and catchy visual anchor. The brand must, however, fulfil its promises. For example, an automobile brand's model, whose essential values are quality and reliability, should not be permanently

lier. Les considérations de prix ne sont plus les uniques critères de choix, il revient aux marques d'orienter les clients. Nous avons tous notre propre perception des sociétés et des produits qu'elles proposent. La plupart des produits que l'on connaît de nos jours n'existent en fait que dans notre esprit, sous forme d'idées. Et cette perception est décisive pour les ventes. De plus, les marques fortes se permettent des prix plus élevés. Ce sont souvent des marques qui ont su combiner qualité et fiabilité (capital confiance) et un élément plus psychologique et d'expérience (capital de sympathie).

Sans identité visuelle distincte, il n'y a pas de marque clairement identifiable. Celui qui veut gagner des parts de marché doit définir une stratégie précise qui se construit sur l'identité de la société. Celle-ci prend alors la forme d'un visuel dynamique et accrocheur. Mais la marque doit bien sûr tenir ses promesses. Un modèle de voiture dont la marque est bâtie sur des valeurs de qualité et de fiabilité ne doit pas figurer constamment en tête des

nicht mehr aus. Marken bieten den Verbrauchern die nötige Orientierung. Sie sind Bilder und Vorstellungen, die im Kopf der Menschen von Unternehmen, ihren Produkten und Dienstleistungen entstehen. Ein Großteil des Produktes, das wir sehen, existiert also lediglich als Vorstellungswelt in unseren Köpfen. Dieses Image ist kaufentscheidend. Starke Marken erzielen im Markt zudem höhere Preise. Häufig sind dies solche Marken, die die Elemente Verlässlichkeit und hohe Qualität („trust mark") mit einem Mehr an Emotion und Erlebnis („love mark") zu koppeln wissen.

Ohne eine klare Corporate Identity gibt es auch keine klare Marke. Wer beim Kunden punkten möchte, muss auf der Identität des Unternehmens aufbauend eine klare Markenstrategie definieren. Diese macht das Corporate Design als eingängige visuelle Klammer in allen Bereichen des Markenauftritts lebendig. Das Versprechen, das die Marke so gibt, muss allerdings auch eingelöst werden. Die Modelle einer Automarke, deren we-

occupying the lower echelons of the breakdown statistics.

Even for countries and regions, brands are becoming more and more important. As a tourist destination and manufacturer they are – as are companies – up against ever increasing competition. This also applies to South Tyrol. With over 300 days of sunshine a year, the autonomous province of South Tyrol in northern Italy is not only a popular holiday destination, but also the origin of numerous quality agricultural products and specialities. In recent years, the economic conditions in which South Tyrol operates have also been steadily intensifying; manufacturers of quality regional products are in intense competition with international brand items and strong trade brands. In addition, they are having to respond to an increasing discounting trend in the market. At the same time, tourism is experiencing stagnating demand. Cheap flight operators are becoming just as noticeable as the competition is between rival Alpine regions. Demands are changing. New target groups must be reached and specialised offers must be more strongly communicated.

A strong umbrella brand for South Tyrol should unify tourism and agriculture along with the manufacturing and service provision sectors associated with them. Smaller businesses profit just as much as the larger ones from a strong umbrella brand. An umbrella brand allows operations to cover all business areas and the exploitation of synergy potential created as a result. The position of South Tyrol as holiday destination and, at the same time, manufacturing centre for a variety of quality products should be given greater competitive strength.

The way to an umbrella brand for South Tyrol

The South Tyrolean economy is characterised by numerous small to medium sized enterprises. These frequently have, as do the holiday regions and even individual holiday resorts, their own logos or brands. Independently of each other,

statistiques de pannes mécaniques.

Même pour les pays et les régions, les marques deviennent de plus en plus importantes. Les destinations touristiques sont, comme les entreprises, soumises à rude concurrence. C'est également le cas du Tyrol du Sud. Avec plus de 300 jours d'ensoleillement par an, la province autonome du Tyrol du Sud, dans le nord de l'Italie, est à la fois une destination de vacances prisée et le lieu de production de nombreux produits agricoles de qualité. Ces dernières années, la situation économique du Tyrol du Sud s'est faite de plus en plus délicate : les producteurs régionaux subissent une grande pression concurrentielle de la part des producteurs internationaux et de grandes marques commerciales et doivent faire face à une tendance croissante du marché discount. Dans le même temps, le tourisme connaît une stagnation de la demande. Les effets des compagnies aériennes à bas prix et de la rivalité entre régions alpines se font de plus en plus sentir. Les demandes changent. Il faut toucher de nouveaux créneaux et mieux promouvoir les offres spécialisées.

Une marque ombrelle forte pour le Tyrol du Sud doit faire le lien entre tourisme et agriculture, et entre les industries et les services qui y sont associés. Les petites sociétés ont autant de bénéfices à tirer d'une marque ombrelle que les grandes. Une marque ombrelle permet de lancer des opérations touchant tous les secteurs d'activité et d'exploiter le potentiel synergique qui en résulte. Comme destination touristique et pôle de production d'une grande variété de produits de qualité, le Tyrol du Sud réclame une plus grande compétitivité.

Vers une marque ombrelle pour le Tyrol du Sud

L'économie du Tyrol du Sud repose sur un maillage de petites et moyennes entreprises. Elles possèdent souvent leur propre marque et leur propre logo, tout comme certaines régions ou stations touristiques. C'est donc indépendamment les unes des autres qu'elles tentent d'attirer l'attention

sentlichste Werte Qualität und Zuverlässigkeit sind, sollten zum Beispiel in der Pannenstatistik nicht ständig die vordersten Plätze belegen.

Auch für Länder und Regionen werden Marken immer wichtiger. Als touristische Ziele und Erzeuger von Produkten stehen sie -analog zu Unternehmen- immer mehr im Wettbewerb. Das gilt auch für Südtirol. Mit seinen 300 Sonnentagen im Jahr ist die Autonome Provinz Südtirol im Norden Italiens nicht nur eine beliebte Urlaubsregion, sondern auch Herkunft zahlreicher landwirtschaftlicher Qualitätsprodukte und Spezialitäten. In den letzten Jahren haben sich allerdings auch die wirtschaftlichen Rahmenbedingungen für Südtirol kontinuierlich verschärft: Die Anbieter von regionalen Qualitätsprodukten stehen im intensiven Wettbewerb mit internationalen Markenartikeln und starken Eigenmarken des Handels. Sie müssen sich zudem auf eine steigende „Aldisierung" bei den Verbrauchern einstellen. Gleichzeitig erlebt der Tourismus eine stagnierende Nachfrage. Die Billigfliegerangebote machen sich genauso bemerkbar wie der Wettbewerb mit konkurrierenden Alpenregionen. Die Ansprüche verändern sich. Neue Zielgruppen müssen erreicht und spezielle Angebote verstärkt kommuniziert werden.

Eine starke Dachmarke Südtirol soll Tourismus, Landwirtschaft und dem damit jeweils verbundenen produzierenden und dienstleistenden Gewerbe gleichermaßen nützen. Die kleinen Unternehmen werden von einer starken Dachmarke ebenso profitieren wie die großen. Mit einer Dachmarke kann branchenübergreifend agiert und können Synergiepotenziale ausgeschöpft werden. Die Position von Südtirol als Urlaubsregion und gleichzeitigem Herkunftsland zahlreicher Qualitätsprodukte soll im Wettbewerb weiter gestärkt werden.

Auf dem Weg zur Dachmarke Südtirol

Südtirols Wirtschaft ist durch zahlreiche kleinst- und mittelständische Betriebe geprägt. Diese verfügen wie die Urlaubsregionen und sogar einzelne Urlaubsorte

therefore, they are trying to attract attention to the region and its products. Two logos or two brands here should be especially emphasised: the Südtirol Marketing Gesellschaft (SMG) enterprise has been operating business image promotion with the logo 'Südtirol – Italia' for a fairly long time in the tourism sector. This well-known symbol has therefore, up until now, been associated exclusively with tourism. In addition, the logo is not protected as a branded name and has therefore appeared in innumerable modified forms. The trademark 'Südtirol' has stood for agricultural products since 1976. However, as a result of new EU regulations, the legal framing conditions for these types of trademarks have changed. The trademark 'Südtirol' was threatened in its previous form by an EU procedure. Furthermore, it was not regarded as suitable as a comprehensive umbrella brand because of its many years of application exclusively for agricultural products.

Against this background, the South Tyrolean regional government set up a

sur la région et ses produits. Examinons ici le cas de deux marques en particulier. Dans le secteur du tourisme, la société Südtirol Marketing Gesellschaft (SMG, société de marketing pour le Tyrol du Sud) gère la promotion de son image avec le logo « Südtirol-Italia » depuis déjà un certain nombre d'années. Jusqu'à présent, ce célèbre symbole a donc été associé exclusivement au tourisme. De plus, le logo n'est pas protégé comme nom de marque, et il apparaît donc sous d'innombrables formes dérivées. La marque « Südtirol », pour sa part, représente les produits agricoles depuis 1976. Cependant, suivant de nouvelles réglementations européennes, le cadre juridique de ce genre de marques a changé. La marque « Südtirol » est menacée sous sa première forme par une procédure européenne. De plus, elle n'a pas été retenue comme marque ombrelle car elle s'est appliquée exclusivement aux produits agricoles pendant de nombreuses années.

C'est dans ce contexte que les autorités régionales ont mis sur pied un groupe de réflexion chargé de concevoir une marque

häufig über eigene Logos oder Marken. Man versucht also unabhängig voneinander, Aufmerksamkeit für die Region und ihre Produkte zu wecken. Zwei Logos beziehungsweise Marken sind dabei sicher besonders hervorzuheben: Die Südtirol Marketing Gesellschaft (SMG) betrieb mit dem Logo „Südtirol – Italia" im touristischen Bereich seit geraumer Zeit Imagewerbung. Das bekannte Zeichen wurde bislang ausschließlich mit dem Tourismusbereich assoziiert. Zudem ist das Logo markenrechtlich nicht geschützt und existierte daher in unzähligen Abwandlungen. Für landwirtschaftliche Erzeugnisse gibt es seit 1976 wiederum die Schutzmarke „Südtirol". Durch neue EU-Bestimmungen haben sich jedoch die rechtlichen Rahmenbedingungen für derartige Schutzmarken verändert. Der Schutzmarke „Südtirol" drohte in ihrer bisherigen Form ein Verfahren der EU. Darüber hinaus kam sie auch aufgrund ihrer jahrelangen Nutzung für ausschließlich landwirtschaftliche Produkte nicht als übergreifende Dachmarke in Frage.

## AltO ADiGE SüDtiROL

Previous page: *series of old logos of the region ///* **Page précédente** *: Série d'anciens logos de la région ///* **Vorherige Seite:** *Reihe alter Logos der Region*

Above: *new typeface applied to the name of a city in the region; region's quality seal ///* **Ci-dessus** *: La nouvelle police de caractères appliquée au nom d'une ville de la région ; le sceau de qualité de la région ///* **Oben:** *Neues Schriftbild für einen Städtenamen in der Region. Qualitätssiegel der Region*

Next spread: *panorama of South Tyrol and its effect in the corporate identity ///* **Double page suivante** *: le panorama du Tyrol du Sud et ses effets sur l'identité d'entreprise ///* **Nächste Seite:** *Panorama von Südtirol und seine Wirkung für die Corporate Identity*

group with the task of developing an umbrella brand for South Tyrol – consisting of members of the regional administration, representatives of the most important agricultural sectors, and the SMG. A previously unique undertaking in European location marketing. It was not, up until now, possible in any country or region to unify tourism and products in this way and in such close association under one roof – especially not in a bilingual region with such a multi-faceted political and cultural background. The group decided to commission the corporate identity agency MetaDesign with the development of the umbrella brand.

In the autumn of 2003, MetaDesign began the complex process of umbrella brand development with an initial workshop on brand identity. The reason for this is that before a design can even be considered, it must be clear what the brand should actually convey and what kind of brand architecture is required for this. In cooperation with the group, the MetaDesign team first analysed the pres-

ombrelle pour le Tyrol du Sud. Ce groupe était constitué de membres de l'administration régionale, de représentants des principaux secteurs agricoles et de représentants de la SMG. C'était une initiative de marketing collectif inédite. Jusqu'à ce jour, il était impensable d'associer aussi étroitement tourisme et agriculture dans n'importe quel pays ou région, et à plus forte raison dans une région bilingue présentant des facettes politiques et culturelles aussi diverses que le Tyrol du Sud. Le groupe décida de faire appel à l'agence de gestion de marque MetaDesign pour la création de la marque ombrelle.

À l'automne 2003, MetaDesign démarra le complexe processus de création d'une marque ombrelle par un atelier préliminaire sur l'identité de la marque. La raison en était qu'avant même d'envisager le moindre travail graphique, il fallait clarifier ce que la marque voulait véhiculer, et définir l'architecture de marque adéquate. En collaboration avec le groupe de réflexion, l'équipe de MetaDesign analysa d'abord la situation de départ. Comment

Vor diesem Hintergrund initiierte die Südtiroler Landesregierung eine Arbeitsgruppe zur Entwicklung einer Dachmarke Südtirol – zusammengesetzt aus Mitgliedern der Landesverwaltung, Vertretern der wichtigsten landwirtschaftlichen Sektoren sowie der SMG. Ein bis dato im europäischen Standortmarketing einzigartiges Vorhaben. War es doch bisher noch keinem Land und keiner Region gelungen, in dieser Form und Geschlossenheit Tourismus und Produkte unter einem gemeinsamen Dach zu vereinen – dazu noch in einer bilingualen Region mit einem derartig vielschichtigen politischen wie kulturellen Hintergrund. Die Arbeitsgruppe beschloss, die Corporate-Identity-Agentur MetaDesign mit der Dachmarkenentwicklung zu beauftragen.

Im Herbst 2003 startete MetaDesign den komplexen Prozess der Dachmarkenentwicklung mit einem ersten Workshop zur Markenidentität. Denn bevor überhaupt an die Gestaltung gedacht werden konnte, musste klar sein, was die Dachmarke

ent situation. How has South Tyrol been presenting itself up until now? What messages have been conveyed? MetaDesign presented the participants with, among other things, previous presentations of South Tyrol by individual tourism associations, hoteliers and by individual products. Additionally, the way the competition positions itself was also considered. All the participants sketched out and finally formulated their vision of the umbrella brand; an important step on the way to clarifying their own market identity. On this basis the group defined the set of values which should in future stand for the essence, character and style of the South Tyrolean umbrella brand. MetaDesign bundled these values together into a hierarchy before arranging them in a brand pyramid. In the apex of the pyramid, there are those values which should give the brand for South Tyrol its unmistakable profile. As a reflection of the people who live in this part of the country, the brand should be welcoming by being friendly with a few endearing imperfections. It is also full of contrasts, as is the natural landscape, and rich in tradition as is the culture of South Tyrol. The intention behind this three-part description is to express the unmistakable features of the region and its products. The core of the brand reflects the brand's culture. These are values which are anchored deep within the brand. The combination of ideas 'Knödel & Spaghetti' is an expression of the richly contrasting symbiosis of alpine and Mediterranean culture. Despite these multi-faceted contrasts, the brand remains charismatic. In South Tyrol, life is something to be enjoyed. The brand should be as credible and as genuine as the region itself. The base of the pyramid is formed of values which give the brand a solid foundation. The material of which the South Tyrolean brand consists is strong and reliable.

In the following workshop, MetaDesign presented the group initial visualisations of the previously defined market identity. So-called mood-boards gave the members new access to an impression of the brand through colours, shapes and images. This

la région s'était-elle présentée jusqu'à ce jour ? Quels messages avaient été transmis ? Pour répondre à ces questions, MetaDesign montra aux participants, entre autres documents, d'anciennes présentations du Tyrol du Sud utilisées par des associations touristiques, par des hôteliers et pour des produits isolés. La façon dont la concurrence se positionne fut également analysée. Les membres du groupe furent ensuite invités à esquisser puis à formuler plus précisément leur vision de la marque ombrelle. C'était une étape importante pour clarifier l'identité commerciale. Sur cette base, le groupe définit l'ensemble des valeurs qui allaient imprégner le style, le caractère et l'essence de la marque du Tyrol du Sud. MetaDesign regroupa alors toutes ces valeurs et les organisa hiérarchiquement dans une pyramide. Les valeurs qui conféraient à la marque son caractère distinctif furent placées au sommet de la pyramide. À l'image des habitants de la région, la marque devait exprimer sa convivialité en étant sympathique, avec quelques imperfections non dénuées de charme. Elle devait également être pleine de contrastes, tout comme le paysage, et riche de tradition, tout comme la culture du Tyrol. La description en trois volets exprimait les traits distinctifs de la région et de ses produits. Le cœur de la marque devait refléter sa culture et concentrer ses valeurs. « Knödel et spaghetti » est l'expression de la symbiose hautement contrastée des cultures alpine et méditerranéenne. Malgré ces contrastes à multiples facettes, la marque devait demeurer charismatique. Dans le Tyrol du Sud, on célèbre le plaisir de vivre. La marque devait être tout aussi crédible et authentique que la région elle-même. La base de la pyramide était constituée des valeurs fondamentales de la marque. Le matériau de base de la marque du Tyrol du Sud est solide et fiable.

Au cours de l'atelier suivant, MetaDesign présente au groupe les premières visualisations des valeurs de marque ainsi définies. Des « tableaux d'humeur » donnent aux participants une nouvelle vision de la marque à travers des couleurs, des formes et des images, qui aident à affiner son portrait. Les valeurs de la pyramide ne

eigentlich transportieren sollte und welche Markenarchitektur dafür in Frage kommt. Gemeinsam mit der Arbeitsgruppe analysierte das Team von MetaDesign zunächst die Ist-Situation. Wie trat Südtirol bis dato auf? Welche Botschaften transportierte man? MetaDesign führte den Teilnehmern unter anderem den bisherigen Auftritt von Südtirol – durch einzelne Tourismusverbände, Hoteliers oder bei einzelnen Produkten – vor Augen. Zusätzlich wurde geprüft, wie sich der Wettbewerb positionierte. Alle Teilnehmer skizzierten und formulierten schließlich ihre Vision von der Dachmarke. Ein wichtiger Schritt auf dem Weg zur Klärung der eigenen Markenidentität. Auf dieser Basis definierte die Arbeitsgruppe das Set jener Werte, die künftig für Ausprägung, Charakter und Stil der Dachmarke Südtirol stehen sollten. MetaDesign bündelte und hierarchisierte diese Werte in einer Markenpyramide. In der Spitze der Pyramide finden sich jene Werte, die der Marke Südtirol ihr unverwechselbares Profil verleihen sollen. Wie die Menschen in diesem Land soll die Marke herzlich, im Sinne von kantig und warm, sein. Dazu ist sie kontrastreich wie die Natur und traditionsreich wie die Kultur Südtirols. Dieser Dreiklang soll das Unverwechselbare der Region und ihrer Produkte zum Ausdruck bringen. Der Markenkern spiegelt die Kultur der Marke wider. Dies sind Werte, die tief in der Marke verankert sind. Das Begriffspaar „Knödel & Spaghetti" ist Ausdruck der kontrastreichen Symbiose aus alpiner und mediterraner Kultur. Trotz dieser vielfältigen Kontraste strahlt die Marke Ruhe aus. Denn in Südtirol genießt man das Leben. Die Marke soll glaubwürdig und unverfälscht wie die Region sein. Das Fundament der Pyramide bilden Werte, die der Marke Halt geben. Die Substanz der Marke Südtirol ist kraftvoll und zuverlässig.

Im folgenden Workshop stellte MetaDesign der Arbeitsgruppe erste Visualisierungen der bisher definierten Markenidentität vor. Die sogenannten Moodboards gaben Mitgliedern der Arbeitsgruppe über Farben, Formen und Bildern einen neuen Zugang zur Wirkung

helped to further bring the brand's profile into focus. The values within the pyramid are not placed randomly alongside each other without any context. Their interaction is that which makes the umbrella brand for South Tyrol so unique. A further, central, step in the umbrella brand process was to find a definition which pithily identifies this textual interplay as brand positioning. The visual aspect in this regard acted simultaneously as catalyst, test criterion and strategic translation instrument. Initial approaches for positioning were generated in this phase and were presented in parallel to the design process up to the final positioning: South Tyrol is the richly contrasting symbiosis of alpine and Mediterranean characteristics, spontaneity and reliability, natural beauty and culture.

The design process

The mood-boards presented in the workshop also laid the foundations for the start of the design process. They provided an initial idea of the direction in which the visual development of the brand could lead. Brand strategies and brand design are closely interwoven and mutually correct each other where necessary as early as during the process of their development.

Within the framework of the umbrella brand process, the development of the logo was an exciting milestone in the teamwork for all participants. MetaDesign compiled 300 drafts in one initial step which the group organised and examined. Four proposals were again examined in more detail by the umbrella brand research group. Two favourites quickly crystallised. Both were based on an individually developed logotype. For both logo environments, MetaDesign designed an appropriate presentation; basic colours and fonts were added to the logo, a design principle developed and examples were created from these in concrete applications such as adverts, brochures or merchandising articles. The group was then able, at a very early stage, to ascertain how well certain design elements would work in their practical implementation. In this regard, special attention needed to be paid

sont pas placées de façon aléatoire, les unes à côté des autres, hors de tout contexte. C'est leur interaction qui rend la marque ombrelle du Sud Tyrol si unique. L'étape suivante, cruciale, est de formuler de façon concise cette interaction textuelle pour en extraire le positionnement de la marque. À cet égard, l'aspect visuel agit simultanément comme catalyseur, comme critère de test et comme outil de transposition stratégique. Nous avons proposé plusieurs axes de positionnement lors de cette phase, parallèlement à l'approche visuelle, jusqu'au concept final : le Tyrol du Sud est la symbiose riche en contrastes de caractéristiques alpines et méditerranéennes, à savoir spontanéité et fiabilité, culture et beauté naturelle.

La phase de design

Les tableaux d'humeur présentés dans le cadre de l'atelier ont également servi de point de départ au processus de design graphique, en fournissant l'orientation générale du développement visuel de la marque. Stratégie de marque et design graphique sont intimement imbriqués et se corrigent mutuellement en cas de besoin, et ce, dès la phase de conception.

Dans le cadre du développement de la marque ombrelle, la création du logo a été un événement captivant pour tous les participants de ce travail collectif. L'équipe de MetaDesign réalisa 300 croquis qu'elle soumit ensuite au groupe pour qu'il les trie et les évalue. Quatre propositions furent réexaminées plus en détail, et deux d'entre elles se démarquèrent rapidement. Elles étaient toutes deux basées sur des logotypes développés individuellement. Après avoir enrichi la présentation de chacun des deux univers avec des couleurs et des typographies de base, MetaDesign appliqua la charte graphique résultante à des exemples concrets de publicités, de brochures et d'articles promotionnels. C'est ainsi que, très tôt dans le processus de création, le groupe fut en mesure de vérifier la validité de certains éléments à travers leur mise en œuvre pratique. Il fallait s'assurer que la marque garde son identité dans

der Marke. Dies half, das Profil der Marke weiter zu schärfen. Denn die Werte innerhalb der Pyramide stehen nicht zusammenhangslos nebeneinander. Ihr Zusammenspiel ist es, was die Dachmarke Südtirol schließlich einzigartig macht. Es war ein weiterer zentraler Schritt des Dachmarkenprozesses, eine Definition zu finden, die dieses inhaltliche Wechselspiel als Positionierung der Marke auf den Punkt bringt. Das Visuelle fungierte hierbei zugleich als Katalysator, Prüfkriterium und strategisches Übersetzungsinstrument. Erste Ansätze für eine Positionierung entstanden bereits in dieser Phase und wurden parallel zum Designprozess bis zur finalen Positionierung präzisiert: *Südtirol ist die kontrastreiche Symbiose aus alpin und mediterran, Spontaneität und Verlässlichkeit, Natur und Kultur.*

Der Designprozess

Die im Workshop vorgestellten Moodboards legten aber auch schon das Fundament für den beginnenden Designprozess. Sie gaben eine erste Vorstellung davon, wohin sich die Marke visuell entwickeln könnte. Markenstrategie und Markengestaltung sind eng miteinander verwoben und korrigieren sich wechselseitig, wo nötig bereits im Prozess ihrer Entwicklung.

Die Entwicklung des Logos war im Rahmen des Dachmarkenprozesses für alle Beteiligten ein spannender Meilenstein der Zusammenarbeit. MetaDesign erarbeitete in einem ersten Schritt 300 Entwürfe, die das Team ordnete und prüfte. Mit vier Vorschlägen ging man schließlich erneut mit dem Arbeitskreis Dachmarke in Klausur. Schnell kristallisierten sich zwei Favoriten heraus. Beide basierten auf einem individuell entwickelten Schriftzug. MetaDesign gestaltete für beide Logo-Welten einen adäquaten Auftritt: Zum Logo wurden Basisfarben und Schriften addiert, ein Gestaltungsprinzip entwickelt und anhand von konkreten Anwendungen wie Anzeigen, Broschüren oder Merchandising-Artikeln beispielhaft übersetzt. So konnte das Team bereits in

to the necessity that the brand retained its identity in both Italian and German. On this basis, the research group made a selection of one of the two available design directions. The corporate design of the umbrella brand for South Tyrol took shape in the following months from application to application.

The new corporate design of the umbrella brand consists of the basic elements of umbrella brand, font, and colours in addition to the South Tyrolean panorama. Each of these basic elements emphasise certain facets of the brand identity. For example, the umbrella brand expresses more strongly, by way of its distinctive, handwritten and authentic character, the underlying core values. The mixture of upper and lower case lettering supports the liveliness of the umbrella brand, the high quality and powerful green tones underline the impression of authenticity and genuineness. A special significance is given to the characteristic house font. The font for South Tyrol, specially designed by MetaDesign's typographer Jürgen Huber,

les deux langues de la région, en allemand comme en italien. Une seule des options de design proposées fut alors retenue sur la base de ce critère, et l'identité visuelle de la marque du Tyrol du Sud prit forme au cours des mois suivants, d'application en application.

Les éléments de base de cette identité visuelle sont la marque, la typographie et les couleurs, ainsi qu'un panorama du Tyrol du Sud. Chacun de ces éléments de base souligne une certaine facette de l'identité de la marque. Par exemple, le caractère original, authentique et « écrit à la main » de la marque ombrelle illustre plus particulièrement les valeurs de base. Le mélange de majuscules et de minuscules souligne le dynamisme de la marque, tandis que les tons de vert profond accentuent l'impression d'authenticité et de naturel. Quant à la police de caractères, elle revêt une importance toute particulière. Spécialement conçue par Jürgen Huber, typographe chez MetaDesign, elle transmet les valeurs de la marque à travers tous les supports de communication, sur

einer sehr frühen Phase prüfen, wie sich bestimmte gestalterische Elemente in der praktischen Umsetzung bewähren würden. Dabei war besonders zu beachten, dass die Marke sowohl auf Italienisch als auch auf Deutsch ihre Identität bewahrt. Der Arbeitskreis traf auf dieser Grundlage eine Entscheidung für eine der beiden zur Disposition stehenden Designrichtungen. Das Corporate Design der Dachmarke Südtirol gewann in den folgenden Monaten nach und nach an Kontur.

Das neue Corporate Design der Dachmarke besteht aus den Basiselementen Dachmarke, Schrift, Farben sowie dem Südtirol-Panorama. Jedes dieser Basiselemente betont bestimmte Facetten der Markenidentität. Die Dachmarke zitiert zum Beispiel durch ihren markanten, handschriftlichen und authentischen Charakter stärker die Substanz- und Kernwerte. Die gemischte Groß- und Kleinschreibweise unterstützt die Lebendigkeit der Dachmarke, die hochwertigen und kraftvollen Grüntöne unterstreichen

conveys the values of the umbrella brand across all communication media. As soon as the house font becomes familiar, the South Tyrolean umbrella brand will benefit each time it is referred to or appears in a headline. The South Tyrolean panorama is also of the highest priority for the differentiating brand values. The synthesis of a Dolomite Alps panorama and a colour scheme specific to South Tyrol acts as a powerful, identifying basic element. While the distinctive panorama itself conveys the angular, strong and confident aspects of the region, the colour composition visualises the lively, richly contrasting and Mediterranean liveliness of South Tyrol. The South Tyrolean panorama has not been arbitrarily or freely invented – the basis for this was a sketch which MetaDesign chief Uli Mayer-Johanssen had prepared many years earlier at Ritten. In interaction therefore, umbrella brand and panorama generate a visualisation of the unique and unmistakable character of South Tyrol.

Since the introduction of the umbrella brand in January 2005, over 1000 enterprises and organisations have licensed the umbrella brand. The umbrella brand for South Tyrol is used in advertising campaigns and in TV spots. How can it be guaranteed, with this kind of diverse and intensive use in the most varied contexts and applications, that the umbrella brand be properly implemented and applied? How can the corporate design be protected against improper use or gross error? In a region such as South Tyrol, a situation is encountered which, if not extremely complex, is comparable to large multinational companies; brand management is in the hands of many different people. In an ideal world, brand management should be as centralised as possible and be conducted autocratically. In practice, this is only possible to a limited degree in the region of South Tyrol.

Instruments for management of an umbrella brand

Strategic brand management is implemented early on in the development of the visual translation. In view of this it

lesquels elle sera utilisée systématiquement. Dès que la police deviendra familière au public, la marque ombrelle du Tyrol du Sud en tirera profit chaque fois qu'elle sera utilisée ou évoquée dans un titre. La silhouette de la chaîne de montagnes est aussi un vecteur de différenciation crucial. Le schéma du massif alpin des Dolomites, dans une palette de couleurs typiques du Tyrol du Sud, agit comme un puissant élément de reconnaissance. Le paysage en lui-même, très caractéristique, reflète les aspects de rusticité, de solidité et de confiance de la région, tandis que les couleurs évoquent son dynamisme et sa vitalité méditerranéenne riche en contrastes. Ce motif n'a pas été inventé pour l'occasion, c'était à l'origine un croquis qu'Uli Mayer-Johanssen, le dirigeant de MetaDesign, avait préparé il y a quelques années à Ritten. Le nom de la marque et le panorama s'allient pour donner une visualisation du caractère unique du Tyrol du Sud.

Depuis la présentation de la marque ombrelle en janvier 2005, plus de 1000 entreprises et associations l'ont exploitée. La marque ombrelle du Tyrol du Sud apparaît dans les spots télévisés et les campagnes d'affichage. Comment garantir, avec une utilisation aussi intensive et diversifiée et dans des contextes d'application aussi variés, que la marque sera correctement véhiculée ? Comment protéger l'identité visuelle d'une utilisation erronée ou abusive ? La situation du Tyrol du Sud, sans être très complexe, ressemble à celle d'une entreprise multinationale, où la gestion de marque est entre les mains de nombreuses personnes différentes. Dans un monde idéal, la gestion de marque devrait être aussi centralisée que possible et être dirigée de façon autocratique. En pratique, cela n'est possible que dans une certaine limite pour la région du Tyrol du Sud.

Outils de gestion de marque ombrelle

La gestion stratégique de marque est mise en œuvre dès le début de la conception de l'identité visuelle. Dès les premières étapes de la création, il est important de définir les exigences, les problè-

den Eindruck des Echten und Unverfälschten. Eine besondere Bedeutung kommt der charakteristischen Hausschrift zu. Die von Jürgen Huber, Typograf bei MetaDesign, eigens entworfene Südtirol-Schrift überträgt die Werte der Dachmarke in alle Kommunikationsanwendungen. Ist die Hausschrift erst einmal bekannt, gewinnt die Dachmarke Südtirol durch jede Headline hinzu. Das Südtirol-Panorama wiederum steht in erster Linie für die differenzierenden Markenwerte. Die Synthese aus einem Dolomiten-Panorama und einem für Südtirol spezifischen Farbklang fungiert als starkes, identitätsstiftendes Basiselement. Während das markante Panorama selbst das Kantige, Kraftvolle und Selbstbewusste der Region transportiert, visualisiert der Farbklang das Lebendige, Kontrastreiche, auch Mediterran-Leichte an Südtirol. Das Südtirol-Panorama ist übrigens nicht beliebig oder frei erfunden – die Basis hierfür bildete eine Skizze, die MetaDesign-Chefin Uli Mayer-Johanssen viele Jahre zuvor vom Ritten aus angefertigt hatte. Im Zusammenspiel visualisieren Dachmarke und Panorama den einzigartigen und unverwechselbaren Charakter von Südtirol.

Seit der Einführung der Dachmarke im Januar 2005 haben über 1000 Betriebe und Organisationen die Dachmarke lizensiert. Die Dachmarke Südtirol wird in Anzeigenkampagnen genutzt oder bei TV-Spots eingesetzt. Doch wie stellt man bei einer derart vielfältigen und intensiven Nutzung in unterschiedlichsten Zusammenhängen und Anwendungen sicher, dass die Dachmarke richtig eingesetzt und genutzt wird? Wie kann man das Corporate Design vor falscher Nutzung und vor groben Fehlern schützen? In einer Region wie Südtirol trifft man auf eine mit großen multinationalen Unternehmen vergleichbare, wenn nicht sogar komplexere Situation: Viele Köpfe und Hände sind Teil der Markenführung. Im Idealfall sollte Markenführung aber möglichst zentral sein und autokratisch erfolgen. In der Praxis ist dies gerade im Fall der Region Südtirol nur sehr bedingt möglich.

is important at the beginning of the process to consider requirements, problems and limits of the applications along with their complexity and diversity. Early on, MetaDesign had already begun to think about the most varied forms implementation of the umbrella brand could take and developed solutions for them. How does the brand work as a modular or fixed application in co-branding? How can the brand be integrated into an existing sign? How can the umbrella brand be positioned on various packaging? What would a new trade fair presentation look like? Strategic brand management gives subsequent users clear guidelines to be followed. These kinds of guidelines, however, are not much help on their own in cases of doubt. However, regulations are rarely broken intentionally; frequently, an offence is committed unwittingly or as a result of a lack of practical help. Every brand regulation must thus be coupled with instruments which facilitate the proper application of the corporate design in practice. MetaDesign has therefore created its own website for the umbrella brand (www.provinz.bz.it/dachmarke/_std/home_de.html). Those interested will find here the essential regulations for the most diverse aspects of use and descriptive examples for proper and improper application. In another forum, users are able to ask those commissioned for the umbrella brand concrete questions about its use. A team within the umbrella brand advisory board can respond quickly to any acute problems which might occur. The website has enjoyed an excellent response since its introduction in February 2005. The possibility of having questions about application answered so quickly has been comprehensively well received. An extra bonus are the download areas reserved for registered users. Within this area there is a wide spectrum of digital samples for private use. This is especially welcome assistance for numerous small enterprises. The sample for an advert in the format A4, for example, comes with completed layout – the user needs only to insert a headline, image and copy text in the appropriate places. This kind of

mes et les limites des applications dans leur diversité et leur complexité. Très tôt, MetaDesign a réfléchi à toutes les différentes implémentations possibles et a proposé des solutions adaptées.
Comment se comporte la marque ombrelle en tant qu'application modulaire ou figée dans le cadre d'une association de marques ? Peut-elle être intégrée à un symbole existant ? Comment appliquer la marque ombrelle à différents emballages ? Quelle serait son apparence dans la présentation d'un salon commercial ? La gestion stratégique de marque propose aux utilisateurs un certain nombre de directives à suivre, aussi claires que possible. Mais ce genre de directives ne suffit pas toujours en cas de doute.
Pourtant, les règles sont rarement brisées volontairement, et les erreurs sont le plus souvent commises par mégarde ou à cause d'un manque d'aide sur certains cas concrets. Cet ensemble de règles doit donc s'accompagner d'instruments qui faciliteront la bonne application de l'identité visuelle dans la pratique. C'est pourquoi MetaDesign a créé son propre site Internet pour la marque ombrelle (www.provinz.bz.it/dachmarke/_std/home_de.htlm). On y trouve les règles essentielles pour une grande variété d'utilisations, ainsi que des exemples décrivant les applications correctes et incorrectes. Sur un autre forum, les usagers peuvent interroger les créateurs de la marque sur des problèmes concrets, et une équipe dépendant du comité consultatif de la marque ombrelle peut apporter rapidement des solutions à tout problème imprévu. Le site Internet a reçu un excellent accueil depuis sa mise en service en février 2005, et son efficacité à résoudre les problèmes a été saluée collectivement. En prime, les utilisateurs inscrits peuvent y télécharger des documents. On y trouve par exemple un large éventail d'échantillons numériques à usage privé. Ce service est particulièrement bienvenu pour de nombreuses petites entreprises. L'échantillon d'une publicité en format A4, par exemple, présente une maquette préétablie, et l'utilisateur n'a plus qu'à ajouter le titre, le texte et l'image dans les champs correspondants. Ce genre d'outil pratique ré-

Instrumente zum Management der Dachmarke

Strategische Markenführung setzt schon in der Entwicklung der visuellen Übersetzung ein. Insofern ist es bereits zu Beginn des Prozesses wichtig, Bedürfnisse, Probleme und Grenzen der Anwendungen sowie deren Komplexität und Vielfalt zu bedenken. MetaDesign hat sich frühzeitig über die unterschiedlichsten Einsatzformen der Dachmarke Gedanken gemacht und dafür Lösungen entwickelt. Wie funktioniert die Marke als modulare oder fixierte Applikation im Co-Branding? Wie kann die Marke in ein bestehendes Zeichen integriert werden? Wie platziere ich die Dachmarke auf unterschiedlichsten Verpackungen? Wie könnte ein neuer Messeauftritt im Corporate Design aussehen? Strategische Markenführung gibt den späteren Anwendern klare Regeln vor, die zu befolgen sind. Doch derartige Richtlinien allein nützen im Zweifelsfall wenig. Selten verletzt jemand absichtlich eine Vorgabe. Häufig geschieht der Verstoß unwissentlich oder mangels praktischer Hilfe. Jedes Markenreglementarium ist demnach mit Instrumenten zu koppeln, die die richtige Anwendung des Corporate Design in der Praxis erleichtern. Daher hat MetaDesign eine eigene Website zur Dachmarke aufgebaut. Zu den unterschiedlichsten Aspekten der Nutzung finden Interessierte hier die wesentlichen Vorgaben sowie anschauliche Beispiele für die richtige wie auch falsche Anwendung. Die Nutzer haben in einem extra Forum die Möglichkeit, an den Dachmarkenbeauftragten der Region Südtirol konkrete Fragen zum Umgang zu stellen. Eine eigene Task-Force innerhalb des Dachmarkenbeirats kann überdies schnell auf akut auftretende Probleme reagieren. Die Website erfreut sich seit ihrer Einführung im Februar 2005 einer großen Resonanz. Die Möglichkeit, konkrete Fragen zur Anwendung schnell klären zu können, wird umfangreich wahrgenommen. Ein besonderes Plus ist der den registrierten Nutzern vorbehaltene Downloadbereich. In ihm findet sich ein breites Spektrum digitaler Vorlagen für den eigenen Gebrauch. Das ist insbesondere für die zahlreichen kleineren Unter-

Sonnenluft atmen!

www.webadresse.info

SÜDTIROL

Südtirol Information · Pfarrplatz 11 · I-39100 Bozen
Telefon +39 0471 999 999 · info@suedtirol.info
www.suedtirol.info

Lorem ipsum irit
www.webadresse.info

SüDTiROL

Musterstraße ··· I-39100 Bozen
Telefon +39 0125 456 789 · info@suedtirol.info
www.webadresse.info

**Left:** *sample of advertising page ///* À
gauche : *page de publicité ///* **Links:**
*Werbeseite*

**Right:** *advertising template ///* À droite :
*modèle de publicité ///* **Rechts:**
*Werbe-Template*

practical help significantly reduces the risk of improper application of the corporate design; nevertheless, it is not possible to exclude it altogether. In order to emphasise how important consistent use of the corporate design is, the umbrella brand advisory board has generated a set of conventions for the allocation and use of the umbrella brand 'Südtirol' and 'Alto Adige'. Whoever wishes to use the umbrella brand must recognise and follow this set of conventions. Regular random checks should ensure proper observation of these conventions. In the case of improper or incorrect use of the umbrella brand, administrative penalties will be imposed. An aspect of the set of conventions demonstrates by example how the umbrella brand can be employed for strategic aims; both for quality products and for services, the set of conventions contains clear guidelines which define what obligations are commensurate with the use of the umbrella brand. Companies which are active in tourism and catering must demonstrate measures to increase the value of, and

duit de manière significative les risques d'application incorrecte de l'identité visuelle, bien qu'il soit impossible de tous les éliminer. Afin de souligner l'importance d'une utilisation cohérente du design, le comité consultatif de la marque ombrelle a publié un ensemble de conventions à respecter dans l'utilisation des marques « Südtirol » et « Alto Adige ». Toute personne désireuse d'utiliser la marque ombrelle doit s'engager à respecter ces conventions. Des contrôles aléatoires réguliers devraient assurer la bonne observation de ces conventions. En cas d'utilisation incorrecte ou abusive de la marque ombrelle, des amendes administratives seront imposées. Une partie de ces conventions explique par l'exemple comment se servir de la marque à des fins stratégiques. Que cela concerne un produit ou un service, la convention indique clairement les obligations associées à cette utilisation. Les sociétés des secteurs du tourisme ou de la restauration doivent démontrer leur engagement à améliorer le positionnement des produits du Tyrol du Sud ou à les

nehmen eine große Entlastung. Die Vorlage für eine Anzeige im Format DIN A4 ist zum Beispiel fertig gelayoutet – der Nutzer muss an den entsprechenden Stellen nur noch Headline, Bild und Copy-Text einsetzen. Solche praxisnahen Hilfen mindern das Risiko einer falschen Anwendung des Corporate Design erheblich – ganz ausschließen können sie sie gleichwohl nicht. Um zu unterstreichen, wie wichtig eine konsistente Nutzung des Corporate Designs ist, hat der Dachmarkenbeirat ein Reglement für die Vergabe und den Gebrauch der Dachmarke „Südtirol" beziehungsweise „Alto Adige" erstellt. Wer die Dachmarke nutzen möchte, muss dieses Reglement anerkennen und befolgen. Regelmäßige Stichprobenkontrollen sollen die Einhaltung des Reglements gewährleisten. Bei unrechtmäßiger oder missbräuchlicher Nutzung der Dachmarke drohen Verwaltungsstrafen. Ein Aspekt des Regelwerks zeigt beispielhaft, wie die Dachmarke für strategische Ziele eingesetzt werden kann: Sowohl für Qualitätsprodukte als auch für Dienstleistungen beinhaltet das

improve the positioning of, South Tyrolean quality products. This means, for example, that specific South Tyrolean products must be on the menu. Within the framework of the branding process, the members of the group for the umbrella brand for South Tyrol have exemplarily implemented the final building block for the success of an umbrella brand such as South Tyrol, which is that the products must deliver exactly what the brand promises. South Tyrol keeps its brand promises – this can be experienced whether on holiday in Vinschgau, Meranerland or Trentino, just as the products can be enjoyed from the table or the glass. Ideal prerequisites, then, for the South Tyrolean umbrella brand to prove itself as a worthwhile investment for the future.

valoriser. Cela implique par exemple d'inclure des produits régionaux spécifiques dans les menus des restaurants. Dans le cadre du processus de gestion de la marque, les membres ont posé la dernière pierre à l'édifice d'une marque d'avenir pour le Tyrol du Sud en adhérant à un principe essentiel et en l'appliquant de façon exemplaire : leurs produits doivent correspondre en tous points aux promesses de la marque. La région tient les promesses de sa marque ombrelle, et l'on s'en rendra compte aisément en passant des vacances à Venosta, à Merano ou à Trente, ou en dégustant les spécialités gastronomiques locales. Les conditions idéales sont donc réunies pour que la marque ombrelle du Tyrol du Sud s'avère un investissement rentable à l'avenir.

Reglement klare Vorgaben, welche Pflichten die Nutzung der Dachmarke mit sich bringt. Unternehmen, die im Tourismus und in der Gastronomie tätig sind, haben Maßnahmen zur Aufwertung und besseren Positionierung der Südtiroler Qualitätserzeugnisse nachzuweisen. So müssen zum Beispiel spezifische Südtiroler Produkte auf der Speisekarte zu finden sein. Die Mitglieder des Arbeitskreises Dachmarke Südtirol haben im Rahmen des Markenprozesses vorbildlich das umgesetzt, was der letzte Baustein für den Erfolg einer Dachmarke wie Südtirol ist: Die Produkte müssen einlösen, was die Marke verspricht. Südtirol hält sein Markenversprechen – das kann man im Urlaub im Vinschgau, Meranerland oder Trentino genauso erleben wie beim Genuss der Produkte auf dem Teller oder im Glas. Ideale Voraussetzungen also, dass die Dachmarke Südtirol sich als lohnenswerte Investition für die Zukunft erweist.

# Neugierig ...
### ... auf die Dachmarke Südtirol?

Alle Informationen unter
www.provinz.bz.it/dachmarke
ab dem 1. Januar 2005

**SÜDTIROL**

# Unschlagbar ...
### ... mit der neuen Dachmarke Südtirol.

Alle Informationen unter
www.provinz.bz.it/dachmarke
ab dem 1. Januar 2005

**SÜDTIROL**

# Volle Kanne gut ...
### ... die neue Dachmarke Südtirol.

Alle Informationen unter
www.provinz.bz.it/dachmarke
ab dem 1. Januar 2005

**SÜDTIROL**

# Unschlagbar mit der neuen Dachmarke

www.provinz.bz.it/dachmarke

## SÜDTIROL

Corporate Typeface - Suedtirol

## Die Magie der Vielfalt

Südtirol ist die kontrastreiche Symbiose aus alpin und mediterran, Spontaneität und Verlässlichkeit, Natur und Kultur.

0123456789

@!?%.;,_-*+'#/

Südtirol-Panorama

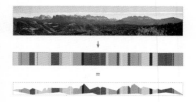

# SÜDTIROL

**Left:** *leaflet promoting the use of the new
identity ///* **À gauche** *: Dépliant de promotion
pour l'utilisation de la nouvelle identité ///*
**Links:** *Broschüre, die für die Verwendung
der neuen Identity wirbt*

# Profile
# (MetaDesign)

**www.metadesign.de**
Location: Berlin, Germany

Awards: Meta Design is an
international, award-winning
design studio, with prizes in

both design and branding
categories

*MetaDesign has been one of Europe's most respected design agencies
for over ten years. Its portfolio of services ranges from strategic brand
management to the design and implementation of complex corporate
identities and images. The company name embodies its philosophy.
Design has become an increasingly important steering instrument for
company success. Visual design is a criterion for defining strategy and
corporate vision, and strategy, for its part, must be reflected in the
visuals in order to generate emotion and minimize interpretative
confusion. The growing significance of identity processes in a dy-
namically changing corporate landscape has made it necessary for
corporate identity to be steered and managed on a meta-level. This is
what MetaDesign stands for.*

*Depuis plus de dix ans, MetaDesign est l'une des agences de design
les plus respectées en Europe. Sa gamme de services s'étend de la gestion stratégique de marque à la conception et à la mise en œuvre
d'identités visuelles élaborées. Le nom de l'agence est une expression
de sa philosophie. Le design est devenu un élément moteur et incon-
tournable du succès commercial d'une marque. La communication
visuelle sert à définir la stratégie et la vision de l'entreprise, qui à
leur tour doivent être reflétées dans les visuels afin de créer de l'émotion et de minimiser l'ambiguïté de l'interprétation. La portée croissante des processus d'identité dans le monde en constante évolution*

*des entreprises implique de gérer l'identité d'une marque à un méta-
niveau. C'est ce concept qu'incarne MetaDesign.*

*MetaDesign ist seit über zehn Jahren eine der renommiertesten
Designagenturen Europas. Ihr Leistungsspektrum reicht vom strategischen Markenmanagement bis zum Design und der Implementierung komplexer Corporate Identitys und Images. Der Firmen-
name verkörpert ihre Philosophie. Design ist ein zunehmend wich-
tiges Steuerungsinstrument für den Erfolg einer Firma geworden.
Visuelles Design ist ein Kriterium für die Definition der Strategie
und Vision einer Firma; die Strategie ihrerseits muss sichtbar
Emotion erzeugen und interpretatorische Verwirrung minimieren.
Die wachsende Bedeutung von Identitätsprozessen innerhalb einer
sich dynamisch wandelnden Firmenlandschaft macht es notwendig,
Corporate Identity auf einem Meta-Level zu steuern und zu mana-
gen. Dafür steht MetaDesign.*

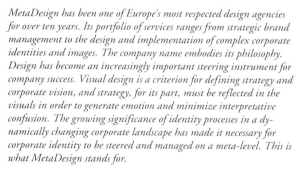

# ACELA: DESIGNED TO MOVE PEOPLE

In 1996, Amtrak began working with the OH&CO and IDEO product development team to design, brand and introduce a completely new train service in the Northeast USA. Everything from train liveries to waiting areas to ticket jackets was completely rethought and redesigned. The approach focused on a comprehensive service strategy that included each aspect of travelers' experience form pre-travel, to in-station, boarding and on-board activities as well as the arrival experience. OH&CO also created a distinctive, new brand to convey this revised travel offering to the American public.

More than just a train: a total travel concept.

As part of an ambitious plan to increase operational self-sufficiency and provide an improved option to travelers in the Northeast, Amtrak was preparing to introduce new high-speed equipment and service between Boston and Washington, DC. This represented a

En 1996, Amtrak s'adresse à l'équipe de gestion de produit de OH&CO et IDEO afin qu'ils conçoivent le design, l'identité visuelle et l'annonce d'un tout nouveau service de transport ferroviaire dans le nord-est des États-Unis. Tout est repensé et remodelé, des couleurs des voitures aux pochettes de billets et aux salles d'attente. La stratégie globale couvre chaque aspect de l'expérience des voyageurs : préparation du voyage, arrivée en gare, embarquement, activités à bord et débarquement. OH&CO conçoit également une marque originale pour incarner cette nouvelle offre de service au public américain.

Plus qu'un simple train : un concept de voyage intégral

Désireuse d'augmenter son autonomie opérationnelle tout en offrant une alternative améliorée aux voyageurs du Nord-Est, Amtrak se prépare à mettre en place un nouveau train express sur la liaison Boston-Washington DC. Pour

1996 begann Amtrak, mit dem Produktentwicklungsteam von OH&CO und IDEO zu arbeiten, um eine komplett neue Marke für einen Bahnservice im Nordosten der USA zu entwerfen und einzuführen. Von den Schaffneruniformen über die Warteräume bis zu den Fahrkartenschaltern wurde alles komplett neu erdacht und entworfen. Der Ansatz konzentrierte sich auf eine umfassende Servicestrategie, die alle Aspekte einer Reise einschließen sollte: von den Reisevorbereitungen über den Aufenthalt auf dem Bahnhof, dem Einstieg und den Aktivitäten in der Bahn sowie die Ankunft. OH&CO schuf außerdem eine unverwechselbare neue Marke, um der amerikanischen Öffentlichkeit dieses überarbeitete Reiseangebot zu vermitteln.

Mehr als nur ein Zug: ein Reisegesamtkonzept.

Teil des ehrgeizigen Plans, die operationale Effizienz zu erhöhen und Reisenden im Nordosten der USA bessere Reisemöglichkeiten zu bieten, war es, einen neuen

In lieu of Light Blue, use 45% PANTONE 5035C or
process 045C 000M 004Y 029K.

In lieu of Green, use PANTONE 368C or
process 065C 000M 100Y 000K.

In lieu of Red, use PANTONE 485C or
process 000C 100M 091Y 000K.

In lieu of Dark Grey, use PANTONE 432C or
process 023C 000M 000Y 079K.

977C process col

GREY  SILVER

## Acela brand pro

05.01.99 release
Interim specifications

### Horizontal brandmark

The horizontal brandma
intentionally aligned to
between the Motion ma
grid shown on this page
correct alignment of elem
output is not available.

⚠ The proportional relationsh
in the horizontal configura
not be altered.

Total width of Motion mark = 3x

The Acela wordmark aligns to the grid
lines from the absolute top and bottom of
the letter "a".

OH&CO
379 West Broadway 5th fl.
New York

major investment for Amtrak and an opportunity. The railway realized that it required a fresh perspective on travel that could outpace the incumbent air shuttles and win over business travelers. Amtrak also understood that the high-speed initiative in the Northeast could help to shift Amtrak internally, from being an operational-focused organization towards servicing travelers with a greater understanding of their needs and desires.

The underlying principle from the beginning was to design a service around the traveler that, to the greatest degree possible, would be balanced with Amtrak's operational requirements and business goals. And so, we put the traveler in the lead from the start. While the high-speed train set design represented a critical task item in the program, our focus shifted predominantly to researching the behavior, needs and desires of the American traveler. Focus groups, audits and more than 20,000 customer interviews provided us with a

l'entreprise, c'est à la fois un investissement majeur et une possibilité d'ouverture. Amtrak doit en effet ouvrir de nouvelles perspectives de voyage pour espérer distancer l'offre des transports aériens et séduire la classe affaires. Cette initiative pouvait en outre contribuer à un changement de politique au sein de l'entreprise elle-même. Les objectifs purement opérationnels seraient délaissés au profit d'un meilleur service à la clientèle, qui tiendrait compte de ses désirs et de ses besoins.

Dès le début, le principe était donc de concevoir un service centré sur le voyageur, qui respecterait autant que possible les exigences opérationnelles et les objectifs commerciaux de l'entreprise. Nous avons donc tout de suite mis le voyageur au premier plan. Le design intérieur du train express était un élément crucial de notre programme, mais nous nous sommes essentiellement attachés à analyser le comportement et les besoins du voyageur américain. Des groupes de discussion, des audits et un

Hochgeschwindigkeitszug und Service zwischen Boston und Washington DC einzurichten. Dies stellte eine bedeutende Investition für Amtrak dar, aber auch eine Chance. Die Bahn realisierte, dass es einer neuen Perspektive des Reisens bedurfte, die den bestehenden Luftverkehr ausstechen und Geschäftsreisende überzeugen konnte. Außerdem war Amtrak klar, dass die Hochgeschwindigkeitsinitiative im Nordosten Amtrak selbst helfen konnte, sich von einer auf den Betrieb konzentrierten Organisation in einen Service zu verwandeln, der besser auf die Bedürfnisse und Wünsche der Reisenden zugeschnitten war.

Das zugrunde liegende Prinzip war von Anfang an die Gestaltung eines Service für den Reisenden, der sich so gut wie möglich mit Amtraks Betriebsanforderungen und Unternehmenszielen vereinbaren ließ. So stand von Beginn an der Reisende im Zentrum unserer Bemühungen.

Während das Design des Schnellzugs eine kritische Aufgabe innerhalb des

**Left & right:** *Conceptual drawings on how the lounges, stores and railway main entrance would look like ///* **Gauche et droite :** *Dessins conceptuels sur l'aspect des salons, des boutiques et de l'entrée principale de la gare ///* **Links & rechts:** *Entwürfe zum möglichen Aussehen der Loungen, der Geschäfte und dem Haupteingang des Bahnhofes*

deep understanding on which we were able to establish a strategy and framework to design each aspect of the service.

Study of travel experiences showed that there is much more to the journey than simply the train ride itself. We were able to identify a sequence of ten interconnected steps that most people navigate as they set out, travel and arrive at their destinations. By understanding each of the steps from the user perspective allowed us to develop an experience map that formed the basis for a connected journey that could be uniquely delivered by the rail mode. Working closely together, IDEO and OH&CO christened the strategy the *Seamless Journey*. An image of a turtle gliding through an infinity of blue water became the metaphorical image for the experience and sensation that was to be projected. This idea was also used to this to deemphasize the idea of speed alone and to dial up the notion of a fluid, connected sensibility. These early ideas shaped the

sondage d'opinion auprès de plus de 20 000 clients nous ont apporté des informations précieuses pour établir une stratégie et concevoir les différents aspects du service. L'analyse des expériences des clients nous a montré que la notion de voyage va au-delà du simple déplacement en train. De la préparation du voyage à son aboutissement, nous avons constaté que l'usager traversait en général une série de dix étapes. En étudiant ces étapes du point de vue du voyageur, nous avons établi une espèce d'itinéraire symbolique dont les caractéristiques n'appartenaient qu'au seul mode de transport ferroviaire. Travaillant en étroite collaboration, IDEO et OH&CO baptisèrent ce concept : le *Voyage continu*. L'image d'une tortue glissant dans le bleu infini fut choisie comme métaphore de la sensation recherchée. Le but était aussi de cesser de mettre l'accent sur la vitesse, au profit des notions de fluidité et de sensibilité. Ce concept préliminaire a guidé toute la conception du nouveau service.

Programms darstellte, konzentrierten wir uns vornehmlich darauf, das Verhalten, die Bedürfnisse und Wünsche des amerikanischen Reisenden zu erforschen. Zielgruppenforschung, Prüfungen und mehr als 20.000 Kundenbefragungen lieferten uns ein gründliches Verständnis dafür, was die Basis für unsere Strategie und den Rahmen jedes Designaspekts des Service sein sollte.

Eine Studie von Reiseberichten zeigte, dass zur Reise viel mehr gehört als nur die Zugfahrt an sich. Wir erkannten eine Abfolge von zehn zusammenhängenden Schritten, die erfolgen, wenn ein Reisender aufbricht, reist und am Ziel ankommt. Aus dem Verständnis dieser Schritte und aus der Kundenperspektive heraus entwickelten wir eine Erfahrungskarte, die die Basis für eine Reiseroute darstellte, die nur per Zug zu bewältigen war. IDEO und OH&CO arbeiteten eng zusammen und weihten *seamless journey* (Nahtlose Reise) ein. Das Bild einer Schildkröte, die durch unendliches, blaues Wasser gleitet, wurde zur

**All images:** *the new Acela brand and the experience it promises include all the details* /// **Toutes les images :** *la nouvelle marque Acela et l'expérience qu'elle promet n'omettent aucun détail* /// **Alle Abbildungen:** *Die neue Acela-Servicemarke und das versprochene Erlebnis beinhalten alle Details*

creation of the new service from the ground up. The Seamless Journey strategy brought true focus to the customer and did a good job of balancing the hard aspects of the service, such as equipment and speed, with the softer dimensions that were so important, such as the behaviors, images and attitude that we wanted the service to have. Furthermore, it provided a complete platform that would guide the many improvements upgrading every step of the journey in the corridor connecting Washington and Boston. Together with Amtrak the team proposed that the Seamless Journey strategy could also be a model other corridors across the nation.

Getting from A to B is now about how you use your time.

As the service strategy was used to inform decisions about the service itself, OH&CO began work on the expression aspects that would communicate the new offering to the public. Once again,

La notion de *Voyage continu* a vraiment recentré la stratégie sur l'usager et a réussi à équilibrer les aspects purement techniques du service, comme les machines et la vitesse, et la dimension humaine que nous cherchions à valoriser à travers de nouvelles images et de nouveaux comportements. Elle a aussi servi de plateforme générale aux améliorations qualitatives de chaque étape du voyage sur la ligne Boston-Washington. Nous avons en outre suggéré à Amtrak d'appliquer ce concept à d'autres lignes dans le pays.

Aller du point A au point B : une autre façon d'employer son temps

Tandis que l'offre de service se modelait sur les impératifs stratégiques, OH&CO réfléchit au moyen de présenter le nouveau service au public. Là encore, notre connaissance des attentes des usagers en matière de petits trajets a nourri notre action. Un nouveau positionnement, *Destination liberté*, s'inspirait de ce que les gens apprécient

Metapher der Erfahrung und Empfindung, die projiziert werden sollte. Die Idee bestand darin, die Vorstellung von Geschwindigkeit allein in den Hintergrund zu rücken, zugunsten der Vorstellung von einer flüssigen, verbundenen Sensibilität. Diese frühen Ideen gaben der Entstehung des neuen Service ihre grundlegende Form.

Die Strategie des „*seamless journey*" konzentrierte sich ganz und gar auf den Kunden. Sie verband die harten Aspekte des Service, wie Ausstattung und Schnelligkeit, mit den weicheren, sehr wichtigen Dimensionen wie das Verhalten, das Image und die Einstellung, die der Service haben sollte. Zusätzlich stellte die Strategie eine Plattform dar, auf der die vielen Verbesserungen der Strecke zwischen Washington und Boston Schritt für Schritt erfolgen konnten. Gemeinsam mit Amtrak schlug das Team vor, das die Strategie der Nahtlosen Reise auch für andere Strecken wegweisend sein könnte.

our learning about what people really want from a short distance travel experience really drove the process. A brand positioning, *Destination Freedom*, was inspired by what people love about train travel: more independence, more comfort and quality time; in short, an enlightened experience in tune with today's values. The positioning strategy promised world-class train service to people who value their time.

*"Time in transit too often feels like time endured, or wasted. But as travel becomes enjoyable and effortless, time turns around. Time is recaptured, restored, redoubled. This kind of heightened perception is embodied in the Acela trains."*
— Travel and Leisure magazine

The new service brand and its identity, Acela, was also a fresh and unexpected departure for Amtrak. Chosen from more than 400 candidates generated by OH&CO, the new name combines acceleration and excellence. The visual identity was designed to convey a sense of and speed freedom of movement — values that are somewhat opposite to those delivered by air travel.

The Acela brand was structured according to a three-tiered service offering. Acela EX at the top for the new high-speed service. And Acela RS and Acela CS for the regional and commuter services that run in the corridor and that make more frequent stops. This configuration of integrated services within the Acela brand presented a setup that customers could readily understand and that Amtrak could deliver more efficiently. The range of features and amenities for each level of service and ticket prices were logically aligned. Existing Amtrak sub brands in the Northeast such as Metroliner and Northeast Direct were retired. This transition represented a significant challenge to Amtrak in that the implementation of this new structure would require an extended period of time and a heightened level of communication with customers about the changes underway as the entire Acela service was being introduced.

dans les voyages en train : plus d'indépendance, plus de confort et de temps pour soi. En résumé, une expérience constructive, en phase avec les valeurs d'aujourd'hui. Cette stratégie de positionnement promettait des prestations haut de gamme aux voyageurs dont le temps est précieux.

*« – Le temps passé dans les transports est trop souvent ressenti comme du temps imposé ou gaspillé. Mais quand voyager devient plaisant et facile, le temps s'écoule autrement. Il est réinvesti, retrouvé et redoublé. C'est cette nouvelle perception qu'incarnent les trains Acela. »* Travel and Leisure Magazine.

La nouvelle marque de service et son identité, « Acela », représentaient aussi un nouveau départ surprenant pour Amtrak. Choisi parmi 400 propositions soumises par OH&CO, le nouveau nom marie accélération et excellence. L'identité visuelle véhicule une notion de vitesse et de liberté de mouvement, des valeurs qui s'opposent quelque peu à celles qui existent dans le transport aérien.

Le concept d'Acela a été articulé selon trois pôles de prestations. Acela EX, le haut de gamme du réseau express, et Acela RS et CS pour le réseau régional et de proche banlieue qui desservait la ligne avec des arrêts plus fréquents. Cette configuration de services intégrés au sein de la marque était facilement compréhensible pour les usagers et facile à mettre en œuvre pour Amtrak. La gamme d'équipements et d'aménagements de chaque niveau de service fut alignée en conséquence, tout comme le prix des billets. Amtrak abandonna aussi les anciennes dénominations Metroliner et Northeast Direct qui existaient dans le Nord-Est. Cette transition était un enjeu de taille pour Amtrak. L'implémentation de cette nouvelle structure allait nécessiter un certain temps d'adaptation et un gros travail de communication en direction des usagers pendant toute la période d'implantation du nouveau service Acela.

Von A nach B zu gelangen hängt nun von ihrer Zeit ab.

Die Servicestrategie informierte über den Service an sich, und OH&CO begannen zu überlegen, wie man das neue Angebot der Öffentlichkeit präsentieren sollte. Wieder wurde der Prozess von den Überlegungen geleitet, was die Leute wirklich von einer Kurzstreckenreise erwarten. Eine Markenpositionierung, *Destination Freedom* (Ziel: Freiheit), wurde davon inspiriert, was Menschen am Reisen lieben: größere Unabhängigkeit, mehr Komfort und Mußestunden, kurz: eine fortschrittliche Erfahrung in Einklang mit den heutigen Werten. Die Positionsstrategie versprach einen Weltklasse-Bahnservice für Menschen, denen ihre Zeit kostbar ist.

*„Zeit auf der Durchreise fühlt sich zu oft wie etwas an, was man erträgt oder wie verschwendet. Aber wenn Reisen angenehm und mühelos wird, dreht sich die Zeit um. Die Zeit wird zurückerobert, wiederhergestellt, verdoppelt. Diese Art erhöhte Wahrnehmung wird von den Acela-Zügen verkörpert."* - Travel and Leisure Magazin.

Die neue Servicemarke und ihr Image, Acela, bedeutete auch einen neuen und unerwarteten Weg für Amtrak. Der Name, aus 400 Vorschlägen von OH&CO ausgewählt, kombiniert Beschleunigung mit Qualität. Das visuelle Image sollte ein Gefühl von Schnelligkeit und Freiheit während der Bewegung vermitteln – Werte, die denen von Flugreisen entgegenstehen.

Die Marke Acela war einem dreistöckigen Serviceangebot gemäß strukturiert: Ganz oben Acela EX für den neuen Schnellzugservice, Acela RS und Acela CS für den regionalen und Pendler-Service mit mehr Haltestellen. Dieser Aufbau zusammenhängender Angebote innerhalb der Marke Acela präsentierte eine Organisation, die schnell vom Kunden verstanden wurde und die Amtrak effizienter liefern konnte. Das Angebot an Funktionen und Möglichkeiten für jede Serviceebene und die Fahrpreise waren logisch miteinander verknüpft. Existierende Amtrak-Marken im Nordosten wie

Designing the journey.

OH&CO helped Amtrak design and implement the new service at every Seamless Journey step. OH&CO together with IDEO and other partners including architects, signage specialists and engineers participated in station improvements and oversaw the design of new and refurbished train interiors to insure that the overall Seamless Journey philosophy would be maintained as each touchpoint was considered. A complete system of service apparel was designed as well. OH&CO also created schedules, employee and stakeholder communications, marketing communications, signage, ticketing interfaces, cafe car designs, on-board service items, and liveries. In the process, a system of secondary identity elements, including a set of consumer-friendly icons, was developed.

The brand launch generated employee excitement; and garnered Amtrak more than $6 million in earned media.

Le design du voyage

OH&CO aida Amtrak dans la conception et la mise en œuvre du nouveau service à chaque étape du *Voyage continu*. OH&CO et IDEO collaborèrent avec des architectes, des ingénieurs et des spécialistes de la signalétique à l'amélioration des gares et supervisèrent l'aménagement intérieur des nouvelles voitures, afin que la philosophie du projet soit respectée en tous points. Tout un ensemble d'uniformes fut également conçu. OH&CO imagina les horaires, la communication aux employés et aux partenaires, la publicité commerciale, la signalétique, l'interface de billetterie, l'architecture des voitures-restaurants, les articles de service à bord et les couleurs. Dans le même temps, un système de vecteurs secondaires d'identité fut développé, dont une série d'icônes conviviales.

Le lancement de la marque suscita l'engouement des employés et rapporta à Amtrak plus de 6 millions de dollars en retombées publicitaires. La création

Metroliner und Northeast Direct wurden aufgegeben. Dieser Übergang stellte eine bedeutende Herausforderung für Amtrak dar, da die Implementierung dieser neuen Struktur einen längeren Zeitraum und zusätzliche Kundenkommunikation bezüglich der Veränderungen des Service verlangen würde.

Der Entwurf der Reise

OH&CO halfen Amtrak Schritt für Schritt bei Design und Implementierung des neuen Service. Gemeinsam mit IDEO und anderen Mitarbeitern, darunter Architekten, Schilderspezialisten und Ingenieure, wirkten sie an Verbesserungen der Stationen mit und überwachten das Design der neuen und renovierten Innenausstattung der Züge, um sicherzustellen, dass die Philosophie des „seamless journey" durchgängig beibehalten wurde. Auch die Servicekleidung wurde komplett neu entworfen. Außerdem erstellte OH&CO Zeitpläne, kommunizierte mit Kunden und Teilhaber, kümmerte sich um Marketing, Beschilderung, Tickets-

Building a customer-oriented service began to change the corporate culture at Amtrak, from an operations-driven agency to a market-driven business. The results were immediate. The first month of Acela service yielded 43,000 new customers. In the rest of the year, route ridership increased 45%, route ticket revenues 76%.

d'un service centré autour de l'usager modifia peu à peu la culture d'entreprise d'Amtrak, qui passa d'une stratégie de rendement à une stratégie de qualité à l'écoute du marché. Les résultats furent immédiats. Le premier mois de mise en service d'Acela attira 43 000 nouveaux clients. Sur le reste de l'année, la fréquentation augmenta de 45 % et les recettes de 76 %.

chalter, das Design der Speisewagen, Servicegegenstände im Zug und die Schaffneruniformen. Währenddessen wurde ein System sekundärer Image-Elemente, wie kundenfreundliche Symbole, entwickelt.

Die Einführung führte zu Aufregung bei den Mitarbeitern und verhalf Amtrak zu mehr als sechs Millionen Dollar. Der Aufbau eines kundenorientierten Service veränderte die Firmenstruktur Amtraks von einem betriebsorientierten Geschäft zu einem marktorientierten Unternehmen. Der Ergebnisse lagen unmittelbar vor: Schon im ersten Monat gewann Acela 43.000 neue Kunden. Im Laufe der Jahres erhöhte sich die Anzahl der Reisenden um 45 Prozent und die Ticketeinnahmen um 76Prozent.

**Left:** *series of service concept launch materials ///* **À gauche** *: Série de documents de lancement du concept du service ///* **Links:** *Serien von Einführungsmaterialien zum Service-Konzept*

**Right:** *Acela backlight in the station ///* **À droite:** *panneau Acela rétroéclairé dans la gare ///* **Rechts:** *Hintergrundbeleuchtung von Acela im Bahnhof*

| KEY PROGRAM COMPONENTS | ÉLÉMENTS CLÉS DU PROGRAMME | SCHLÜSSELKOMPONENTEN DES PROGRAMMS |
|---|---|---|
| Strategy | Stratégie | |
| • *Target market research* | • *Analyse du marché cible* | Strategie |
| • *Service strategy development* | • *Développement de la stratégie de service* | • *Zielgruppenforschung* |
| • *Positioning and image platform* | • *Positionnement et image de marque* | • *Entwicklung einer Servicestrategie* |
| • *Brand auditing* | • *Audit de marque* | • *Positionierung und Image* |
| • *Brand architecture* | • *Architecture de la marque* | • *Markenprüfung* |
| • *Marketing strategy* | • *Stratégie commerciale* | • *Markenarchitektur* |
| • *Brand management strategy* | • *Stratégie de gestion de marque* | • *Marketingstrategie* |
| | | • *Markenmanagementstrategie* |
| Creative/Design | Design/Aspect Créatif | |
| • *Name and secondary nomenclature development* | • *Création du nom principal et de la nomenclature secondaire* | Kreativ/Design |
| • *Brand identity design* | • *Conception de l'identité visuelle* | • *Entwicklung von Name und sekundärer Nomenklatur* |
| • *Brand identity guidelines and management tools* | • *Outils de gestion et de référence design* | • *Design des Markenimage* |
| • *Brand application to equipment exteriors, interiors, station and other environments as well as communications* | • *Application à l'équipement intérieur, extérieur, aux gares et autres environnements, ainsi qu'à la communication* | • *Imageleitfäden und Managementinstrumente* |
| • *Brand launch communications* | • *Annonce de lancement de la marque* | • *Anwendungen der Marke zur Außen- und Innenausstattung, des Bahnhofs und anderen Ausstattungen und Kommunikationen* |
| | | • *Markeneinführung-Kommunikationen* |

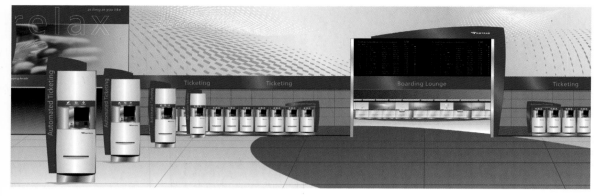

**Below:** *The graphic icons identify the ten journey steps and become part of the overall Acela visual identity system ///* **Ci-dessous** : *Les icônes graphiques identifient les dix étapes du voyage et font partie intégrante du système général d'identité visuelle d'Acela ///* **Unten:** *Die Grafiksymbole bestimmen die Identity der zehn Reiseschritte und wurden ein Teil des gesamten visuellen Identity-Systems von Acela*

**Left:** *illustration of the new Acela EX equipment ///* **À gauche :** *Illustration du nouvel équipement Acela EX ///* **Links:** *Darstellung der neuen Acela EX Ausstattung*

**Right:** *website designed to instruct the use of the new brand ///* **À droite :** *Le site Internet conçu pour enseigner l'utilisation de la nouvelle marque ///* **Rechts:** *Webseite zum Gebrauch der neuen Servicemarke*

# Biography
# Brent Oppenheimer (OH&CO)

www.oh-co.com
Location: New York, USA
Year of foundation: 1999

Position: Co-founder &
Principal

Awards: IDEA award together    high-speed rail service
with project partner IDEO for
the design of Amtrak's Acela

*Brent Oppenheimer is the Principal of OH&CO, a New York-based brand consulting and design firm that he founded in 1999. Under his direction, OH&CO has conducted a wide range of branding programs geared to well established businesses that have typically needed to revitalize and leverage their brands such as Amtrak, IBM, Viacom, Clear Channel, Skadden and The Wallace Foundation. Brent was born and educated in South Africa where he received a bachelor's degree in graphic design. He then set off to Switzerland where he worked for the French advertising agency, Publicis Groupe in Lausanne. Thereafter he joined Addison Design Consultants in London as an associate director. Brent has been appointed to serve on the advisory council of Red Dot Americas. The personal pursuits that Brent is passionate about include travel, photography and adventure motorcycling.*

*Brent Oppenheimer est le dirigeant de OH&CO, la société new-yorkaise de conseil en gestion de marque et de design qu'il a fondée en 1999. Sous sa direction, OH&CO a réalisé une grande variété de projets pour le compte d'entreprises établies qui désiraient revitaliser et recentrer leur image, telles que Amtrak, IBM, Viacom, Clear Channel, Skadden et la Fondation Wallace. Brent est né et a suivi ses études en Afrique du Sud, où il a obtenu une licence en design graphique. Il s'est ensuite installé en Suisse où il a travaillé pour une*

*agence de publicité française à Lausanne, le groupe Publicis. Puis il a rejoint Addison Design Consultants à Londres comme directeur adjoint. Il a également été nommé pour siéger au conseil consultatif de Red Dot Americas. Ses passe-temps favoris sont les voyages, la photographie et la randonnée en moto.*

*Brent Oppenheimer ist der Direktor von OH&CO, ein Markendesign- und Consulting-Unternehmen in New York, das er 1999 gründete. Unter seiner Führung leitete OH&CO ein breites Spektrum an Markenprogrammen, die auf alteingesessene Firmen abzielten, die ihre Marken neu beleben und ankurbeln wollten, wie zum Beispiel Amtrak, IBM, Viacom, Clear Channel, Skadden oder The Wallace Foundation. Brent Oppenheimer wurde in Südafrika geboren und erhielt dort seinen Bachelor in Grafikdesign. Von dort zog er in die Schweiz, wo er für die französische Werbeagentur Publicis Groupe in Lausanne arbeitete. Anschließend wurde er stellvertretender Direktor von Addison Design Consultants in London. Er wurde in den Beirat der Red Dots in den USA berufen. Brent Oppenheimers persönliche Interessen sind Reisen, Fotografie und Motorradfahren.*

# MORE THAN MEETS THE EYE. DESIGNING THE GUARDIAN

At the end of the 1980s, the redesign of the Guardian raised the question of whether a new look influences the quality and tone of the paper's editorial stance.

For so long, journalists designed newspapers. Even in the 80s, the age of specialists, this tradition lived on in some quarters, with journalists being trained in page layout, printing and typography, as well as in shorthand and keyboard skills. It was implicit that the journalist automatically designed to respect the paper's editorial values.

However, journalists fell short in prime design talent and objectivity. With design consultants being regularly commissioned by the newspaper industry, more imaginative and disciplined design skills were brought to bear. But the external designer had to tread very carefully. Everyone in the newspaper industry thinks they know about design, and easily claims that a consultant's objectivity is ignorance. So the designer un-

À la fin des années 1980, la refonte du *Guardian* pose la question de l'influence d'une nouvelle forme sur le contenu rédactionnel et la qualité d'un journal.

Pendant longtemps, les journalistes se sont chargés de la mise en forme des journaux. Même dans les années 1980, où règne la spécialisation, cette tradition perdure dans certains secteurs, et les journalistes sont formés à la mise en page, à l'impression et à la typographie, ainsi qu'à la sténographie et à l'informatique. Implicitement, le journaliste doit adopter une mise en forme respectueuse des valeurs rédactionnelles du journal.

Cependant, les journalistes ne sont pas forcément à la hauteur en termes de créativité et d'objectivité. Les journaux font alors régulièrement appel aux conseils de designers, qui apportent leur savoir-faire technique et artistique. Mais le designer indépendant doit marcher sur des œufs. Dans le monde de la presse écrite, tout le monde se targue d'être compétent en design, et taxe souvent d'ignorance l'ob-

Mit dem geänderten Design des *Guardian* Ende der 1980er-Jahre kam die Frage auf, ob ein neues Aussehen Einfluss auf Qualität und Stil der redaktionellen Einstellung haben könnte.

Lange Zeit wurden Zeitungen von Journalisten gestaltet. Sogar in den 1980er-Jahren, einer Zeit der Spezialisten, wurde diese Tradition an einigen Orten beibehalten: Journalisten wurden in Seitenlayout, Druck, Typografie und Stenografie geschult. Es wurde vorausgesetzt, dass ein Journalist das Design automatisch im Hinblick auf die redaktionellen Werte der Zeitung gestaltete.

Allerdings mangelte es Journalisten an grundlegendem Designtalent und Objektivität. Mit der regelmäßigen Beauftragung von Designberatern durch die Zeitungsbranche entstanden fantasievollere, diszipliniertere Designs. Allerdings musste ein externer Designer vorsichtig sein: Jeder in der Zeitungsbranche glaubt, etwas von Design zu verstehen, und legt die Objektivität eines Beraters

dergoes rigorous scrutiny of his understanding for a newspaper's editorial
stance, before he can prove his ability to
make a considered contribution to it —
one that might prove crucial to a newspaper's fortunes.

The decision to redesign a newspaper is
often a matter of when to do it and how
far to go. For decades, weak management had allowed a system of archaic,
inflexible and very expensive production to become entrenched, giving the
unions control of production. In the
mid 1980s, The Times, Telegraph and
Guardian were being put together as
they had been since the 1920s.
Newspaper publishing had become a
status symbol and tax-loss vehicle for
rich proprietors mainly interested in the
power it gave them.

But some brave men had had enough.
Gradually the power of the unions was
broken, Fleet Street became history and
all national papers moved to new buildings equipped with new technology. No

jectivité du consultant. Celui-ci subit
ainsi une analyse rigoureuse de sa compréhension de la ligne éditoriale avant de
pouvoir démontrer la pertinence de sa
contribution, qui on le sait, peut s'avérer
cruciale pour le succès du journal.

La refonte d'un journal implique de définir le moment opportun, et le degré de
modification désiré. Des décennies de
mauvaise gestion avaient engendré un
système de production rigide, archaïque
et onéreux, entièrement contrôlé par les
syndicats. Au milieu des années 1980, le
*Times*, le *Telegraph* et le *Guardian* étaient
encore produits comme en 1920. L'édition de presse offrait un statut social et
une réduction d'impôts à de riches indus-
triels qui y voyaient surtout un instrument de pouvoir.

Mais quelques hommes courageux réagi-
rent. Le pouvoir des syndicats fut peu à
peu démantelé, les bureaux de Fleet
Street se vidèrent, et les grands journaux
nationaux emménagèrent dans des im-
meubles modernes dotés de nouveaux

schnell als Ignoranz aus. So wird der
Designer einer genauen Prüfung unterzo-
gen, ob er Verständnis für die redaktio-
nelle Einstellung der Zeitung hat, bevor
er seine Fähigkeit, einen durchdachten
Beitrag zu liefern, unter Beweis stellen
kann – einen Beitrag, der für die Zukunft
des Blattes ausschlaggebend sein könnte.

Die Entscheidung, das Erscheinungsbild
einer Zeitung zu ändern, hängt oft vom
Zeitpunkt ab und davon, wie weit die
Änderungen gehen. Jahrzehntelang
herrschte ein schwaches Management,
unter dem sich eine archaische, unflexible
und sehr teure Produktion etabliert hatte
und den Gewerkschaften die Kontrolle
über die Produktion gab. Mitte der
1980er-Jahre schlossen *The Times*,
*Telegraph* und *Guardian* zusammen und
wurden zum Statussymbol und zur Steuer-
erleichterung für reiche Eigentümer, die
hauptsächlich an Macht interessiert waren.

Einige waren jedoch dagegen. Nach und
nach wurde die Macht der Gewerkschaften
gebrochen, Fleet Street wurde Geschichte,

**Left:** *Outdoor in London associating the new identity and the newspaper ///* **À gauche :** *Panneaux d'affichage en extérieur à Londres, associant la nouvelle identité et le journal ///* **Links:** *In London beim Assoziieren der neuen Identity der Zeitung*

**Right:** *The new The Guardian in the newstand ///* **À droite :** *Le nouveau The Guardian dans un kiosque ///* **Rechts:** *Der neue The Guardian am Zeitungskiosk*

one could afford to be left off the band-wagon. The Guardian had always stood apart from the other 'qualities', having been born and bred in Manchester, not London. This and its traditional appeal to the more radical reader gave it special status among the British press. When the Fleet Street revolution broke, the time was right to reaffirm its radical reputation through redesign.

Our first task was to assess the history, market and competition. The Independent was brand new and had adopted a traditional-looking design – because it didn't have a tradition. Only an established newspaper can break new ground in design terms and The Times and Telegraph showed no signs of doing so. The Manchester Guardian of the 1950s was a classic, with a design that survived a move to London and renaming as the Guardian. A new distinctive look was introduced in the 60s, attracting much praise and remaining until the beginning of 1987. So we had a golden opportunity to maintain a worthy de-

moyens techniques. Aucun journal ne pouvait se permettre de rester sur la touche. Le *Guardian* s'était toujours distingué des autres quotidiens de qualité, car il était né et avait grandi à Manchester, non à Londres. En outre, le fait qu'il s'était adressé dès l'origine à un lectorat politiquement à gauche lui conférait une place particulière au sein de la presse britannique. Quand Fleet Street fit sa révolution, l'heure sonna pour le journal de réaffirmer sa réputation radicale à travers un nouveau design.

Notre première tâche fut d'étudier l'historique du journal, son marché cible et sa concurrence. L'*Independent* était tout récent et avait adopté une maquette traditionnelle, pour compenser un manque de tradition historique. Seul un journal qui a de l'ancienneté peut se permettre d'innover dans la forme, et le *Times* et le *Telegraph* n'en montraient pas l'intention. Le *Manchester Guardian* des années 1950 était un classique, et sa maquette avait survécu à un déménagement à Londres et au changement de nom en

und alle nationalen Zeitungen zogen in Gebäude um, die mit neuer Technologie ausgerüstet waren. Niemand konnte es sich leisten, zurückzubleiben. Der *Guardian*, in Manchester statt London entstanden, hatte schon immer einen anderen Standpunkt. Außerdem verlieh ihm seine Anziehungskraft auf radikalere Leser eine besondere Stellung innerhalb der britischen Presse. Bei Ausbruch der Revolution in der Fleet Street war es an der Zeit, diesen radikalen Ruf durch eine Neugestaltung zu bestätigen.

Unsere erste Aufgabe war die Beurteilung von Geschichte, Markt und Wettbewerb. Der *Independent* war brandneu und vertrat ein traditionelles Design. Nur eine etablierte Zeitung kann in Bezug auf Design neue Wege beschreiten, und weder *The Times* noch der *Telegraph* machten Anstalten in diese Richtung. Der *Manchester Guardian* der 1950er-Jahre war ein Klassiker – mit einem Design, das den Umzug nach London überstand und sich in den *Guardian* umtaufte. In den 1960er-Jahren wurde ein neues, unverwechsel-

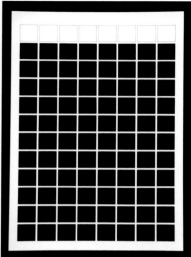

sign tradition, enabling the Guardian to distinguish itself yet again.

The work commenced with early exploratory meetings with Peter Preston, the editor. Having analysed the background and the market, we set five design criteria to guide our efforts: readable, well organised, clean, simple to put together, distinctive.

Readability is a matter of respecting the way the eye moves around the page, starting at the top left and moving down and across. Most newspapers had forgotten this, with headlines following a column of text. We put the headline above the text, at the beginning, and led the reader through the story and then to the next headline.

Introduction of new technology at the time helped ensure the new paper was well organised. We were able to back-set the paper – printing each edition in two sections, preparing some pages beforehand. This was common practice in the

*Guardian*. La nouvelle maquette adoptée dans les années 1960 avait été saluée par la critique et avait perduré jusqu'au début de l'année 1987. Nous avions donc une occasion en or de maintenir une digne tradition esthétique, tout en permettant au *Guardian* de se démarquer une fois de plus.

Le travail a débuté par des réunions préliminaires avec le rédacteur en chef Peter Preston. Après analyse du marché et de l'historique, nous nous sommes fixés cinq critères pour guider nos efforts : lisibilité, efficacité, clarté, simplicité d'assemblage et originalité.

La lisibilité tient au respect du mouvement des yeux le long de la page, en commençant en haut à gauche pour finir en bas à droite. Beaucoup de journaux négligeaient ce détail, et plaçaient des titres à la suite d'une colonne de texte. Nous avons rétabli le titre au-dessus du texte, en première place, encourageant le lecteur à lire l'article jusqu'en bas, où venait alors le titre suivant.

bares Layout eingeführt, das viel Lob erhielt und bis Anfang 1987 bestehen blieb. Daher hatten wir die einmalige Gelegenheit, eine wertvolle Designtradition weiterzuführen, indem wir dem *Guardian* dazu verhalfen, sich durch eine Neugestaltung wieder vom Rest abzusetzen.

Die Arbeit begann mit Sondierungsgesprächen mit dem Herausgeber Peter Preston. Nach einer Analyse von Hintergrund und Markt legten wir fünf Designkriterien fest, nach denen wir uns richten wollten: lesbar, gut organisiert, sauber, einfach zusammenzusetzen, unverwechselbar. Die Lesbarkeit orientiert sich an der Art und Weise, wie sich das Auge auf der Seite bewegt: links oben beginnend und dann die Seite hinauf und hinunter. Die meisten Zeitungen ignorierten dies und ließen eine Überschrift auf eine Textspalte folgen. Wir setzten die Überschrift an den Anfang, über den Text, sodass der Leser den Artikel bis zur nächsten Überschrift lesen konnte.

Die Einführung einer neuen Technologie

**Left:** *The grid extracted from the old newspaper ///* À gauche : *La grille de l'ancien journal ///* **Links:** *Das Raster der alten Zeitung wird entfernt*

**Right:** *Sketch of the new grids ///* À droite : *Croquis de la nouvelle grille ///* **Rechts:** *Entwurf des neuen Rasters*

USA but revolutionary in the UK, and allowed the paper to be organised more rationally.

Producing a clean design is a matter of discipline and careful use of white space. Making the paper simple to produce was a task of re-education. We had to devise a simple system of handling forty-eight pages produced by new technology. This involved some basic layout training for sub-editors, without ignoring existing skills.

Perhaps most importantly, being distinctive concerned winning the battle of the news stands. The masthead was our main gambit here. After early criticism, its radical device of trailers and photos at the top of the paper has become a standard.

The development of the new design was carried out in two phases. The first involved creating a series of options — defining what was really wanted by finding out what wasn't. This included

L'arrivée de nouvelles technologies nous permit de mieux organiser le journal. Nous avons pu le fragmenter, en imprimant chaque édition en deux sections, et en préparant certaines pages à l'avance. C'était une pratique commune aux États-Unis, mais c'était révolutionnaire en Grande-Bretagne, et cela permettait d'organiser le journal de façon plus rationnelle.

La clarté d'une maquette repose sur l'utilisation méthodique et équilibrée des espaces blancs. Faciliter la production du journal fut un travail de rééducation. Il nous fallait donc inventer un système simple pour gérer les 48 pages nées de la nouvelle technologie. Les rédacteurs de chaque rubrique reçurent par conséquent une formation complémentaire en composition.

L'aspect le plus délicat consistait à imposer son originalité dans les kiosques. Nous avions principalement misé sur la manchette. Après quelques débuts critiques, le bandeau de photos en haut de page est devenu un classique.

zu jener Zeit trug dazu bei, die Zeitung gut zu organisieren. Wir konnten das Papier zurücksetzen: Jede Ausgabe wurde in zwei Teilen gedruckt, wobei einige Seiten im Vorhinein vorbereitet wurden. Diese Methode war in den USA geläufig, für England jedoch revolutionär und erlaubte es, das Papier rationeller zu organisieren.

Ein klares Design erfordert Disziplin und den vorsichtigen Gebrauch von Leerstellen. Wir mussten zudem ein einfaches System ausarbeiten, um 48 Seiten mit neuer Technologie zu produzieren. Dies beinhaltete eine Grundausbildung in Layout für die Redakteure, ohne deren vorhandene Fähigkeiten zu ignorieren.

Unverwechselbar zu sein ist vielleicht das Wichtigste: Man musste den Kampf bei den Zeitungsauslagen gewinnen. Das Inhaltsverzeichnis war hierbei unser bedeutendster Schachzug. Trotz einiger Kritik zu Beginn ist seine radikale Anordnung von Vorschau und Fotos über dem Titel zum Standard geworden.

a design that challenged British precon-
ceptions about tabloids as downmarket.
While I did not convince the editor that
the time was right for this approach, the
events of 2000 have borne out my in-
stincts! Having made some of the basic
decisions, we carried out comparative
development, translating real pages into
the new design to prove viability.

The second phase involved all
Guardian staff translating the designs
into a real working system, based on an
excellent training manual produced in-
house, communicating design objec-
tives to over fifty journalists and subs.
Each spent three hours a week at a computer terminal testing the process,
while continuing to produce their regular edition. Teaching the new computer
the rules was quite another thing. The
success of translating the design into
code, while completely retaining its
integrity, was entirely due to Davis
Watts at the paper. Thus the basic layout and design rules did not have to be
remembered by the team but were made
automatically.

As the launch date approached, a complete dummy edition was produced
alongside the regular edition for the
streets. Old attitudes about headlines
were refusing to lie down and the use of
white space, and how to break a column
of text, were entirely new skills that
only became second nature after days of
practice.

The intent to redesign was announced
to the public only a month before
launch and we soon knew we wouldn't
please everyone. In fact the new design
was such a closely guarded secret that
nothing was seen in public until the
morning of the launch, 12 February
1988, when posters went up on hoard-
ings, the sign on the Guardian building
was changed, and some readers were
bemused not to recognise their paper as
an old friend in new clothes. It also had
less production staff, more journalists,
better coverage and improved finances.
Technology helped, but it was the people who did it.

La conception du nouveau design a été
menée en deux étapes. La première
consistait à définir une série d'options, en
établissant ce que voulait ou ne voulait
pas le client. L'un des designs proposés
allait à l'encontre du principe qui veut
que la presse populaire soit bas de gamme. Je n'ai pas réussi à convaincre le rédacteur en chef de l'opportunité de cette
approche, mais les événements de l'année
2000 ont confirmé mes intuitions ! Une
fois prises les décisions principales, nous
avons fait un essai comparatif et testé la
viabilité du nouveau design en l'appliquant à une édition antérieure.

La seconde étape a vu la participation de
tout le personnel du Guardian. Il s'agissait de faire de la nouvelle maquette un
vrai outil de fonctionnement, grâce à un
excellent manuel de formation conçu en
interne, qui exposait les objectifs du projet à plus de cinquante journalistes et
rédacteurs. Chacun a passé trois heures
par semaine à tester le procédé sur un
ordinateur, tout en continuant à produire
ses articles. Transmettre à l'ordinateur les
nouvelles données a été une autre paire de
manches. Le succès de la programmation
informatique, qui devait respecter chaque
élément du design, est entièrement dû à
David Watts, qui travaille au journal.
Grâce à lui, l'équipe n'était pas obligée de
connaître par cœur les éléments de mise
en page, les corrections adéquates étant
faites automatiquement.

À l'approche de la date de lancement,
nous avons sorti un numéro zéro en
même temps que l'édition normale. Les
vieilles habitudes concernant la titraille,
l'usage des blancs et les formats de co-
lonnes étaient très ancrées, et il fallut
quelques jours de pratique avant que les
nouvelles normes soient appliquées de
façon naturelle.

Le projet d'une nouvelle maquette ne fut
annoncé au public qu'un mois avant le
lancement et nous avons vite compris que
nous ne pourrions pas plaire à tout le
monde. La nouvelle maquette fut un secret si bien gardé que rien ne filtra jusqu'au jour du lancement, le 12 février
1988 au matin. Les panneaux publicitai-

Die Entwicklung der Neugestaltung fand
in zwei Phasen statt. Die erste beinhaltete
die Herstellung einer Reihe von Optionen
– man musste herausfinden, was man
wollte, indem man überlegte, was man
nicht wollte. Das hieß ein Design, das der
britischen Vorstellung, Tageszeitungen
seien weniger anspruchsvoll, entgegentrat.
Zwar konnte ich den Herausgeber damals
nicht überzeugen, dass die Zeit für diesen
Ansatz reif war – die Ereignisse im Jahr
2000 bestätigten jedoch meinen Instinkt!
Nachdem wir einige grundlegende Entscheidungen getroffen hatten, erstellten
wir einen Vergleich, indem wir existierende Seiten in das neue Design umsetzten,
um dessen Durchführbarkeit zu beweisen.

Die zweite Phase betraf die gesamte
Mitarbeiter des Guardian, die das Design
in ein funktionierendes System übertragen
musste. Die Basis dafür war ein Leitfaden,
der im Haus produziert wurde und die
Ziele des neuen Designs über 50
Journalisten und Redakteuren kommunizierte. Jeder verbrachte pro Woche drei
Stunden damit, den Prozess am Computer
zu testen, während er gleichzeitig die regu-
läre Ausgabe produzierte. Die neuen
Regeln auch den Computern beizubringen
war eine andere Angelegenheit. Dank
Davis Watts gelang es, das Design fest zu
installieren. Auf diese Weise mussten weder das grundlegende Layout noch die
Designregeln vom Team auswendig ge-
lernt werden, sondern erfolgten
automatisch.

Als der Termin der Einführung näher
rückte, wurde eine komplette Dummy-
Ausgabe neben der regulären Ausgabe für
die Öffentlichkeit produziert. Alte
Einstellungen gegenüber Überschriften,
dem Gebrauch von Leerstellen und dem
Umbruch von Textspalten erforderten
eine völlig neue Herangehensweise, die
schon nach wenigen Tagen Praxis zur
zweiten Natur wurde.

Die Absicht, die Zeitung neu zu gestalten,
wurde erst einen Monat vor der
Einführung publik gemacht, und es war
bald klar, dass wir nicht jeden damit er-
freuen würden. Tatsächlich war das neue
Design ein so wohlgehütetes Geheimnis,

Did the Guardian change editorially? The new design certainly attracted new and different readers – three years after introduction, readership among fifteen to twenty-four year old had risen by 33 per cent. The paper changed more than just its design. For us as designers, for the readers and professional media watchers, and for the team at the Guardian itself, there was much more to the redesign than met the eye.

res se couvrirent d'affiches, on posa une nouvelle enseigne au siège du journal, et les lecteurs eurent du mal à reconnaître leur ancien journal dans ses nouveaux atours. L'entreprise possédait également plus de journalistes, moins d'ouvriers à la production, une meilleure distribution et des finances plus saines. La technologie y avait contribué, mais c'était surtout le résultat du travail des hommes.

Le contenu rédactionnel du *Guardian* a-t-il changé ? La nouvelle maquette a incontestablement rajeuni le lectorat – trois ans après son introduction, le lectorat des 15-24 ans avait augmenté de 33 %. Le journal a modifié davantage que sa maquette. De l'avis des designers, des lecteurs, des observateurs des médias, et de l'équipe du *Guardian* elle-même, le nouveau design a modifié bien plus que la simple apparence.

dass bis zum 12. Februar 1988 nichts an die Öffentlichkeit geriet. An diesem Morgen wurden Poster an Plakatwänden aufgehängt, das Schild auf dem Guardian-Gebäude ausgetauscht, und einige Leser standen der Tatsache ratlos gegenüber, dass sie ihre Zeitung nicht wie einen alten Freund im neuen Gewand erkannten. Das Blatt benötigte außerdem weniger Mitarbeiter in der Produktion, mehr Journalisten, beinhaltete bessere Berichterstattung und erzielte höhere Einkünfte. Die Technik war eine große Hilfe, aber letztendlich waren es die Menschen, die dies bewerkstelligt hatten.

Hat sich der *Guardian* redaktionell verändert? Sicherlich zog das neue Design neue und andere Leser an – drei Jahre nach der Einführung stieg die Zahl der 13- bis 24-jährigen Leser um 33 Prozent. Das Blatt änderte mehr als nur sein Design. Für uns als Designer, für die Leser und professionellen Medienbeobachter, und für das *Guardian*-Team selbst, änderte sich mit dem neuen Design mehr, als das Auge sieht.

**Previous spread:** *Newspaper old and new* /// **Double page précédente** : *Le nouveau journal et l'ancien* /// **Vorherige Seite:** *Die alte und die neue Zeitung*

**Left:** *The different segments of the new The Guardian* /// **À gauche** : *les différentes sections du nouveau The Guardian* /// **Links:** *Die unterschiedlichen Segmente des The Guardian*

# Biography / Profile
# David Hillman / Pentagram

**www.pentagram.co.uk**
Location: London, United Kingdom

Awards: Gold and silver awards from D&AD for the widely acclaimed English

Sunrise book among many others

*Educated at the London School of Printing, David began his career as a design assistant at the Sunday Times Magazine. At the same time he began work on the redesign of the Sunday Times newspaper. In 1975 he set up his own design practice in London. Since joining Pentagram as a partner in 1978, he has continued his editorial design work on publications including De Volkskrant, Il Sole 24ore, and The Guardian. David has served on the juries of a number of major international competitions including D&AD, the New York One Show, and the BBC Design Awards. Pentagram is an independent award-winning design firm founded in 1972 with offices in London, New York, San Francisco, Austin and Berlin. With a multidisciplinary team, Pentagram is involved in a wide variety of projects from graphic to product design, from interior design to architecture.*

*David a fait ses études à la London School of Printing, et a commencé sa carrière en tant qu'assistant designer au Sunday Times Magazine. Il a dans le même temps commencé à travailler à la révision du design du journal le Sunday Times. En 1975, il a monté son propre cabinet de design à Londres. Depuis qu'il est devenu associé chez Pentagram en 1978, il poursuit son travail de design éditorial pour des publications telles que De Volkskrant, Il Sole 24ore et The Guardian. David a été membre du jury pour de nombreuses compétitions internationales de premier ordre, dont*

*D&AD, le New York One Show et les BBC Design Awards. Pentagram est une société de design indépendante qui a été récompensée de nombreux prix. Elle a été fondée en 1972 et elle est présente à Londres, New York, San Francisco, Austin et Berlin. L'équipe multidisciplinaire de Pentagram travaille sur une grande variété de projets, du design graphique au design de produit et de la décoration d'intérieur à l'architecture.*

*Ausgebildet an der London School of Printing startete David seine Karriere als Designer beim Sunday Times Magazine. Gleichzeitig begann er mit der Neugestaltung der Zeitung Sunday Times. 1975 gründete er seine eigene Designagentur in London. Nachdem er 1978 Pentagram Partner wurde, hat er seine redaktionellen Designarbeiten kontinuierlich in Publikationen wie De Volkskrant, Il Sole 24ore und The Guardian veröffentlicht. David fungierte in etlichen internationalen Wettbewerben als Jurymitglied, wie zum Beispiel D&AD, die New York One Show und die BBC Design Awards. Pentagram ist eine unabhängige preisgekrönte Designagentur. Sie wurde 1972 gegründet und unterhält Niederlassungen in London, New York, San Francisco, Austin und Berlin. Mit einem interdisziplinären Team ist Pentagram an breitgefächerten Designprojekten beteiligt, vom Grafikdesign über das Produktdesign bis hin zur Architektur.*

# THE HOMECHOICE MANUAL: TOTAL CORPORATE IDENTITY

### THE BRIEF

To redesign the Homechoice brand and corporate identity, which had originally been created in-house. The new look and feel required a comprehensive and flexible set of graphic elements for all marketing communications, with a more distinctive and desirable personality for its target market (25-35 early adopters of "cool" new broadband and multichannel TV as well as 30-45 families in search of a flexible, value-for-money home communications and entertainment service).

The new brand personality needed an iconographic image and modular system that would be simple, warm, modern, personal and highly focused. Brand guidelines would be required to cover all aspects of Homechoice visual implementation, including on-screen, online, print, signage, uniforms and all advertising.

### LA MISSION

Remodeler l'image et l'identité visuelle de Homechoice, qui avaient été à l'origine conçues en interne. La nouvelle image devait se composer d'un ensemble flexible d'éléments graphiques adaptés à toute la communication commerciale, et d'une personnalité originale et séduisante pour son marché cible (la tranche des 25-35 ans qui avaient adopté l'Internet haut débit et la télévision numérique et les couples entre 30 et 45 ans à la recherche d'un service économique combinant téléphonie et audiovisuel).

La nouvelle identité de marque nécessitait une représentation iconographique et un système modulaire simple, chaleureux, moderne, personnel et très ciblé. Elle devait s'accompagner de directives pratiques couvrant tous les aspects de la mise en œuvre visuelle, qu'il s'agisse de signalétique, d'habillage, ou de publicité imprimée, électronique ou télévisée.

### DER AUFTRAG

Die Marke Homechoice und deren Corporate Identity war ursprünglich intern entworfen worden und sollte nun neu gestaltet werden. Der neue Look erforderte ein umfassendes und flexibles Set grafischer Elemente für alle Marketing-kommunikationen, mit einer unverwechselbaren und begehrenswerten Persönlichkeit für seine Zielgruppe (25–35 frühe Anwender von „coolen" neuen Breitband-und Mehrkanal-Fernsehern und 30–45 Familien auf der Suche nach einem flexiblen, preiswerten Kommunikations-und Unterhaltungsservice für daheim).

Das neue Image sollte ikonografisch und ein modulares System sein, das einfach, modern, persönlich und sehr gezielt sein musste. Um alle Aspekte der visuellen Implementierung von Homechoice einzufangen – auf dem Bildschirm, online, gedruckt, auf Schildern, Uniformen und die gesamte Werbung – war ein Markenleitfaden gefordert.

# brand language spectrum
## corporate

corporate | mainstream | modular | playful

The corporate language uses essentially fixed elements in terms of colour, organisation, position and typography.

homechoice
digital
home
network

homechoice
digital
home
network

homechoice
digital
home
network

| areas of application | attributes |
|---|---|
| stationery | utility |
| signage | secure |
| documents | warm |
| small sign-off on | reliable |
| atl/btl ads, dm | reassuring |
| sponsorship | simple |
| events | business-like |
| product | |

---

# colour chart

core branding colour | secondary branding colours | special metallic colours | special fluorescent colours

| Pantone 285c | Pantone 285c | Pantone 156c | Pantone 465c | Pantone 156c | Pantone 286c | Pantone 180c | Pantone 180c | Pantone 398c | Pantone 266c | Pantone | Silver Metallic Pantone 8400c | Gold Metallic Pantone 8400c | Fluorescent Pink Pantone 802c | Fluorescent Pink Pantone 806c |
|---|---|---|---|---|---|---|---|---|---|---|---|---|---|---|
| C = 90% M = 40% Y = 0% K = 0% | C = 30% M = 0% Y = 100% K = 0% | C = 0% M = 0% Y = 100% K = 0% | C = 30% M = 0% Y = 100% K = 0% | C = 0% M = 0% Y = 100% K = 0% | C = 0% M = 100% Y = 0% K = 0% | C = 0% M = 100% Y = 100% K = 30% | C = 0% M = 75% Y = 100% K = 0% | C = 0% M = 75% Y = 100% K = 20% | C = 76% M = 0% Y = 100% K = 20% | | | | | |
| R = 0 G = 118 B = 198 | R = 191 G = 215 B = 47 | R = 255 G = 235 B = 0 | R = 135 G = 195 B = 58 | R = 243 G = 240 B = 32 | R = 240 G = 0 B = 96 | R = 177 G = 16 B = 45 | R = 150 G = 141 B = 0 | R = 75 G = 71 B = 139 | | | | | | |
| Hex #0080C6 | Hex #BFD72F | Hex #FFE000 | Hex #C3A33I | Hex #F3F020 | Hex #F067A6 | Hex #B10F15 | Hex #968D00 | Hex #4B478B | | | | | | |
| Web Safe 0066CC | Web Safe CCCC00 | Web Safe FFCC00 | Web Safe CC9933 | Web Safe FFCC00 | Web Safe FF6699 | Web Safe 990000 | Web Safe 666600 | Web Safe 330033 | | | | | | |

homechoice digital home network

**Previous page:** *corporate identity manual ///* **Page précédente :** *manuel d'identité d'entreprise ///* **Vorherige Seite:** *Corporate Identity Leitfaden*

**Above:** *identity's flexible color scheme ///* **Ci-dessus :** *le thème de couleurs flexible de l'identité visuelle ///* **Oben:** *Die flexible Farbzusammenstellung der Identity*

**Right:** *application on a device and remote control ///* **À droite :** *application sur un appareil et sur une télécommande ///* **Rechts:** *Anwendung auf einer Fernbedienung*

| THE SOLUTION | LA SOLUTION | DIE LÖSUNG |
|---|---|---|
| As a fan of Neville Brody's work, Giusti felt that his uncluttered and direct approach to both print and electronic art would be an ideal fit for an organization with a pioneering spirit that had a need to communicate externally and internally in an informal, yet invigorating style. Brody and Giusti worked very closely throughout the new brand's development. | Admirateur du travail de Neville Brody, Giusti estime que son approche limpide et directe du design graphique et de l'infographie conviendrait parfaitement à l'esprit pionnier d'une société qui devait communiquer de façon interne et externe dans un style informel mais dynamique. Brody et Giusti vont collaborer étroitement au cours de l'élaboration de la marque. | Als Fan von Neville Brodys Arbeiten war Giusti klar, dass seine ordentliche und direkte Herangehensweise an Druck- und elektronische Kunst ideal zu einer Organisation passte, die Pioniergeist besaß und sowohl extern als auch intern einen informellen, aber erfrischenden Stil kommunizieren musste. Brody und Giusti arbeiteten bei der Entwicklung der neuen Marke eng zusammen. |
| Brody's vision was for the Homechoice brand to represent the centre of the home not just in name but also in iconographic terms, but without becoming boring, predictable and mainstream. "We need to find a new visual vocabulary," was his starting point for the project. | L'idée de Neville Brody est de placer la marque Homechoice au cœur de la maison, non seulement par les mots mais aussi en termes iconographiques, mais sans devenir ennuyeux, prévisible et conventionnel. «Inventer un nouveau langage visuel » devient le point de départ du projet. | Nach Brodys Vision sollte die Marke Homechoice das Zentrum des Heims nicht nur dem Namen nach, sondern auch in ikonografischer Hinsicht repräsentieren, ohne langweilig, vorhersehbar und durchschnittlich zu werden. „Wie müssen ein neues visuelles Vokabular entwickeln", war sein Ansatzpunkt für dieses Projekt. |
| From a starting point of over fifty designs, a shortlist of three routes were fully explored with the clear winner being the current corporate image that was launched on 1st September 2005. This was deemed to best capture the essence, spirit and aspirations of Homechoice as a business. | Partant d'une base de plus de 50 dessins, trois directions sont explorées et le gagnant s'avère être le logo actuel lancé le 1er septembre 2005. De l'avis général, c'est celui qui symbolise le mieux la nature, l'esprit et les aspirations de la société Homechoice. | Ausgehend von über 50 Entwürfen wurde eine Auswahl von drei Richtungen getroffen. Klarer Sieger war das gegenwärtige Firmenimage, das am 1. September 2005 eingeführt wurde. Man hielt es am besten |

Brody's approach resulted in a strong yet flexible identity programme that, although anchored in a definite design language, could also incorporate an unprecedented degree of personalisation (for a corporate company) which was both exciting and challenging for Homechoice to adopt.

The main logo itself further reinforces the home aspect of the organisation by (loosely) representing a plan of a room, with an open and inviting entrance in the top right. The big idea however, occurs at the centre of this room representation with "the square", which represents the core of the room. This can be any of ten different colours, with each one representing a Homechoice-enabled state of being that you (the customer or employee) can identify with. The nature of the central element also changes depending on the application representing an active space.

A fundamental benefit of Brody's design mastery was his understanding of the

La démarche de Brody donne naissance à un système identitaire fort et flexible, qui malgré son ancrage dans un langage visuel bien défini, peut aussi incorporer un niveau inédit de personnalisation pour une société, et dont l'adoption s'avère à la fois excitante et stimulante pour Homechoice.

Le logo principal renforce l'aspect domestique de l'offre de service. C'est une adaptation assez libre d'un plan de pièce, avec une entrée accueillante dans l'angle supérieur droit. L'idée maîtresse, cependant, est au centre de ce cadre, sous la forme d'un carré. Il peut être décliné en dix couleurs différentes, chacune représentant un état auquel l'usager ou l'employé peut s'identifier. L'élément central est un espace actif qui change aussi de nature selon l'application désirée.

Grâce à sa grande expérience professionnelle, Neville Brody a acquis la compréhension des défis qu'une nouvelle marque doit surmonter sur le marché. Dans le cas de Homechoice, il a proposé que la définition de « Réseau domestique numéri-

dafür geeignet, Essenz, Geist und Bestrebungen von Homechoice als Unternehmen einzufangen.

Brodys Ansatz resultierte in einem starken, aber flexiblen Imageprogramm, das zwar fest in einer Designsprache verankert war, aber auch auf beispiellose Art und Weise Individualisierungsmöglichkeiten (für eine Firma) beinhaltete, die aufregend und herausfordernd für Homechoice waren. Das Hauptlogo selbst stützt den Heimaspekt der Organisation, indem es den Umriss eines Raumes zeigt, mit einem einladenden, offenen Eingang rechts oben. Die entscheidende Idee erscheint jedoch in der Mitte dieser Raumdarstellung in Form „des Quadrats", das das Herz des Raumes repräsentiert. Es kann in zehn verschiedenen Farben erscheinen, von denen jede einen durch Homechoice verursachten Zustand repräsentiert, mit dem sich ein Kunde oder Mitarbeiter identifizieren kann. Die Erscheinung dieses zentralen Elements ändert sich dem jeweiligen Verwendungszweck entsprechend und repräsentiert so einen aktiven Raum.

challenges that a new brand name in this market would have to surmount – in the case of Homechoice, he proposed using the phrase "Digital Home Network" as part of the core language. Based on his idea of Homechoice being at the centre of the "Digital Home" and "Home Network", he decided to incorporate this directly and permanently into the design. This is key in defining, instantly, what type of a company and organisation Homechoice isn't.

The whole corporate identity programme was conceived around four key voices – corporate (industry-facing image), mainstream (standard customer-facing image), modular (for objects and concepts) and playful (which offers a more extreme, youth-oriented, urban image). These states allow the Homechoice brand to vary visually according to the different needs demanded of it.

The resulting brand, (which is individual, honest, fun, innovative, human and simple) is neither shy nor timid, in both its

que » fasse partie du vocabulaire identitaire. Plaçant Homechoice à la croisée de la « maison numérique » et du « réseau domestique », il incorpore ce concept dans le design de façon directe et permanente. C'est une façon immédiate de définir ce que Homechoice n'est pas, en tant que service et entreprise.

Tout le programme de gestion d'identité visuelle a été conçu selon quatre axes. Une image commerciale (destinée aux professionnels), une image grand public (destinée aux usagers), une image modulaire (pour les produits et les concepts) et une image ludique (destinée aux jeunes citadins branchés). Ces différents niveaux permettent des variations visuelles selon les objectifs recherchés.

La marque qui en résulte (individuelle, honnête, drôle, innovante, humaine et simple) n'est timide ni dans son apparence ni dans son message. Elle se positionne en challenger, avec une empreinte audacieuse mais accessible dans un marché saturé.

Ein wesentlicher Vorteil von Brodys gestalterischem Meisterwerk war sein Verständnis für die Herausforderungen, die sich einem neuen Markennamen auf diesem Markt stellen würden – im Falle von Homechoice schlug er vor, die Phrase „Digital Home Network" als Teil der Kernsprache zu benutzen. Basierend auf der Idee, dass Homechoice im Zentrum des „Digital Home" und „Home Network" steht, integrierte er dies direkt und dauerhaft in das Design. Das ist der direkte Schlüssel zur Definition, was für eine Art Unternehmen und Organisation Homechoice nicht ist.

Das gesamte Corporate-Identity-Programm ist um vier Schlüsselpunkte konzipiert – Firma (firmenorientiertes Image), durchschnittlich (normales, kundenorientiertes Image), modular (für Objekt und Konzepte) und spielerisch (verleiht ein extremeres, jugendorientiertes, urbanes Image). Diese Zustände erlauben es der Marke Homechoice, je nach den verschiedenen erforderlichen Bedürfnissen visuell zu variieren.

**Left & right:** *iconography and its application in the identity ///* **Gauche et droite :** *l'iconographie et son application dans l'identité ///* **Links & Rechts:** *Ikonografie und ihre Anwendung bei der Identity*

look and feel, as well as through its messaging, and positions Homechoice as a challenger product, with a bold, yet accessible imprint in a crowded market place.

Based on Research Studios' Visual Language – a corporate identity document that outlines the design of all the fundamental Homechoice visual building blocks, the full design implementation was undertaken by Giusti's internal creative department who had been involved from conception. This collaborative way of working between Brody's Research Studios and Giusti's[1] team meant not only that the short timescales could be met but also that Homechoice retained creative influence.

Grâce au Langage Visuel de Research Studios, un guide de gestion d'identité visuelle qui contient les références de tous les visuels fondamentaux, la mise en œuvre générale a été prise en charge par le service créatif interne dirigé par Giusti, qui s'est impliqué dès le départ. Cette collaboration entre l'équipe de Giusti[1] et le Research Studios a permis de respecter l'échéancier et de maintenir l'influence créative de Homechoice.

Die daraus resultierende Marke (individuell, ehrlich, lustig, innovativ, menschlich und einfach) ist bezüglich Erscheinung und Botschaft weder schüchtern noch ängstlich und positioniert Homechoice als herausforderndes Produkt – mit einem kühnen, aber zugänglichen Gepräge innerhalb eines engen Marktes. Mit der Visual Language (visuelle Sprache) der Research Studios als Basis – ein Corporate-Identity-Dokument, dass das Design aller fundamentalen visuellen *building blocks* von Homechoice umreißt – wurde die gesamte Implementierung des Designs durch Giustis interne kreative Abteilung geleistet, die von der Konzeption an einbezogen waren. Diese Zusammenarbeit zwischen Brodys Research Studios und Giustis[1] Team stellte nicht nur sicher, dass die engen Zeitpläne eingehalten wurden, sondern auch, dass Homechoice weiterhin kreativen Einfluss ausüben konnte.

1  2005 new corporate identity commissioned by Video Networks (Homechoice) Creative Director Marco Giusti and created by Neville Brody's Research Studios.

1  Nouvelle identité visuelle 2005 commanditée par le directeur de création Marco Giusti pour Video Networks (Homechoice) et réalisée par le Research Studios de Neville Brody.

1  2005 wurde vom Kreativdirektor der Video Networks (Homechoice), Marco Giusti, ein neues Firmenimage in Auftrag gegeben und von Neville Brodys Research Studios entwickelt.

# brand language spectrum
## playful

corporate | mainstream | modular | playful

The playful, or extreme area is largely based on skate or snowboard language and allows the brand to express its individuality and urban qualities. The mark is based on an outline 3d, and contains a monochrome icon within the frame.

areas of application
web
merchandise
guerilla campaigns
stickers
ads
dm
specials
on-screen

attributes
dynamic
youthful
fun
technological
urban
skate/snow
surprising/maverick
not utility or corporate
young/hip/urban

# general typography and layout

There are no strict grids.

Use the three Knockout weights for large texts and headlines.

Use Helvetica for all body copy below 14pt.

Layout should be clean, with a dynamic use of typography. Scale should be utilised.

Alignment of elements should be dynamic.

use corporate palette for brand signature

Dotted lines, iconic images, vertical type and white space plus a creative use of colour in type all help create the Homechoice design space.

*NB: Text and copy are only an example and should not be used in any Homechoice communication, it is purely a guide for typography and layout. Text and font sizes are not to scale.

Please note: kern all word space in headlines -10%.

Knockout Ultimate for headlines and numbers. | Knockout Junior for large texts. | Iconic imagery. | Helvetica body copy. | Modular line drawings. | Corporate logo.

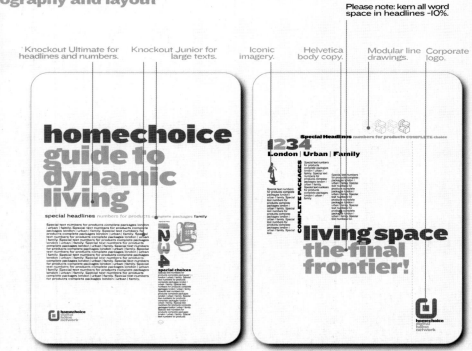

# btl and dm typography, C.I. and layout

Knockout should be used playfully, within a clean but bold and dynamic typographic layout. Always maintain a dynamic use of white space. the sign-off should be selected from the corporate monochrome versions.

Knockout Ultimate for headlines and numbers.

Knockout Junior for large texts.

Use coloured backgrounds where useful.

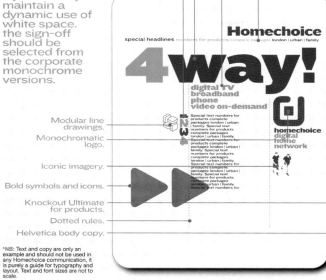

Modular line drawings.

Monochromatic logo.

Iconic imagery.

Bold symbols and icons.

Knockout Ultimate for products.

Dotted rules.

Helvetica body copy.

*NB: Text and copy are only an example and should not be used in any Homechoice communication, it is purely a guide for typography and layout. Text and font sizes are not to scale.

## building signage

The Homechoice icon is raised from the back plate. The center square is changed monthly for a new colour from the Homechoice colour palette.

Homechoice corporate colour palette level one

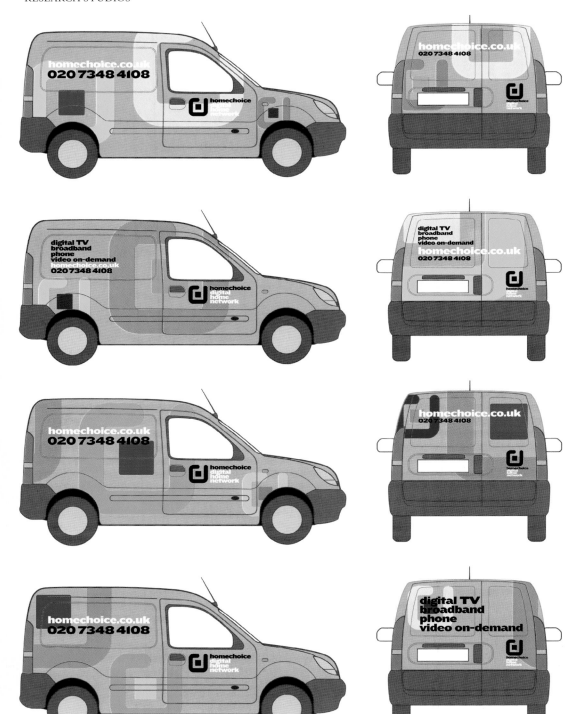

**Previous spread:** *Corporate identity manual*
*/// **Double page précédente** : Manuel*
*d'identité d'entreprise /// **Vorherige Seite:***
*Corporate Identity Leitfaden*

**Left:** *Transportation with logos applied /// À*
**gauche** : *Véhicules avec logos /// **Links:***
*Transporter mit angebrachten Logos*

# Biography
# Neville Brody (Research Studios)

www.researchstudios.com       Year of foundation: 1994       Awards: Multiple
Location: London, United       Position: Founder/
Kingdom                        Creative Director

*The legendary designer Neville Brody, together with business partner Fwa Richards, opened the very first Research Studios in London during 1994. Since then, many designers have worked at the London studio, both on a temporary and a full time basis. Some of them have even gone on to establish other studios that make up the Research. A key difference in working with Research Studios is the approach. A small team infrastructure brings some of the best creative visual communications experience to a streamlined and direct design process. Exploratory development is at the heart of the Studio's being, and the award-winning communication languages that are created are vital, challenging and evolutionary. Research Studios has been highly influential in the visual communications industry, and has generated many ground-breaking ideas.*

*Le légendaire designer Neville Brody et son associé Fwa Richards ouvrent les premiers Research Studios à Londres en 1994. Depuis, de nombreux designers ont travaillé avec eux, que ce soit de façon ponctuelle ou permanente. Quelques-uns ont même monté par la suite d'autres studios rattachés à ceux de Londres. La singularité des Research Studios tient à leur démarche. Une petite infrastructure met son étonnante créativité visuelle au service d'un processus de fabrication direct et rationalisé. L'expérimentation formelle est au cœur de l'existence des Studios et les langages visuels qui en résultent*

*ont été primés pour leur aspect dynamique, provocant et avant-gardiste. Les Research Studios ont beaucoup d'influence dans le domaine de la communication visuelle et sont à l'origine de nombreuses idées novatrices.*

*Der legendäre Designer Neville Brody eröffnete das erste Research Studio zusammen mit seinem Geschäftspartner Fwa Richards 1994 in London. Seitdem haben viele Designer in diesem Studio gearbeitet, sowohl Teilzeit als auch Vollzeit. Einige von ihnen haben sogar weitere Studios eröffnet, die Research komplett machen. Der Hauptunterschied bei der Arbeit mit Research Studios liegt im Ansatz. In einem kleinen Team entsteht durch die beste kreative und visuelle Kommunikationserfahrung ein geradliniger und direkter Designprozess. Die Arbeit des Studios liegt in der sondierenden Entwicklung, und die entstehenden Kommunikationssprachen, die schon Preise gewannen, sind lebendig, herausfordernd und revolutionär. Research Studios hat großen Einfluss auf die visuelle Kommunikationsindustrie genommen und viele bahnbrechende Ideen erzeugt.*

117

# THE
# REBRANDING
# OF CORBIS

Graphic design, print advertising, logos, catalogs, annual reports, brochures, corporate identities, posters and new media are not the only things Segura Design does, but they are some of the things they do best. Whatever the medium, they create marketing messages that people notice and respond to, with a distinctive sense of style and simplicity that stands the test of time.

Founder and principal Carlos Segura, an award-winning designer whose work is well-respected in the local, national and international design communities, brings over a decade of advertising experience with him, being a successful art director for many of the advertising giants such as Young & Rubicam, Ketchum, HCM Marsteller, Bayer Bess Vanderwacker, FCB and BBDO, prior to establishing Segura Inc. in 1991. Despite the size, Segura Inc. is now considered to be one of the top design firms in the USA.

When [T-26] Digital Type Foundry was first introduced in 1994, it received instant welcome from designers. Founder of

Le design graphique, la publicité imprimée, les logos, les catalogues, les rapports annuels, les brochures, la gestion de marque, les affiches et les nouveaux supports multimédia ne sont pas les seules cordes à l'arc de Segura Design, mais c'est dans ces domaines que l'agence a réalisé ses plus beaux projets. Quel que soit le support, elle crée des messages que les gens remarquent et auxquels ils réagissent, dans un style simple et original qui résiste à l'épreuve du temps. ·

Le fondateur et dirigeant Carlos Segura, designer primé qui jouit du respect de la profession à l'échelle internationale, est riche d'une décennie d'expérience publicitaire et a été directeur artistique chez de nombreux géants de la publicité comme Young & Rubicam, Ketchum, HCM Marsteller, Bayer Bess Vanderwacker, FCB et BBDO, avant de monter Segura Inc. en 1991. Malgré sa taille modeste, Segura Inc. est aujourd'hui considérée comme une des meilleures agences de design des États-Unis.

Grafikdesign, Printwerbung, Logos, Kataloge, Jahresberichte, Broschüren, Corporate Identitys, Poster und neue Medien das spektrum der Aufgaben von Segure Design ist nicht nur breit gefächert und vielfältig, die Firma führt ihre Arbeiten auch in hervorragender Weise aus. Egal mit welchem Medium – sie entwickeln Marketingbotschaften, die Aufmerksamkeit erregen und Reaktionen hervorrufen, mit einem unverwechselbaren Gespür für zeitlosen Stil und Einfachheit.

Gründer und Direktor Carlos Segura, ein preisgekrönter Designer, dessen Arbeit in lokalen, nationalen und internationalen Designergemeinden anerkannt wird, bringt über ein Jahrzehnt Erfahrung in der Werbung mit: Bevor er Segura Inc. 1991 etablierte, war er erfolgreicher Art-Direktor für viele Werbegiganten wie Young & Rubicam, Ketchum, HCM Marsteller, Bayer Bess Vanderwacker, FCB und BBDO. Trotz seiner geringen Mitarbeiteranzahl wird Segura Inc. heute als eine der Top-Designfirmen in den USA angesehen.

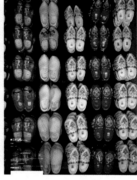

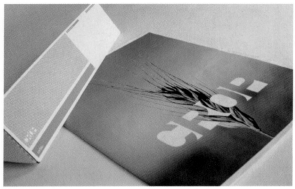

this company, Carlos Segura, a designer originally from Cuba, began to establish [T-26] among designers by introducing experimental and cult design. Discounts to students and other users increased their interest in [T-26] and incorporating these users in production made [T-26] indispensable in their work. [T-26] is currently providing more than 400 typefaces designed by more than 100 designers around the world. Carlos Segura says that the success of [T-26] lies beyond the subject of 'fonts'.

*"When we started [T-26] in 1994, it was at the beginning of an experimentation period that changed the face of design."*

"With that in mind, we wanted to offer tools and ideas that would contribute to that effort, and we wanted [T-26] to be the 'place to get it.' It was quite difficult to find these tools prior to 1994 without going through an extensive search."

Couple years ago Corbis Images ap-

Quand la « fonderie » de polices de caractères numériques (Digital Type Foundry) [T-26] a été créée, en 1994, elle a reçu d'emblée un accueil chaleureux de la part des designers. Carlos Segura, son concepteur cubain, s'impose dans la profession grâce à un design expérimental et bientôt culte. Les rabais accordés aux étudiants et autres usagers augmentent la popularité de [T-26], et leur contribution active à la production fait bientôt de [T-26] un outil indispensable dans leur travail. [T-26] offre actuellement plus de 400 polices de caractères dessinées par plus de 100 designers du monde entier. Carlos Segura estime que le succès de [T-26] dépasse le simple domaine des « fontes ».

*« Quand nous avons lancé [T-26] en 1994, c'était le début d'une période d'expérimentation qui allait bouleverser le monde du design. »*

« Notre objectif était de proposer des outils utiles à l'effort collectif, et nous

Als das Schriftenhaus [T-26] 1994 eingeführt wurde, wurde es von Designern sehr begrüßt. Der Gründer dieses Unternehmens, Carlos Segura, gebürtiger Kubaner, begann [T-26] bei Designern zu etablieren, indem er experimentelles und kultiges Design einführte. Rabatte für Studenten und andere Nutzer erhöhte deren Interesse an [T-26], und die Integration dieser Nutzer in die Produktion machte [T-26] für ihre Arbeit unentbehrlich. [T-26] stellt derzeit über 400 Schrifttypen bereit, die von über 100 Designern weltweit entworfen wurden. Laut Carlos Segura liegt der Erfolg von [T-26] jenseits der „Fonts".

*„Als wir 1994 mit [T-26] begannen, war dies zu Beginn einer Experimentierphase, die das Gesicht des Designs veränderte."*

„Dies im Hinterkopf, wollten wir Werkzeuge und Ideen anbieten, die zu dieser Entwicklung beitragen würden, und wir wollten, dass [T-26] der Ort war, wo diese zu finden waren. Vor 1994 war es

Opening: *Spreads of the first catalogue of the series* /// Ouverture : *Doubles pages du premier catalogue de la série* /// Anfang: *Seiten des ersten Katalogs der neuen Serien*

From left to right: *Package and cover of the CROP editions 1, 2, and the CD collection* /// De gauche à droite : *Emballage et couverture des éditions 1 et 2 de CROP, et la collection de CD* /// Von links nach rechts: *Verpackung und Abdeckung der CROP Edition 1, 2, und die CD Sammlung*

proached Segura Inc. with a re-branding idea, that should involve no only the re-design of the logo, but also include other promotional material that would revamp the brand. "Corbis had many years of bad habits under their belt. Their perception in the marketplace from a "creative's" perspective was dismal. Our challenge was to change that. Not an easy task when you are speaking to (what I believe is) a very sophisticated target. One who is most aware of all visual qualities in most categories. From design to architecture to furniture to automobile to fashion and so on.

*We wanted to create materials that would not only tackle our competition, but also compete with the everyday onslaught of sensory input we get all day. There is very little room to "carve" out a place in our "experience."*

We all remember the best "car," the best "movie" the best "computer" the best

voulions que [T-26] devienne la « boîte à outils » idéale. Avant 1994, à moins de se lancer dans des recherches fastidieuses, il était très difficile de se procurer ce genre d'outils. »

Il y a quelques années, Corbis Images s'est adressé à Segura Inc. pour un projet de rénovation de marque, qui concernait non seulement le remodelage d'un logo, mais aussi d'autres formes de promotion desti-nées à stimuler la marque. « Corbis était alourdi par des années de mauvaises habi-tudes. Son image de marque d'un point de vue créatif était épouvantable. Notre mis-sion était de changer cette situation. Ce qui est loin d'être aisé lorsqu'on s'adresse (comme je le crois) à une cible très infor-mée, un public sensible aux qualités esthé-tiques des produits quel que soit le do-maine. Design, architecture, mobilier, automobile, mode et j'en passe.

*Nous voulions créer des visuels qui s'attaqueraient à la concur-rence d'une part, et qui d'autre part se démarqueraient du ma-*

ziemlich schwierig, ohne eine weitschwei-fige Suche an diese Hilfsmittel zu kommen."

Vor zwei Jahren fragte Corbis Images bei Segura Inc. bezüglich einer neuen Markenidee an, die nicht nur ein verän-dertes Logodesign, sondern auch zusätz-liches Werbematerial beinhaltete, das die Marke aufpeppen würde. „Corbis hatte viele Jahre schlechter Angewohnheiten auf dem Buckel. Die Wahrnehmung auf dem Markt war, von einem kreativen Blickwinkel aus betrachtet, miserabel. Unsere Herausforderung bestand darin, dies zu ändern. Keine leichte Aufgabe, wenn man von einer (wie ich glaube) sehr anspruchsvollen Vorgabe spricht. Von Design über Architektur und Möbeln zu Automobilen und Mode und so weiter.

*Wir wollten Material entwerfen, dass nicht nur unserer Kon-kurrenz die Stirn bietet, sondern auch mit dem täglichen Bombar-dement an Sinneseindrücken konkurrieren kann. Es ist schwie-*

"experience." And, we wanted to be in that league. When you (or at least I) think of the best computer, I think of Apple. When I think of the best car, I think of Audi (among others). Now, when most think of the best stock photo company (which in itself, is a major step forward that they are thinking of us at all, They think of Corbis."

*So Carlos Segura led the team and created a completely new logo for Corbis, which expressed the sense of modernity the brand needed. But to be remembered as the best stock photo company, a new logo was not enough, and they developed the "CROP" magazine.*

"CROP" is a large format product catalog series for Corbis Stock Photography. There have been 7 produced to date. "CROP" is also part of a re-branding effort Segura has been involved for about 2 years. While these are free, they are very limited runs of 30,000 and include an extraordinary amount of different papers, printing techniques and varied content, all in specially produced packaging. "CROP" has been awarded numerous prizes, including the Red Dot "Grand Prix," which is in essence Europe's best of show "Oscar," Communication Arts Annual, Print Design Annual, and AIGA.

*traquage quotidien de stimuli sensoriels dont nous sommes la cible. Il reste peu d'espace libre à conquérir dans notre "univers".*

Nous avons tous une image de la meilleure voiture, du meilleur film, du meilleur ordinateur, de la meilleure aventure. Et nous voulions nous inscrire dans cette lignée. Quand on pense (ou moi du moins) au meilleur ordinateur, je pense à Apple. Quand je pense à la meilleure voiture, je pense à Audi (entre autres). Aujourd'hui, quand on pense à la meilleure banque d'images (et le fait qu'on y pense est un énorme progrès en soi), on pense à Corbis. »

*Carlos Segura et son équipe conçoivent alors un tout nouveau logo pour Corbis, qui exprime la modernité dont la marque avait besoin. Mais pour être mémorable, un logo est insuffisant, et c'est ainsi que naît le magazine « Crop ».*

« Crop » est une série de catalogues grand format de produits de la banque d'images Corbis. Sept numéros ont été édités à ce jour. « Crop » fait également partie du programme de gestion de marque dans lequel Carlos Segura s'est engagé depuis deux ans. Ces catalogues gratuits ne sont tirés qu'à 30 000 exemplaires, et offrent une extraordinaire variété de contenu, de papiers et de techniques d'impressions et ont tous un emballage unique. « Crop » a reçu de nombreuses récompenses, dont le Grand Prix de Red Dot (un équivalent des Oscars pour le cinéma), et des récompenses de Communications Arts Annual, Print Design Annual et AIGA.

*rig, einen Platz in unsere ‚Erfahrung' zu ‚meißeln'.*

Wir erinnern uns an das beste ‚Auto', den besten ‚Film', den besten ‚Computer', die beste ‚Erfahrung'. In dieser Liga wollten wir spielen. Wenn Sie (oder ich zumindest) an den besten Computer denken, denke ich an Apple. Wenn ich an das beste Auto denke, denke ich an Audi (unter anderen). Wenn die meisten an die beste Bilddatenbank denken (es ist schon an sich ein großer Schritt, dass sie überhaupt an uns denken), denken sie an Corbis."

*Also leitete Segura das Team und gestaltete ein komplett neues Logo für Corbis, das den Modernitätssinn ausdrückte, den die Marke benötigte. Um aber als die beste Bilddatenbank zu gelten, reichte ein neues Logo nicht aus: Das „CROP"-Magazin wurde geboren.*

„CROP" ist eine großformatige Serie von Produktkatalogen für die Corbisbilddatenbank. Bisher wurden sieben Ausgaben produziert. „CROP" ist auch Teil der Anstrengungen der neuen Markenbildung, an der Segura seit zwei Jahren arbeitet. Die Kataloge sind zwar kostenlos, aber die Auflage auf 30.000 Stück begrenzt. Sie enthalten außergewöhnlich viele unterschiedliche Papiersorten, Drucktechniken, abwechslungsreichen Inhalt und extra produzierte Verpackungen. „CROP" erhielt zahlreiche Preise, unter anderem den Red Dot „Grand Prix", Communication Arts Annual, Print Design Annual und AIGA.

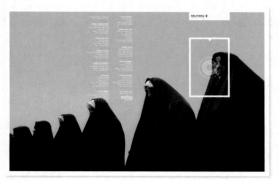

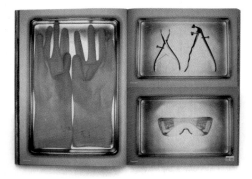

# Biography
# Carlos Segura (Segura Inc.)

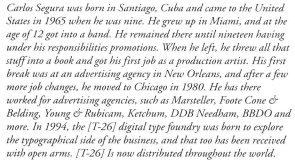

**www.segura-inc.com**
Location: Chicago, USA

Position: Founder/Creative
Director

Awards: Communications Art,
AIGA, Red Dot Award

*Carlos Segura was born in Santiago, Cuba and came to the United States in 1965 when he was nine. He grew up in Miami, and at the age of 12 got into a band. He remained there until nineteen having under his responsibilities promotions. When he left, he threw all that stuff into a book and got his first job as a production artist. His first break was at an advertising agency in New Orleans, and after a few more job changes, he moved to Chicago in 1980. He has there worked for advertising agencies, such as Marsteller, Foote Cone & Belding, Young & Rubicam, Ketchum, DDB Needham, BBDO and more. In 1994, the [T-26] digital type foundry was born to explore the typographical side of the business, and that too has been received with open arms. [T-26] Is now distributed throughout the world.*

*Carlos Segura est né à Santiago de Cuba. Il arrive aux États-Unis en 1965, à l'âge de neuf ans. Il grandit à Miami et intègre un orchestre à l'âge de douze ans. Il vit là-bas jusqu'à l'âge de dix-neuf ans, où il est chargé de la promotion de l'orchestre. Avant de quitter la région, il rassemble son expérience dans un book et décroche son premier emploi comme illustrateur. Il perce ensuite dans une agence de publicité de la Nouvelle-Orléans, et après quelques changements de postes, il s'installe à Chicago en 1980. Il travaille dès lors pour des agences de publicité comme Marsteller, Foote Cone & Belding, Young & Rubicam, Ketchum, DDB Needham, BBDO et autres.*

*En 1994, il crée la police de caractère numérique [T-26] dans le but d'explorer l'aspect typographique du design, et il reçoit un accueil enthousiaste. La police de caractère [T-26] est aujourd'hui distribuée dans le monde entier.*

*Carlos Segura wurde in Santiago, Kuba, geboren und kam 1965 mit neun Jahren in die Vereinigten Staaten. Er wuchs in Miami auf und wurde mit zwölf Jahren Schlagzeuger einer Band, für deren Promotion er verantwortlich war, bis er neunzehn wurde. Als er die Band verließ, stellte er die von ihm gestalteten Flyer zu einem Buch zusammen und bekam so seinen ersten Job in einer Werbeagentur in New Orleans. 1980 zog er nach Chicago, wo er unter anderem für Werbeagenturen wie Marsteller, Foote Cone & Belding, Young & Rubicam, Ketchum, DDB Needham und BBDO arbeitete. Er befasste sich mit den typografischen Aspekten des Grafikdesigns und gründete 1994 das Schriftenhaus [T-26], mit dem er offene Türen einrannte. [T-26]-Fonts werden heute weltweit vertrieben.*

# THE REBIRTH OF A CLASSIC

## GERMAN TV SERIES

Interview with Pia Kemper, creative director of Simon & Goetz Design.

Entretien avec Pia Kemper, directrice de création chez Simon & Goetz Design.

Interview mit Pia Kemper, Kreativdirektorin von Simon & Goetz Design.

**T:** How does it work with a briefing for you? Who gets the briefing the first time and how does it reach the creative team?
**PK:** *First of all, the account manager gets the client's briefing. Then he meets with his design team, which will work on the job. The most important points are discussed and the team thinks about ways to work on it. Further on the timing is set up.*

**T :** Comment les briefings se passent-ils chez vous ? Qui assiste au premier briefing, et comment est-il transmis à l'équipe de créatifs ?
**PK :** *Tout d'abord, le client fait un briefing au responsable du compte, qui réunit ensuite l'équipe de design qui travaillera sur le projet. Ils examinent ensemble les points essentiels, et l'équipe réfléchit aux moyens de les réaliser. Puis on dresse un échéancier.*

**T:** Wie funktioniert das Briefing bei Ihnen, wer erhält es zuerst, und wie erreicht es das Kreativteam?
**PK:** *Als Erstes erhält der Kundenberater das Briefing. Er setzt sich mit dem Designteam zusammen, das den Job bearbeiten wird. Man klärt die wichtigsten inhaltlichen Fragen, überlegt schon, in welche Richtungen es gehen könnte, und setzt zusammen einen Zeitplan auf.*

**T:** How many people work on an identity proposal?
**PK:** *It depends on the project's complexity. But it always makes sense that at least two designers work on a project in order to inspire each other.*

**T :** Combien de personnes travaillent sur un projet d'identité visuelle ?
**PK :** *Cela dépend de sa complexité. Mais il est toujours bon de faire collaborer au moins deux designers, afin qu'ils s'inspirent mutuellement.*

**T:** Wie viele Personen arbeiten an einem Vorschlag?
**PK:** *Das hängt vom Umfang des Projektes ab. Aber es macht Sinn, dass mindestens zwei Leute zusammenarbeiten, die sich gegenseitig inspirieren.*

**T:** How many alternatives are generated before you come back to the client the first time?
**PK:** *In the developing process of a logo, it is possible to have up to a hundred variations — depending on the timing, the team and their motivation to work on it. Of course not all of*

**T :** Combien d'alternatives concevez-vous avant de retourner voir le client pour la première fois ?
**PK :** *Dans le processus de conception d'un logo, on peut avoir jusqu'à une centaine de variations, selon le délai dont on dispose, le*

**T:** Wie viele Alternativen werden entwickelt, bevor Sie die Ergebnisse dem Kunden präsentieren?
**PK:** *Bei der Entwicklung eines Logos können schon je nach Zeitumfang, Mitarbeitern und Motivation bis zu hundert Varianten entste-*

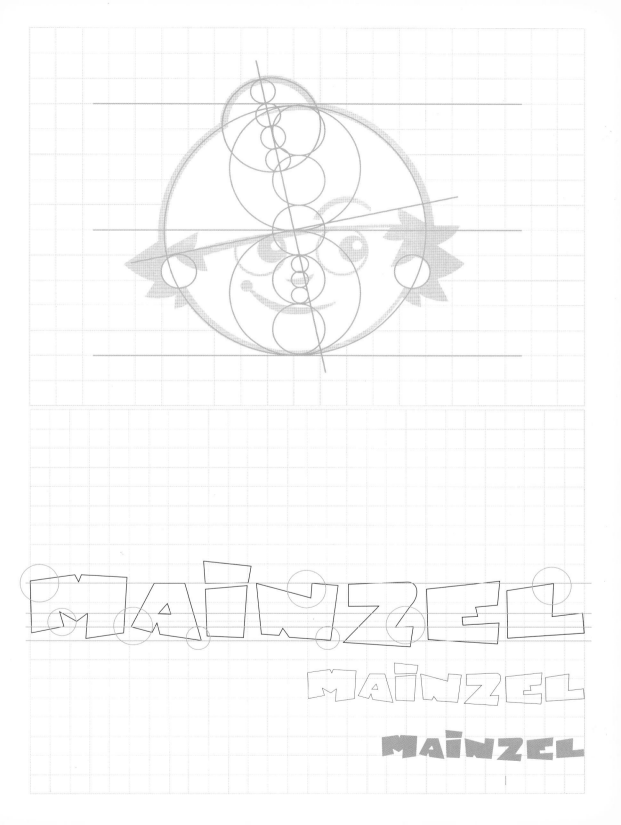

them are presented to the client. The client only gets the best of them – usually about 10 preliminary studies that show the developing process and one definite logo recommendation.

**T:** How do you work with the selection inside the studio, before showing something to the client?
**PK:** *In the development phase we always have an exhibition in our design studio. The designers put their scribbles and layouts on boards, which are then surveyed, graded or sorted out. In this way, we have the best overview of our work and the whole agency knows what is going on and may give their opinion or integrate themselves in ongoing projects.*

**T:** What is the most difficult part of the corporate identity? Is it the logo design?
**PK:** *The logo design is definitely the biggest challenge, because it has to be the most important form of corporate communication. Moreover, it has to function in the long run, whereas the graphic language can be a bit more flexible.*

talent et la motivation de l'équipe responsable. Bien entendu, on ne les présente pas toutes au client. On ne lui soumet que les meilleures, en général une dizaine d'études préliminaires qui rendent compte de la progression du travail, ainsi qu'une recommandation d'un logo en particulier.

**T :** Comment procédez-vous à la sélection, avant de montrer les résultats au client ?
**PK :** *Dans la phase de conception, nous organisons toujours une exposition dans nos locaux. Les designers affichent leurs croquis et leurs maquettes sur des panneaux, nous les étudions, les notons et trions les meilleurs. Nous avons ainsi une vue d'ensemble de notre travail et tous les collaborateurs de l'agence sont au courant de ce qui se passe. Ils peuvent donner leur opinion, voire s'intégrer au projet en cours.*

**T :** Qu'est-ce qui réclame le plus de travail ? La conception du logo ?
**PK :** *Le design du logo est incontestablement le plus gros enjeu, car c'est la forme la plus importante de la communication de l'entreprise. De plus, il doit fonctionner sur le long*

hen. Dem Kunden präsentieren wir natürlich nur die besten Ergebnisse – ca. zehn Vorstudien, die den Entwicklungsprozess aufzeigen, und eine definitive Logoempfehlung.

**T:** Wie arbeiten Sie mit den verschiedenen Entwürfen innerhalb des Studios, bevor Sie dem Kunden etwas präsentieren?
**PK:** *In der Entwicklungsphase findet bei uns in den Räumen des Designstudios immer eine Ausstellung statt. Jeder hängt seine Scribbles und Entwürfe an die Wand, die dann begutachtet, sortiert oder aussortiert werden. So hat man den besten Überblick, und die ganze Agentur kriegt etwas davon mit und kann ihre entsprechenden Kommentare abgeben.*

**T:** Was ist der schwierigste Teil der Corporate Identity? Das Logodesign?
**PK:** *Das Logodesign ist auf jeden Fall die größte Herausforderung, da ein Logo die komprimierteste Form der Unternehmenskommunikation darstellen sollte. Es muss langfristig funktionieren, wobei die Gestaltungswelt etwas flexibler sein kann.*

T: How many applications do you generate for a client (T-shirt, cards, papers, office material, etc)?

PK: *It depends on the client's branch of trade and its budget. When a final logo has been chosen, we develop a concept for the graphic world. Then we start working on the stationary, image- or product brochures and the corporate design manual. At the end we adopt the new corporate design on advertising material.*

T: Taking *Mainzelmännchen* as an example, you do a lot of variations within the same theme, in that case a character. Do you always try to do the same with every project?

PK: *The many variations result, because we usually are not satisfied easily and we always go on trying new things. This way of working has been proved of value in the past.*

T: Finally, would you give us a definition of what is the importance of a logo in the world today.

PK: *A good logo plays a significant role in building up a strong brand:*

- **It has to have a strong visual impact**
- **It has to be independent, characteristic and timeless**
- **It has to be easily recognizable and functional**
- **It has to communicate the positioning idea clearly**

*terme, alors que le langage graphique peut être un peu plus flexible.*

T: T-shirts, cartes, papeterie, articles de bureau… Quels sont les domaines d'application que vous proposez ?

PK : *Cela dépend de la branche d'activité du client, et de son budget. Quand nous avons choisi le logo définitif, nous développons le concept pour la chaîne graphique. Puis nous travaillons sur la papeterie, les plaquettes de produit et le manuel de référence. Pour finir, nous adaptons le nouveau design aux différents supports publicitaires.*

T: Dans l'exemple de *Mainzelmännchen*, on retrouve un grand nombre de déclinaisons à partir d'un même thème, dans ce cas un personnage. Essayez-vous d'appliquer ce système à tous vos projets ?

PK : *Les différentes variations viennent du fait que nous avons du mal à être satisfaits, donc nous essayons toujours de nouvelles choses. Et cette façon de travailler a prouvé son efficacité dans le passé.*

T : Pouvez-vous nous donner une définition de l'importance du logo dans le monde d'aujourd'hui ?

PK : *Un bon logo joue un rôle essentiel dans la construction d'une marque solide :*

- **Il doit avoir un impact visuel fort**
- **Il doit être personnel, original et intemporel**
- **Il doit être fonctionnel et aisément identifiable**
- **Il doit véhiculer clairement le positionnement de la marque**

T: Wie viele Verwendungen entwickeln Sie für einen Kunden (T-Shirt, Karten, Papier, Büromaterial etc.)?

PK: *Das ist sehr abhängig von der Kundenbranche und des entsprechenden Budgets. Nachdem ein Logo verabschiedet wurde, entwickeln wir erst einmal ein Konzept für die Gestaltungswelt. Danach wird meistens die Geschäftsausstattung, Image- oder Produktbroschüren oder ein CD-Manual erstellt.*

T: Bei den Mainzelmännchen zum Beispiel variieren Sie viel innerhalb eines Themas, in diesem Fall ist es ein Charakter. Verfahren Sie bei jedem Projekt auf diese Weise?

PK: *Die vielen verschiedenen Variationen kommen zusammen, weil wir uns nie so schnell zufriedengeben und immer noch etwas ausprobieren wollen. Diese Art zu arbeiten hat sich bis jetzt bestens bewährt.*

T: Können Sie uns abschließend eine Definition zur Bedeutung des Logos in der heutigen Welt geben?

PK: *Ein gutes Logo trägt zum Aufbau einer starken Marke bei:*

- **Es muss einen starken visuellen Impact besitzen.**
- **Es muss eigenständig, charakteristisch und zeitlos sein.**
- **Es muss leicht erkennbar und funktional sein.**
- **Es muss die Positionierungsidee klar kommunizieren.**

**Left:** *Complete family of characters and design sketches /// * **À gauche :** *La famille complète de personnages et des croquis conceptuels /// * **Links:** *Komplette Familie der Figuren*

**Right:** *Complete logo and the grid /// * **À droite :** *Le logo et la maquette /// * **Rechts:** *Fertiges Logo und Raster*

# Profile
# Simon & Goetz Design

**www.simongoetz.de**
Location: Frankfurt, Germany
Year of foundation: 1991.

*Founded by Mathias Simon and Rüdiger Goetz in 1991, Simon & Goetz is a leading design and communication company in Frankfurt, Germany. As an integrated enterprise with independent business units for strategic brand management, communications and corporate design, the company has always targeted solutions for integrated communications. Simon & Goetz Design is a fundamental part of this concept by creating comprehensive Corporate Design for domestic and international companies – ranging from the naming, the logo, the stationary, the graphic language to packaging: the formal implementation to build a strong brand. The design unit employs currently over 20 people in Frankfurt.*

*Fondée par Mathias Simon et Rüdiger Goetz en 1991, Simon & Goetz est une agence renommée de design et de communication située à Francfort, en Allemagne. Composée de différentes branches autonomes consacrées à la gestion stratégique, à la communication et au design industriel, la société a toujours encouragé les solutions de communication globale. Simon & Goetz Design applique ce concept en créant des identités visuelles polyvalentes pour une clientèle nationale et internationale. Le nom, le logo, les articles de papeterie, l'emballage et la communication visuelle, tout est conçu pour valoriser l'impact d'une marque. Le service de design emploie aujourd'hui plus de 20 personnes à Francfort.*

*Simon & Goetz, 1991 von Mathias Simon und Rüdiger Goetz gegründet, ist ein führendes Design- und Kommunikationsunternehmen in Frankfurt, Deutschland. Als integriertes Unternehmen mit unabhängigen Firmeneinheiten für strategisches Markenmanagement, Kommunikations- und Corporate Design hat die Firma stets auf Lösungen für integrierte Kommunikation abgezielt. Simon & Goetz Design ist ein fundamentaler Bestandteil dieses Konzepts: Es entwickelt umfassendes Corporate Design für inländische und internationale Unternehmen, von Namensgebung und Logo über Geschäftsausstattung und Grafik bis zur Verpackung: Die formale Implementierung zum Aufbau einer starken Marke. In der Designabteilung in Frankfurt sind derzeit über 20 Mitarbeiter beschäftigt.*

# UNILEVER: ADDING VITALITY TO LIFE

Consumers around the world choose Unilever products 150 million times every day. Yet most of them are unaware of it. As a company Unilever is 'blue chip' by any standards, but as a brand it is almost invisible in most western countries. An obvious question to ask was whether the Unilever brand could be developed to galvanise the organisation and help it achieve future growth.

Until now the Unilever brand has only really talked to the investment community – in part because the majority of Unilever's operating companies around the world are not actually called Unilever. If you looked on the back of a pack of Persil or Dove the 'corporate' brand names you'd find are Lever Fabergé and Lever Brothers. Even inside the company, when any of the 240,000 employees thought of Unilever they probably pictured the head-quarter buildings in Rotterdam and London – the 'bank' at the centre. Unilever started thinking seriously about its corporate brand around the time of the Persil Power 'fiasco' as it

Les consommateurs du monde entier choisissent des produits Unilever 150 millions de fois par jour. Et pourtant, la plupart l'ignorent. Comme entreprise, Unilever est par bien des côtés une valeur de premier ordre, mais comme marque elle est quasiment invisible dans la plupart des pays occidentaux. La question était : la marque Unilever peut-elle être développée afin de stimuler sa productivité et de lui garantir une croissance future ?

Jusqu'ici, la marque Unilever n'était connue que de la communauté des investisseurs, en partie parce que la majorité de ses filiales internationales ne s'appellent pas Unilever. Si l'on regarde au dos d'un baril de Persil ou d'un savon Dove, on trouve le nom Lever Fabergé ou Lever Brothers. Au sein même de l'entreprise, lorsque l'un des 240 000 employés pense à Unilever, il se représente probablement les sièges de Rotterdam et de Londres, les « banques » du groupe. Unilever s'est mis à réfléchir sérieusement à son image de marque à l'occasion de ce qui fut appelé le « fiasco » de Persil, quand le fait de savoir

Verbraucher aus aller Welt verwenden durchschnittlich150 Millionen Mal täglich Unilever-Produkte – aber die meisten sind sich dessen nicht bewusst. Als Unternehmen ist Unilever in jeder Hinsicht erstklassig, aber als Marke ist die Firma in den westlichen Ländern nahezu unsichtbar. Daher lag die Frage nahe, ob die Marke Unilever dahingehend entwickelt werden konnte, der Organisation frischen Wind zu geben und ihr zu größerem Wachstum zu verhelfen.

Bisher hat die Marke Unilever tatsächlich nur mit der Investitionsgemeinde kommuniziert – das liegt zum Teil daran, dass die Mehrzahl der von Unilever betriebenen Firmen weltweit gar nicht Unilever heißen. Suchte man auf der Verpackung von Persil oder Dove nach Firmennamen, stieß man auf Lever Fabergé und Lever Brothers. Sogar innerhalb des Unternehmens denken die 240.000 Mitarbeiter bei Unilever bei de Nennung des Firmennamens wohl eher an die Hauptgebäude in Rotterdam und London – die „Bank" im Zentrum. Unilever begann

Lemon

Lemon

STILL SOFT DRINK
WITH TEA EXTRACT
AND LEMON JUICE.

Unilever

Lipton

unfortunately became known, when the debate over whether it rotted clothes became a tabloid news story. The prevailing wisdom at the time was that having a 'hidden' owner brand insulated individual product brands from each other within Unilever's portfolio. Of course it took the media a nanosecond to make the link, and the story became not a Persil story, or even a Lever Brothers story but a Unilever story. The Unilever chairman at the time, Niall FitzGerald, says that this confirmed what he had already begun to suspect – that the main argument for not doing more with the Unilever brand was a myth.

By the time Wolff Olins began working with Unilever, early in 2002, the decision had been made to make more of the Unilever brand. The first task was to find a way to articulate what the business stood for – something that could be an anchor and touchstone for Unilever in the future. Since 1999 Unilever had been working through its five-year strategic plan, Path to Growth, which has

si la lessive faisait moisir ou non les vêtements fit la une des journaux à scandale. On pensait à l'époque que le fait d'avoir une marque mère « cachée » protégeait la réputation de chaque sous-marque du portefeuille de Unilever. Bien sûr, il ne fallut à la presse qu'une nanoseconde pour faire le lien, et le scandale ne fut plus le scandale Persil, ni le scandale Lever Brothers, mais le scandale Unilever. Niall FitzGerald, alors PDG du groupe, pense que cet esclandre a confirmé ce qu'il soupçonnait déjà, à savoir que négliger de valoriser la marque Unilever est une erreur stratégique.

C'est pour y remédier que l'entreprise fait appel à l'agence Wolff Olins au début de l'année 2002. Leur premier travail consiste alors à trouver une façon d'exprimer les valeurs du groupe, et d'en faire un point d'ancrage pour l'avenir. Depuis 1999, Unilever a appliqué son plan stratégique quinquennal, intitulé « Chemin de la croissance », et celui-ci a déjà transformé l'entreprise sous plusieurs aspects. Unilever est à présent une organisation

beim unglücklichen Persil-Power-Fiasko, erstmals ernsthaft über seine Firmenmarke nachzudenken, als die Debatte darüber, ob sie Kleider verfaulen ließen, Thema der Boulevardpresse wurde. Damals herrschte die Meinung vor, dass eine „versteckte" Eigentümermarke die individuellen Produktmarken innerhalb von Unilevers Geschäftsbereich voneinander abgrenzte. Natürlich erkannten die Medien diese Verbindung in einer Nanosekunde, und die Geschichte wurde keine Geschichte über Persil oder die Brüder Lever, sondern eine Geschichte über Unilever. Der damalige Vorsitzende von Unilever, Niall Fitzgerald, sagte, dass dies seinen schon geschürten Verdacht bestätigte: Das Hauptargument, warum nicht mehr für die Unilever-Marke getan wurde, war ein Mythos. Als Wolff Olins Anfang 2002 begann, mit Unilever zusammenzuarbeiten, war die Entscheidung, mehr aus der Marke Unilever zu machen, schon gefallen. Als Erstes musste man artikulieren, wofür das Unternehmen stand – man musste einen Ankerpunkt und Prüfstein für die Zukunft von Unilever finden.

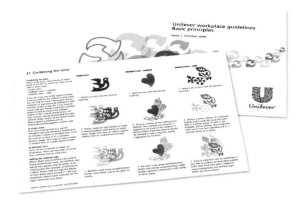

**Left and right:** *Website and printed material created to support the correct use of the new logo /// Gauche et droite : Le site Internet et les documents imprimés créés pour encourager une utilisation correcte du nouveau logo /// Links und rechts: Webseite und Druckmateriel zum Wechsel des Logos*

transformed the business in many ways. Unilever is now a much more focused organisation, marketing only 400 brands rather than the 1,600 or so it had five years ago.

*Gone are the businesses left over from the days when conglomerates were fashionable, and gone are most of the smaller single country product brands, leaving the multinational brands such as Knorr and Hellmann's and only the biggest 'local jewels' like Persil.*

The restructuring has slimmed the business down, but Unilever is still a vast organisation operating in over 150 countries. The challenge in finding a core idea for such a diverse business was, well, a challenge.

When we first met Unilever they told us stories to introduce us to the company – stories they were proud to tell. Stories about helping establish and train a distri-

plus recentrée, et ne commercialise plus que 400 marques, au lieu de 1600 il y a cinq ans.

*Peu de sociétés ont survécu à la mode des conglomérats, les petites entreprises locales sont en voie de disparition, et hormis quelques « joyaux nationaux » comme Persil, tout est entre les mains de marques multinationales comme Knorr et Hellmann.*

La restructuration a dégraissé les effectifs, mais Unilever reste un énorme groupe qui opère dans plus de 150 pays. Trouver une idée fédératrice pour une compagnie aussi tentaculaire était une vraie gageure.

Lors de notre première rencontre, les dirigeants de Unilever nous racontèrent des histoires pour nous présenter la compagnie, des histoires qui faisaient leur fierté. Celle de la mise en place d'un réseau de distribution local en Asie grâce à des femmes qui vendent les produits Unilever à leurs voisins, arrondissant ainsi leurs reve-

Von 1999 an arbeitete sich Unilever durch seinen strategischen Fünf-Jahres-Plan, „Path to Growth" (Weg zum Wachstum), der das Unternehmen veränderte. Unilever ist nun eine stärker zentrierte Organisation, die nur noch 400 Marken statt der 1600 vor fünf Jahren vertreibt.

*Die Unternehmen, die aus Zeiten übriggeblieben waren, in denen man gerneKonglomerate bildete, gab es nicht mehr; genau so wenig wie die kleineren, nationalen Produktmarken. Übrig blieben multinationale Marken wie Knorr oder Hellmanns und nur die größten „lokalen Schmuckstücke" wie Persil.*

Durch die neue Struktur ist das Unternehmen schlanker geworden, aber Unilever ist immer noch eine riesige, in über 150 Ländern tätige Organisation. Die Herausforderung, eine Kernidee für ein so vielfältiges Unternehmen zu finden, war nun – eine Herausforderung.

bution network of local women in Asian markets who sell Unilever products to their neighbours, earning extra income for their families. Stories about setting up the Marine Stewardship Council with WWF in order to source sustainable fish stocks. Stories about their tea plantations that grow their own eucalyptus trees to use as a renewable fuel for the tea driers.

*It was clear that social responsibility was more than a veneer – it was part of the Unilever DNA.*

Of course it's easy to get overly sentimental about this stuff - after all Unilever is in the business of making and selling things all over the world, and the brand has to tell that story as well. We needed to find a big idea that would drive the portfolio of consumer brands, but perhaps we could find one that also embraced Unilever's very real sense of responsibility.

Through a process of workshops and discussions with the leadership team, the

nus. Celle de la création du Marine Stewardship Council, sous l'égide de la WWF, qui a pour vocation de renouveler les réserves poissonnières. Celle où des plantations d'eucalyptus servent de combustible renouvelable pour le séchage du thé...

*Il était clair que l'engagement citoyen était plus qu'un vernis, il était dans les gènes d'Unilever.*

Gardons-nous cependant de tout sentimentalisme, car après tout Unilever fabrique et vend des produits dans le monde entier, et la marque doit aussi vendre cette histoire. Nous devions donc trouver une idée générale qui valoriserait le portefeuille de marques d'Unilever, tout en reflétant l'authentique sens des responsabilités du groupe.

Lors d'ateliers de discussions avec l'équipe dirigeante, le concept de vitalité émergea pour définir la marque Unilever, ainsi que sa nouvelle mission : « donner de la vitalité à la vie ». L'idée de vitalité allait

Als wir mit Unilever zum ersten Mal in Kontakt kamen, erzählten sie uns Anekdoten, um uns mit der Firma vertraut zu machen – Geschichten, auf die sie stolz waren: Darüber, wie sie den Aufbau eines Verteilernetzwerks in Asien unterstützten, wo einheimische Frauen Unilever-Produkte an ihre Nachbarn verkaufen und dieses zusätzliche Einkommen ihren Familien zugute kommt. Über die Errichtung des Marine Stewardship Council mit WWF, um erneuerbare Fischvorräte zu beschaffen. Geschichten über ihre Teeplantagen, wo ihre eigenen Eukalyptusbäume wachsen, um als erneuerbare Energie für Teetrockner verwendet zu werden.

*Soziale Verantwortung war offensichtlich mehr als nur äußerer Schein – sie war Teil der Unilever-DNA.*

Darüber kann man leicht gefühlsselig werden – aber letztendlich ist Unilever ein Unternehmen, das Produkte herstellt und weltweit vertreibt, und auch diese

Left to right: *New identity applied to the environment in the offices ///* **De gauche à droite** : *La nouvelle identité appliquée à l'environnement des bureaux ///* **Von links nach rechts:** *Neue Identity wird in der Büroumgebung angewendet*

concept of 'vitality' emerged as the idea to build the Unilever brand around, captured in the new Unilever mission – 'adding vitality to life'. The idea of vitality would sit at the heart of Unilever's brands and its behaviour.

*Vitality is about feeling good, looking good and getting more out of life – consumer needs that many of Unilever's consumer brands meet. Flora Pro-Activ helps you feel good because it lowers cholesterol. Dove is all about beauty from the inside, not just moisturising.*

Ben & Jerry's is all about enjoyment of life – 'joy for the belly and soul' as they say in Vermont. Vitality firstly gives a focus for Unilever's portfolio of 400 brands. It embraces the business today and it gives the company a clear focus for the future – for innovation, for investment and even for future acquisitions. Put simply, Unilever believes that the more the portfolio delivers vitality,

être au cœur de la marque et de son comportement.

*La vitalité est associée à l'épanouissement, au bien-être physique et mental, des qualités dont se réclament un grand nombre de produits Unilever. Le Pro-Activ fait du bien car il réduit le taux de cholestérol et, non content d'hydrater la peau, Dove révèle la beauté intérieure.*

Quant à Ben & Jerry, c'est le plaisir de vivre, « de la joie pour le corps et pour l'âme » comme on dit dans le Vermont. La vitalité serait le point de ralliement des 400 marques de Unilever. Elle définirait l'activité présente et donnerait au groupe un but dans l'avenir, pour l'innovation, l'investissement et même les futures acquisitions. Autrement dit, Unilever pensait que plus son portefeuille dégagerait de vitalité, plus il gagnerait en croissance. Cette nouvelle politique permettait aussi d'englober la véritable vocation citoyenne qui anime la société. Unilever sait que les

Geschichte muss erzählt werden. Wir mussten eine großartige Idee haben, die den Geschäftsbereich der Konsumgüter vorantrieb; aber vielleicht konnten wir einen Plan entwickeln, der dem tatsächlichen Verantwortungssinn Unilevers Rechnung trug. In Workshops und Diskussionen mit dem leitenden Team entstand das Konzept „Vitalität", das den Rahmen der Marke Unilever sichtbar machen sollte, indem es die neue Unilever-Mission darstellte – „mehr Vitalität fürs Leben". Diese Idee der Vitalität sollte den Kernpunkt der Marken von Unilever darstellen.

*Bei Vitalität geht es um Wohlbefinden, gutes Aussehen und darum, mehr aus seinem Leben zu machen – Kundenbedürfnisse, denen viele Unilever-produkte gerecht werden: Flora Pro-Activ verstärkt das Wohlbefinden, indem es den Cholesterinspiegel senkt. Bei Dove geht es um innere Schönheit, nicht bloß um eine Feuchtigkeitscreme.*

the more Unilever grows. The mission also has the potential to embrace the genuine passion for social and environmental responsibility that we observed running through the business. Unilever knows that consumers are increasingly acting as 'citizens' in the choices they make about brands. And that is where perhaps the greatest future potential lies - in establishing Unilever as a brand that adds vitality to life in the way it behaves as a company. Unilever has traditionally been quite reticent in talking about its 'CSR (Corporate Social Responsability)' programmes – a term that suggests these things are disconnected from the day-to-day business - precisely the opposite of what Unilever believes they must be to be effective. Its commitment to communities and the environment is backed by strong operational commitments and supply chain programmes that address vitality head-on.

Then of course there are the outward symbols of change. A Unilever that is coming out of hiding and standing for

consommateurs agissent de plus en plus en citoyens dans leur choix de marques. Et c'est peut-être là que se trouve le plus grand potentiel de croissance, dans le fait d'établir Unilever comme une marque qui donne de la vitalité à la vie, dans son comportement en tant que société. Unilever a par tradition toujours été réticent à parler de ses projets de responsabilité sociale, terme qui suggère que ces actions sont annexes à son activité principale, ce qui est l'inverse du message que le groupe désire véhiculer. Son engagement envers les hommes et l'environnement est soutenu par des programmes d'aide au développement qui abordent de front le concept de vitalité.

Viennent ensuite les symboles extérieurs de changement. Unilever qui sort de l'ombre pour incarner la vitalité doit avoir une identité visuelle à sa mesure. À de nombreux égards, l'identité visuelle allait donner le ton aux employés et même aux consommateurs. Si Unilever adoptait une identité qui tendait vers la vitalité sans l'embrasser totalement, les sceptiques à

Bei Ben & Jerry's geht es darum, das Leben zu genießen – „Freude für Leib und Seele", wie man in Vermont sagt. Vitalität verschafft der Unilever-Kollektion von 400 Marken ein Zentrum. Es erfasst das heutige Unternehmen und hält der Firma ein klares Zukunftsziel vor Augen – Innovation, Investition und sogar zukünftigen Erwerb. Kurz gesagt: Je mehr Vitalität seine Kollektion liefert, um so mehr wird Unilever wachsen. Die Mission hat außerdem das Potenzial, der aufrichtigen Begeisterung für soziale und umweltpolitische Verantwortung Rechnung zu tragen, die wir innerhalb des Unternehmens wahrgenommen hatten. Es ist Unilever bewusst, dass Kunden mehr und mehr als „Bürger" handeln, wenn es darum geht, Marken auszuwählen. Hier liegt vielleicht das größte Potenzial für die Zukunft – Unilever als Marke zu etablieren, die dem Leben in derselben Weise Vitalität hinzufügt, in der es sich als Unternehmen verhält. Traditionell hat sich Unilever zurückgehalten, wenn es darum ging, über seine „CSR (Corporate Social Responsability)"-Programme zu sprechen;

**Left to right:** *Parts of the logo turned into objects in the Unilever training center ///* De gauche à droite : *Des parties du logo transformées en objets dans le centre de formation Unilever ///* Von links nach rechts: *Abbildungen des Logos werden auf Objekten im Unilever Training Center angewendet*

vitality needs an identity that lives up to this. In many ways the identity would set the tone for employees and even consumers. If Unilever tried to 'get away' with a new identity that leaned towards vitality but didn't embrace it fully, the sceptics inside and outside the company would be quick to find the fault-lines.

When we were initially asked our views on the old Unilever 'U' identity, we asked ourselves 'would you put this on your body or in your body?' The old identity was designed primarily to talk to a corporate audience. The challenge we faced was to create a new identity that begins to tell the vitality story.

*The 25 individual icons that make up the new U symbolise the vitality story. The fish represents products like fish fingers, and also Unilever's sustainable fish policies. Bees of course make honey, an ingredient in many food products, and also symbolise nature and the environment.*

l'intérieur comme à l'extérieur de la compagnie allaient s'empresser de relever la moindre défaillance.

Quand on nous a interrogés sur notre perception de l'ancienne identité « U » d'Unilever, nous nous sommes demandé : « Avons-nous envie d'arborer cette marque, ou d'ingérer ses produits ? » L'ancienne identité avait été essentiellement conçue pour s'adresser aux professionnels. Il nous fallait donc créer une nouvelle identité qui transmettrait à tous le principe de vitalité.

*Les 25 icônes qui composent le nouveau U ont été choisies dans ce but. Le poisson représente à la fois les aliments surgelés et la politique de renouvellement des ressources dans le domaine de la pêche. Les abeilles font bien sûr du miel, un ingrédient entrant dans la composition de nombreux produits alimentaires, et elles symbolisent aussi la nature et l'écologie.*

ein Begriff, der andeutet, dass diese Dinge nicht zum alltäglichen Geschäft gehören – das genaue Gegenteil dessen, was tatsächlich der Fall ist und wie sie sein wollen, um effektiver zu sein. Ihre Verpflichtung gegenüber den Gemeinden und der Umwelt wird durch starke operative Verbindlichkeiten und Verbraucherketten-Programme gestützt, die unmittelbar Vitalität ansprechen.

Außerdem gibt es natürlichen die äußeren Symbole einer Veränderung. Unilever, das aus der Versenkung auftaucht und für Vitalität steht, braucht ein Image, dass dieser Erwartung entspricht. In vielerlei Hinsicht bestimmt das Image das Ansehen des Unternehmens bei den Mitarbeitern und Kunden. Würde Unilever versuchen, mit einem Image „durchzukommen", das sich nicht zu 100 Prozent dieser Vitalität verschrieben hat, würden die Skeptiker innerhalb und außerhalb der Firma schnell hinter ihre Schwächen kommen.

Als wir zunächst über das alte „U"-Image von Unilever diskutieren, fragten wir uns

Getting buy-in to an identity as bold and innovative as this would be a challenge in any organisation – let alone the one of the scale and diversity of Unilever. As it's a truly global company we had to ensure that no offence or hidden meaning existed in any other religions, languages or cultures.

*We consulted many, many experts along the way. Religious experts advised us to turn what was a six-pointed star into the seven-pointed star. Cultural advisors suggested we made the icon of the hand next to the flower clearer to avoid it being misunderstood as the sole of a foot and so cause offence in countries such as Thailand.*

We also had to ensure that even when looked at upside down or say, reflected in a mirror, none of the individual icons could be misread as offensive in any language.

*We even consulted a graphologist who advised us that the Unilever signature in an earlier version sloped too much to the left – which apparently isn't good. And along the way of course we had to get the buy-in of the hundreds of important stakeholders in the brand - the leaders of the business all over the world, representatives of the rest of the employees, external opinion formers, the investment community, and of course consumers.*

The outcome is that the Unilever name and logo will appear on brands in supermarkets from Shanghai to Seattle. Although the vitality mission and the new identity have now been launched the real work is only just beginning.

If Unilever is truly to stand for vitality and if Unilever's employees are truly to embrace the new mission then the idea has to weave its way into everything that Unilever does - the decisions peo-

Obtenir l'adhésion à une identité innovante et audacieuse est un défi pour n'importe quelle organisation, alors imaginez la difficulté quand il s'agit d'un groupe de la taille d'Unilever ! La compagnie étant internationale, il fallait s'assurer que les visuels ne contenaient aucun message caché ou offensant quelle que soit la religion, la langue ou la culture.

*Nous avons consulté beaucoup, beaucoup d'experts en cours de route. Les spécialistes en religion nous conseillèrent de transformer l'étoile à six branches en étoile à sept branches. Des conseillers culturels nous suggérèrent de mettre en valeur l'icône de la main près de la fleur afin qu'elle ne soit pas confondue avec un pied, pour ne pas offenser certains pays comme la Thaïlande.*

Il fallait aussi s'assurer que lorsque l'on regarderait l'emblème à l'envers, ou reflété dans une glace, aucune des icônes ne pourrait être interprétée comme offensante, quelle que soit la langue.

*Nous avons même consulté un graphologue, qui nous a indiqué que la signature de Unilever dans une précédente version penchait trop vers la gauche, ce qui apparemment n'était pas bon signe. Et bien sûr, nous avons dû obtenir l'adhésion des centaines de gros actionnaires du groupe, des décideurs du monde entier, des représentants des employés, des leaders d'opinion, de la communauté des investisseurs, et bien sûr des consommateurs.*

Le nom et le logo de Unilever peuvent aujourd'hui s'afficher sur une grande variété de produits, dans les rayons des supermarchés de Shanghai comme de Seattle.

Bien que le concept de vitalité et la nouvelle identité visuelle soient à présent lancés, le vrai travail ne fait que commencer. Pour que la marque incarne la vitalité, et que les employés du groupe s'approprient

Folgendes: „Würden wir dies auf oder in unserem Körper haben wollen?" Das alte Image war vorwiegend auf Firmenkunden ausgerichtet. Die Herausforderung, die sich uns stellte, war die Entwicklung eines neuen Images, das beginnt, die Geschichte der Vitalität zu erzählen.

*Die 25 individuellen Symbole, die das neue U ausmachen, versinnbildlichen die Vitalitätsstory. Der Fisch repräsentiert sowohl Produkte wie Fischstäbchen als auch Unilevers Firmenpolitik bezüglich der Aufrechterhaltung der Fischbestände. Bienen stellen nicht nur Honig her, sondern symbolisieren auch Natur und Umwelt.*

Ein so kühnes und innovatives Image wäre für jede Organisation eine Herausforderung – von Größe und Vielfältigkeit Unilevers mal ganz abgesehen. Da es ein globales Unternehmen ist, mussten wir sicherstellen, dass nirgendwo eine Beleidigung oder versteckte Bedeutung steckt, die in anderen Religionen, Sprachen oder Kulturen Anstoß erregen könnte. Wie ließen wir uns von zahlreichen Experten beraten. Religionsexperten rieten uns, einen sechs-zackigen Stern in einen sieben-zackigen zu ändern. Kulturratgeber wiesen darauf hin, das Symbol der Hand neben der Blume deutlicher zu machen, damit man es nicht mit einer Fußsohle verwechseln konnte, was in Ländern wie Thailand als Beleidigung aufgefasst werden könnte.

Außerdem mussten wir gewährleisten, das keines der einzelnen Symbole in irgendeiner Sprache missverständlich war – sei es von oben oder unten oder im Spiegel betrachtet. Wir befragten sogar einen Grafologen, der uns darauf hinwies, dass sich die Unilever-Signatur in einer früheren Version zu weit nach links neigte – was offenbar nicht gut ist. Zur gleichen Zeit mussten wir die Übernahme des Konzepts durch Hunderte von wichtigen Teilhabern der Marke sicherstellen: die Geschäftsführer weltweit, Repräsentanten der restlichen Mitarbeiter, externe Meinungsmacher, die Investorengemeinde und natürlich die Kunden.

Corporate material with new logo and identity applied /// Document d'entreprise avec le nouveau logo et la nouvelle identité /// Firmenmaterial mit neuem Logo und Identity

ple make, the new ideas they create and the future commitments they make.

*In five or ten years' time we hope to look back at this as the beginning of a new era of growth for Unilever – one where a previously hidden brand stepped out of the shadows and showed its true colours.*

le nouveau concept, l'idée doit imprégner toutes les actions d'Unilever : ses décisions, ses orientations, et ses engagements futurs.

*Dans cinq ou dix ans, nous espérons regarder en arrière et voir en cette aventure le début d'une nouvelle ère de croissance pour Unilever, le moment où la marque est sortie de l'ombre pour se montrer sous son vrai jour.*

Als Resultat wird der Name Unilever samt Logo auf Supermarktartikeln von Shanghai bis Seattle erscheinen. Obwohl das Konzept der Vitalität und das neue Image nun weltweit eingeführt sind, beginnt die wirkliche Arbeit erst jetzt. Wenn Unilever wirklich für Vitalität und Unilevers Mitarbeiter wirklich dahinterstehen sollen, dann muss sich die Idee durch alles ziehen, was Unilever tut – die Entscheidungen, die getroffen werden, die neuen Ideen, die entwickelt werden, und die zukünftigen Verpflichtungen, die man eingeht.

*In fünf oder zehn Jahren hoffen wir, auf diese Phase als den Beginn einer neuen Ära des Wachstums von Unilever zurückzublicken – eine Phase, in der eine bis dahin versteckte Marke aus der Versenkung trat und ihr wahres Gesicht zeigte.*

**Below:** *Package displaying the logo ///*
**Ci-dessous :** *Le logo sur un emballage*
*///* **Unten:** *Verpackung mit Logo*

# Biography
# Lee Coomber (Wolff Olins)

**www.wolff-olins.com**
Location: London, United
Kingdom

Year of foundation: 1965
Position: Executive Creative
Director

*Lee is responsible for the quality of Wolff Olins' creative output. He is a visionary thinker able to marry creativity and strategic insight. Lee has created many outstanding brands for clients from a wide range of sectors and geographies. His recent work includes the new corporate brand for Unilever and clients such as Cadillac, BT, Suez, Linklaters, Tesco, World Gold Council. Lee is passionate about how creativity and design can change and re-invent organisations. He is a frequent commentator in the media on design. He also serves on many design excellence awards. Lee joined Wolff Olins in 1993. Trained originally in theatre design Lee has had a rich and varied career, working in the US and Asia, he began his career designing exhibitions at the British Design Council.*

*Lee Comber est responsable de la qualité de la production créative chez Wolff Olins. C'est un visionnaire capable de marier créativité et intuition stratégique. Lee a créé de nombreuses marques remarquables pour des clients dont les origines et les activités sont très diverses. Il a récemment travaillé sur la nouvelle identité visuelle d'Unilever et compte parmi ses clients Cadillac, BT, Suez, Linklaters, Tesco et World Gold Council. Lee est convaincu que le design et la créativité peuvent modifier et réinventer les entreprises. Il est régulièrement invité par les médias pour commenter les nouveautés en design. Il participe aussi à de nombreux jurys de concours professionnels.*

*Formé initialement à la scénographie, il a débuté en concevant des expositions pour le British Design Council. Son domaine d'intervention est aujourd'hui très large, et il exerce tant aux États-Unis qu'en Asie. Il a rejoint Wolff Olins en 1993.*

*Lee ist für die Qualität von Wolff Olins kreativen Leistungen verantwortlich. Als visionärer Denker verknüpft er Kreativität mit strategischer Einsicht. Lee hat viele herausragende Marken für Kunden verschiedener Sektoren und Orte entwickelt. Seine jüngsten Arbeiten umfassen die neue Firmenmarke für Unilever und Kunden wie Cadillac, BT, Suez, Linklaters, Tesco und World Gold Council. Lee ist ein leidenschaftlicher Verfechter der Meinung, dass Kreativität und Design eine Organisation verändern und neu erfinden können. Er ist mit seinen Kommentaren zu Design regelmäßig in den Medien vertreten; außerdem ist er Jurymitglied bei zahlreichen herausragenden Designwettbewerben. Lee, der eigentlich in Theaterdesign ausgebildet ist, arbeitet seit 1993 für Wolff Olins. Zu Beginn seiner abwechslungsreichen Karriere arbeitete er in den USA und Asien, wo er Ausstellungen im British Design Council entwarf.*

# CREATIVE INDUSTRY

DESIGNERS AND DESIGN OFFICES, ARCHITECTS AND ARCHITECTURE OFFICES, PHOTOGRAPHERS, ADVERTISING AGENCIES, BRANDING COMPANIES, ARTISTS, INDUSTRIAL & PRODUCT DESIGNERS, ILLUSTRATORS, FILM PRODUCTION COMPANIES

cook·e

0001

ditto¨

0002

0003

0004

CRUSH

0005

0006

yo5ho

0007

RBA

0008

DOT

0009

MOMKAI

0010

CLAT

0011

SLANG

0012

---

**0001.** Cookie / Cookie  **0002.** Ditto / Department 3  **0003.** Circus / Superbüro  **0004.** Caótica / Caótica  **0005.** Crush / Crush  **0006.** Liquid / Yomar Augusto  **0007.** Yosho / Segura Inc.  **0008.** RBA / Milkxhake  **0009.** Dot Studio / Default  **0010.** Momkai / Momkai  **0011.** ALRT / AN3A  **0012.** Slang / Slang

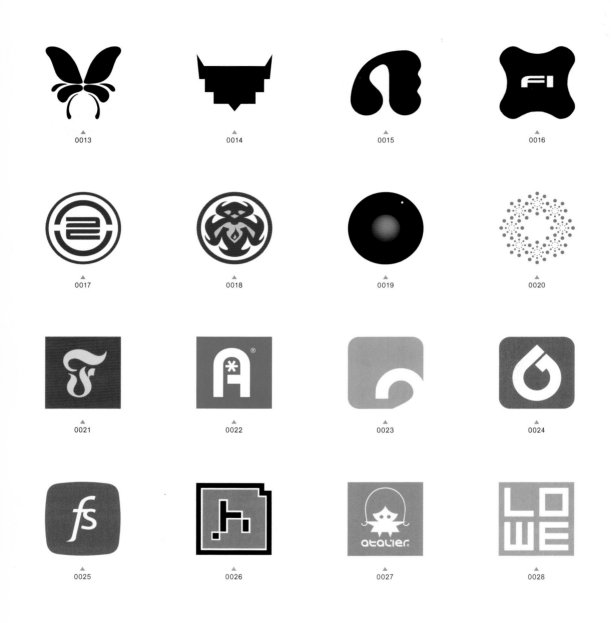

0013

0014

0015

0016

0017

0018

0019

0020

0021

0022

0023

0024

0025

0026

0027

0028

**0013.** Yonderland / Yonderland  **0014.** Fulguro / Fulguro  **0015.** Andreas Emenius / Andreas Emenius  **0016.** Fantasy Interactive / Fantasy Interactive  **0017.** 2Advanced Studios / 2Advanced Studios  **0018.** DHM Graphic Design / DHM Graphic Design  **0019.** DoubleYou / DoubleYou  **0020.** Pod Interior Design / Mattisimo  **0021.** 4vs5 / 4vs5  **0022.** Asterik Studio / Asterik Studio  **0023.** Hydra / Adrenalab  **0024.** GLU / Fluoro  **0025.** Fahrenheit Studio / Fahrenheit Studio  **0026.** Jh Design / Estudiotres  **0027.** Atalier / Atalier  **0028.** Lowe / Carter Wong Tomlin

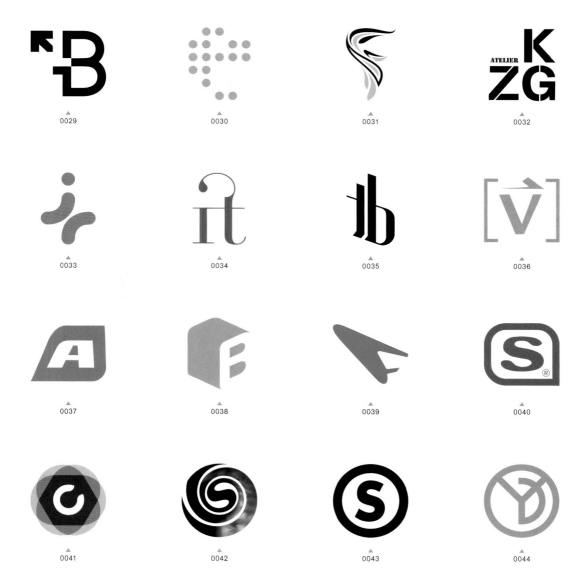

0029     0030     0031     0032

0033     0034     0035     0036

0037     0038     0039     0040

0041     0042     0043     0044

**0029.** Bikini Design Collective / Bikini Design Collective **0030.** Erwowe Design / 9Myles **0031.** Full Fat / DHM Graphic Design **0032.** KZG / Coast **0033.** Identy / Identy **0034.** IT Design / Fulguro **0035.** Thiago Barros / Yomar Augusto **0036.** Velocity Studio & Associates / Velocity Studio & Associates **0037.** Adrenalab / Adrenalab **0038.** Brandsmiths / CDT Design **0039.** Forma / Mattisimo **0040.** SightTwo / SightTwo **0041.** Les Chinois / Les Chinois **0042.** Spindoctors Media / DHM Graphic Design **0043.** Sagmeister / Sagmeister **0044.** Yeeda Design / Yeeda Design

0045

0046

PHOTOGRAPHY

0047

architektur+leben

0048

0049

0050

0051

0052

0053

0054

0055

0056

0057

0058

0059

0060

---

**0045.** Marc Herold / Marc Herold  **0046.** UTG / BLK/MRKT  **0047.** Paul Aresu / Marcos Leme  **0048.** Ja Ja / Transporter  **0049.** The Oesterle / Formikula  **0050.** Freisteller / Formikula  **0051.** Marc Herold / Marc Herold  **0052.** Central Groucho / Studio FM Milano  **0053.** Barfutura / Barfutura  **0054.** Caracol Diseño & Multimedia / Alberto Cerriteño  **0055.** Jacqueline Callaghan / The Consult  **0056.** A Small Percent / asmallpercent  **0057.** BCO / Simon & Goetz  **0058.** Cinecue / Dual  **0059.** Bloc-A / Atelier Télescopique  **0060.** Studio Thoughtcrimez / Grand Creative

0061

0062

0063

0064

0065

0066

0067

0068

0069

0070

0071

0072

0073

0074

0075

0076

---

**0061.** Synopsis / Synopsis Media  **0062.** Hoet & Hoet / Hoet & Hoet  **0063.** Velocity / Estudiotres  **0064.** Hitchwood / Ten4 Design
**0065.** Longa025 / Bikini Design Collective  **0066.** GMW Architects / CDT Design  **0067.** Full On Films / Crush  **0068.** Sevenstamp / Seven
**0069.** Bandage / Bandage  **0070.** Fake I.D. / Fake I.D.  **0071.** Illuminate Labs / 802  **0072.** Milkxhake / Milkxhake  **0073.** Tettamanti /
Fulguro  **0074.** Similis / Bionic Systems  **0075.** Celcius Films / Segura Inc.  **0076.** Soter Design / Soter Design

0077

0078

0079

0080

0081

0082

0083

0084

**0077.** Superbüro / Superbüro   **0078.** Newpollution / Newpollution   **0079.** Viagrafik / Viagrafik   **0080.** Medusa / Medusa   **0081.** Machinas / Machinas   **0082.** Mattisimo / Mattisimo   **0083.** Dtoxx / Yomar Augusto   **0084.** Matador / Coast

0085

0086

COMPUTERCAFE
ANIMATION AND VISUAL EFFECTS

0087

pure communication

0088

THE  SYNDICATE

0089

Becker Giseke
Mohren Richard
Landschafts-
architekten

0090

0091

0092

---

**0085.** Bluelounge / Bluelounge  **0086.** Twisted Interactive / Twisted Interactive  **0087.** CafeFX / Segura Inc.  **0088.** Pure Communication / Pure Communication  **0089.** The Syndicate, CafeFX / Segura Inc.  **0090.** BGMR / Adler & Schmidt  **0091.** Mattisimo / Mattisimo **0092.** Bionic Systems / Bionic Systems

0093

0094

0095

0096

**0093.** Zip Design / Zip Design   **0094.** Klaus Vedfelt / Bandage   **0095.** U.C.A.A. / Default   **0096.** Zion Graphics / Zion Graphics

elevation®

0097

**heavyform.com**

0098

sighttwō

0099

nerv®

0100

**DMC**GROUP

0101

ateLieR TéLeSCOPiQue

0102

PUSH

0103

**ANA COUTO** BRANDING&DESIGN

0104

red ant

MEDIAGROUP, INC.

0105

DIVERSID'ARTE

0106

eōe

PRODUÇÕES

0107

6D ESTŪDIO

0108

---

**0097.** Elevation, CafeFX / Segura Inc.  **0098.** Heavyform / Heavyform  **0099.** SightTwo / SightTwo  **0100.** NervMedia / NervMedia  **0101.** DMC Group / DMC Group  **0102.** Atelier Télescopique / Atelier Télescopique  **0103.** Push / Popglory  **0104.** Ana Couto Branding & Design / Ana Couto Branding & Design  **0105.** Red Ant / Simon & Goetz  **0106.** Diversid'Arte / 6D Estúdio  **0107.** Zoe / Oestudio  **0108.** 6D Estúdio / 6D Estúdio

0109

0110

0111

0112

**0109.** Sonar Media & Design / Sonar Media & Design   **0110.** Terior / The Consult   **0111.** Alberto Cerriteño / Alberto Cerriteño   **0112.** *self-promo* / Zip Design

0113

0114

0115

0116

0117

0118

0119

0120

0121

0122

0123

0124

---

**0113.** AN3A / AN3A **0114.** Bionic Systems / Bionic Systems **0115.** Locals / Bandage **0116.** Econa / Cookie **0117.** Fishouse / Zanon Design **0118.** Sevencrest / Seven **0119.** Yonderland / Yonderland **0120.** Al-Mussavir / Mule Industry **0121.** NeuBau / Mule Industry **0122.** Thilde Jensen / Bandage **0123.** Klaus Thymann / Bandage **0124.** BLK/MRKT Visual Communications / BLK/MRKT

0125

0126

0127

0128

MULLER • LEE

0129

0130

0131

0132

0133

0134

0135

0136

---

**0125.** Made / Made **0126.** Opale / Opale **0127.** Vo6 / Yomar Augusto **0128.** Tom Muller / Tom Muller **0129.** Muller & Lee / Tom Muller
**0130.** Yann Mingard / Fulguro **0131.** Punk Films / Grand Creative **0132–0136.** Buck / Buck

0137

0138

0139

0140

0141

0142

0143

0144

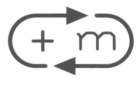

0145

0146

0147

0148

0137. Vinnie / Zip Design   0138. Hooek / SightTwo   0139. Artless Inc. / Artless Inc.   0140. CafeFX / Segura Inc.   0141. 14bits / 14bits   0142. Formul 8 / Formul 8   0143. I Love 3Deluxe, *self-promo* / 3Deluxe   0144–0145. Move Design / Move Design   0146. Tak! Design / Tak! Design   0147. Circus / Shamrock Int.   0148. Soap Creative / Soap Creative

0149

0150

0151

0152

0153

0154

0155

0156

0157

0158

0159

0160

**0149.** Eboost Media / DHM Graphic Design   **0150.** Christoph Kappl / Formikula   **0151.** Rohr Shultze / Mattisimo   **0152.** BrandSlam / 9Myles   **0153.** Duprez Dolores / The Cocoe Conspiracy   **0154.** Treeline Studios / Mattisimo   **0155.** FX Schmidt Spiele / Simon & Goetz   **0156.** Futurefarmers / Futurefarmers   **0157.** Mar Design / Mar Design   **0158.** Fisher Homes / Mattisimo   **0159.** Fake I.D. / Fake I.D.   **0160.** Springtime / Simon & Goetz

0161

0162

0163

0164

0165

0166

0167

**E3 : RGB**

0168

**E3 : CMYK**

0169

0170

0171

0172

**0161–0163.** Mezzetty / Clusta  **0164–0166.** Agent8 Design / Agent8 Design  **0167.** Estudiotres / Estudiotres  **0168–0169.** Estudiotres, *applications* / Estudiotres  **0170–0172.** Estudiotres, *variations* / Estudiotres

**SAYIMSORRY™**

0173

FULTON MARKET FILMS

0174

MAAK ROBERTS FOTOGRAPHIE

0175

studioV

0176

mecano

0177

exopolis

0178

KENT WILLIAMS

0179

basement media ™

0180

**0173.** Sayimsorry / 123Buero   **0174.** Fulton Market Films / Segura Inc.   **0175.** Maak Roberts Fotographie / 123Buero   **0176.** Studio V / Clusta
**0177.** Mecano / Mecano   **0178.** Exopolis / Exopolis   **0179.** Kent Williams / Tom Muller   **0180.** Basement Media / SightTwo

0181

0182

0183

**0181.** Hi-There / NSSgraphica   **0182.** Buck / Buck   **0183.** Corbin Bronze / Blacktop Creative

0184

0185

0186

0187

0188

0189

0190

0191

0192

0193

0194

0195

---

**0184.** Popglory / Popglory   **0185.** ImageNow / ImageNow   **0186.** Studio Thoughtcrimez / Grand Creative   **0187.** Popglory / Popglory   **0188.** ImageNow Films / ImageNow   **0189.** Studio Thoughtcrimez / Grand Creative   **0190.** Zanon & Partners / Zanon Design   **0191.** The Oesterle / Formikula   **0192.** Mule Industry / Mule Industry   **0193.** Zanon & Partners / Zanon Design   **0194.** The Oesterle / Formikula   **0195.** Mule Industry / Mule Industry

 TV

0196

 LINK

0197

 TOUCH

0198

0199

0200

0201

0202

0203

0204

0205

0206

0207

0196–0198. IMM / Mata Limited  0199–0201. T26 / Segura Inc.  0202–0204. The Kern / Yonderland  0205–0207. Also Design / Also Design

0208

0209

0210

0211

0212

0213

0214

0215

---

**0208.** Transporter / Transporter  **0209.** Ultrart / D.Workz  **0210.** Machbar / Machbar  **0211.** Amodesign / Amodesign  **0212.** Zum Kuckuck / Zum Kuckuck  **0213.** CTRLSpace / Transporter  **0214.** Airside / Airside  **0215.** Clark Studios Graphic Design / Clark Studios Graphic Design

BATTERY STUDIOS

0216

0217

virtualideas™

0218

supperstudio®

0219

FIRESTORM PC

0220

THE VILLAGE
*motion* group

0221

superieurgraphique

0222

expo
crew   messe deko event

0223

**0216.** Battery Studios / Yonderland   **0217.** Attak / Attak   **0218.** Virtual Ideas / Fluoro   **0219.** Supperstudio / Supperstudio   **0220.** Firestorm PC / Fantasy Interactive   **0221.** The Village / Twisted Interactive   **0222.** Superieur Graphique / Superieur Graphique   **0223.** Expo Crew / Superieur Graphique

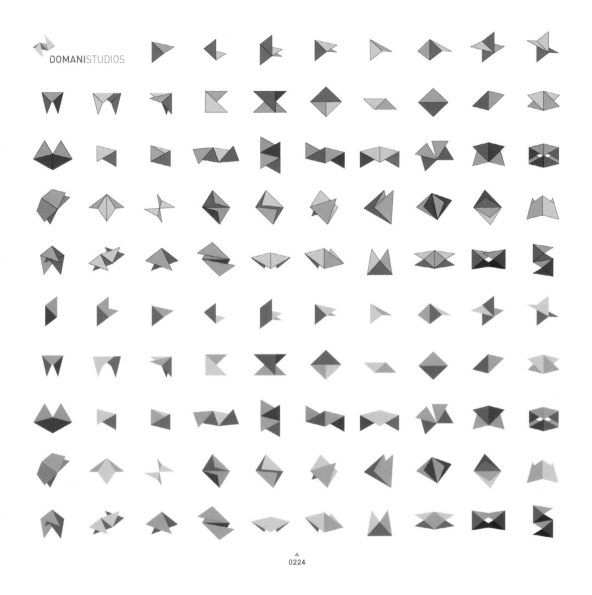

0224

**0224.** Domani Studios / Domani Studios

0225

0226

0227

0228

**0225–0226.** Evil Architecture / Domani Studios   **0227.** Bandage / Bandage   **0228.** Evil Architecture / Domani Studios

0229

0229. Sagmeister / Sagmeister

0230

0230. Formul 8 / Formul 8

# EVENTS & ENTERTAINMENT

## AWARDS, CHAMPIONSHIPS, CONTESTS, TRADE FAIRS, FESTIVALS, MEETINGS, PARTIES, SHOWS, THEATRE COMPANIES

0231

0232

0233

0234

0235

0236

0237

0238

0239

0240

0241

0242

0243

0244

0245

0246

---

**0231.** Stanford Art Department MFA Show / Futurefarmers  **0232.** Rio Cidade Estado / Oestudio  **0233.** Calabash International Literary Festival 2003 / Ricardo Leme Lopes  **0234.** Net Driver Online Magazine  / SightTwo  **0235.** 40 Jahre Videokunst / dWork  **0236.** Ministry of Foreign Affairs, The Netherlands / Studio Dumbar  **0237.** Museum of Design Zurich  / Martin Woodtli  **0238.** United Nations  / SightTwo  **0239.** Net Driver Online Magazine  / SightTwo  **0240.** RTV Awards / Airside  **0241.** Petrobrás Surf Competition / Bruno Richter  **0242.** Culture Department (Brazil), House of World Cultures (Berlin) / Felipe Taborda  **0243.** Auckland Readers and Writers Festival / Seven  **0244.** Lunes party / 2pix  **0245.** Melt / Caótica  **0246.** Nyenrode, Gummo.nl / Shamrock Int.

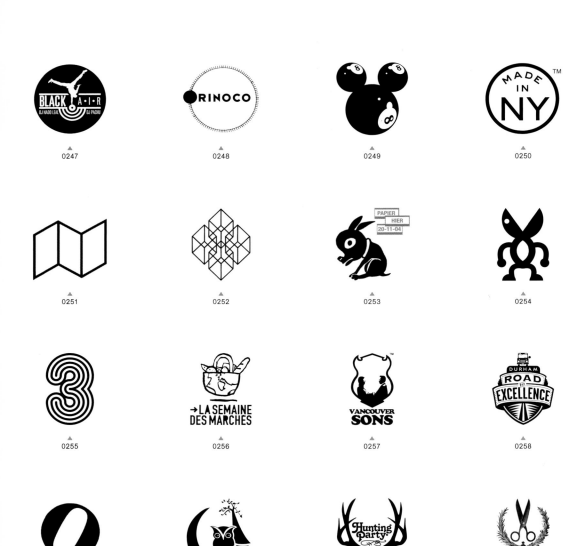

0247

0248

0249

0250

0251

0252

0253

0254

0255

0256

0257

0258

0259

0260

0261

0262

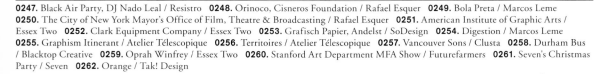

**0247.** Black Air Party, DJ Nado Leal / Resistro   **0248.** Orinoco, Cisneros Foundation / Rafael Esquer   **0249.** Bola Preta / Marcos Leme
**0250.** The City of New York Mayor's Office of Film, Theatre & Broadcasting / Rafael Esquer   **0251.** American Institute of Graphic Arts /
Essex Two   **0252.** Clark Equipment Company / Essex Two   **0253.** Grafisch Papier, Andelst / SoDesign   **0254.** Digestion / Marcos Leme
**0255.** Graphism Itinerant / Atelier Télescopique   **0256.** Territoires / Atelier Télescopique   **0257.** Vancouver Sons / Clusta   **0258.** Durham Bus
/ Blacktop Creative   **0259.** Oprah Winfrey / Essex Two   **0260.** Stanford Art Department MFA Show / Futurefarmers   **0261.** Seven's Christmas
Party / Seven   **0262.** Orange / Tak! Design

0263

0264

0265

0266

0267

0268

0269

0270

0271

0272

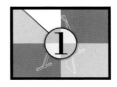

0273

0274

**0263.** Oprah Winfrey / Essex Two   **0264.** Tistu / Marcos Leme   **0265.** French Government / Base Design   **0266.** Mi Yo / Yomar Augusto
**0267.** Soup, Pry / Zetalab   **0268.** Galerie Neurotitan / Slang   **0269.** Adobe Design Achivement Awards / Mucca Design   **0270–0274.** Adobe Design Achivement Awards, *applications* / Mucca Design

0275

0276

0277

0278

0279

**0275.** Forum Barcelona 2004 / Area 3   **0276.** Nu'Sessions party, DJ Nado Leal / Resistro   **0277.** Madame, Scarlet 5 / Marcos Leme
**0278.** Organic Electronics / 3Deluxe   **0279.** Saturday Night Ride / 3Deluxe

**0280.** Leeds Youth Opera, *logo system* / Brahm Design

Calabash 2004

0281

0282

0283

0284

0285

0286

0287

---

**0281.** Calabash International Literary Festival 2004 / Ricardo Leme Lopes  **0282.** Calabash International Literary Festival 2005 / Ricardo Leme Lopes, Marcos Leme  **0283-0287.** Calabash International Literary Festival 2003 / Ricardo Leme Lopes

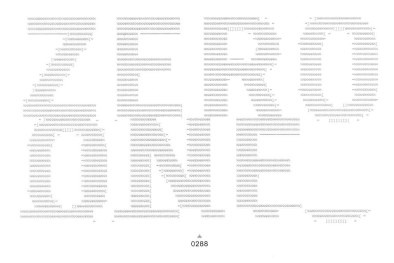

0288

0289

0290

**0288.** Zero One, San Francisco Museum of Modern Art / Move Design    **0289.** HN05, Dutch Corporate Identity Award 2005 / SoDesign
**0290.** Viessmann Werke, ISH Trade Fair / Stankowski+Duschek

0291

0292

0293

0294

0295

0296

0297

0298

**0291.** Noise Pop vs Giant Robot / Kaliforniarepublik **0292.** Renaissance Communications / 3rd Edge **0293.** Blu Soul / Image Now
**0294.** Hokupoku / Miles Newlyn **0295.** ASTEJ / Fulguro **0296.** Milano Film Festival / Zetalab **0297.** Coastboy / Superieur Graphique
**0298.** Technoheadz / Resistro

0299

0300

0301

0302

---

**0299.** Bos theater / DBXL   **300.** Expresso Productions / Resistro   **301.** H*RT, Myra Driessen / Shamrock Int.   **302.** WUSA / 9Myles

0303

0303. Mind the Gap / Brahm

SILVERSTONE

0304

**0304.** Octagon Motorsport / Carter Wong Tomlin

# swissincheese +

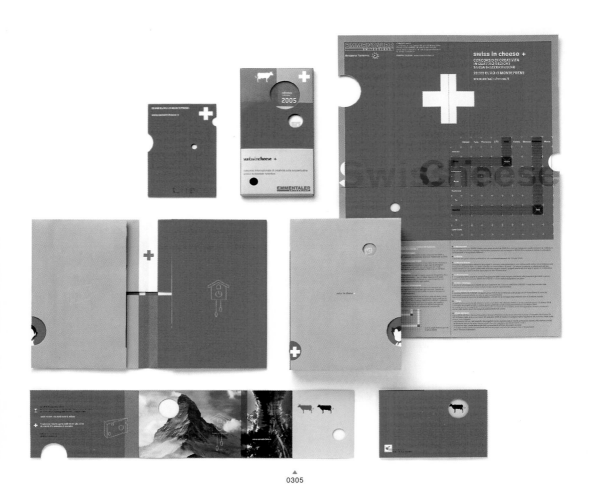

0305

---

**0305.** Connexine / Studio FM Milano

0306

0306. Connexine / Studio FM Milano

0307

**0307.** XV Pan American Games Rio 2007 Organizing Committee / Dupla Design

0308

**0308.** XV Pan American Games Rio 2007 Organizing Committee, *iconographic system* / Dupla Design

# FASHION & APPAREL

## CLOTHING, FOOTWEAR, EYEWEAR, ACCESSORIES

0309

0310

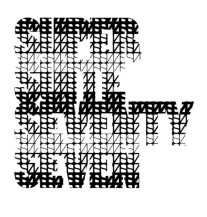

0311

0312

**0309.** Pow Clothing / Buck **0310.** Icarus Clothing, T-shirt / Twisted Interactive **0311.** SuperSuite77 / 2x4 Inc. **0312.** Liberty Department Store, T-Shirt / Zip Design

0313

0315

0314

0316

0317

0318

0319

---

**0313.** Cantão / Oestudio   **0314.** Sta Ephigênia / Yomar Augusto   **0315.** Icarus Clothing, T-shirt / Twisted Interactive   **0316.** Rina Rich / SightTwo   **0317.** Nine to Go / 6D Estúdio   **0318.** No Limite / Oestudio   **0319.** Rockitqueen / Grand Creative

vento
OSKLEN SUMMER 05

0320

0321

0322

0323

0324

0325

*Konhof*

0326

ZOOGAMI

0327

ZORREL

0328

nuala

0329

Hinoki

0330

CODY

0331

---

**0320.** Osklen / Comparsas  **0321.** Wassingue / Atelier Télescopique  **0322.** Porcaputtana Streetwear / Truly Design  **0323.** Schoger / Mule Industry  **0324.** Vollinsky / Zanon Design  **0325.** J Shoes / Bluelounge  **0326.** Konhof / Sille Bjarnhof  **0327.** Zoogami / Zanon Design **0328.** Zorrel / Polychrome  **0329.** Nuala, Puma Inc. / Base Design  **0330.** Hinoki / Atelier Télescopique  **0331.** Cody Eyewear / Bluelounge

0332

0333

0334

0335

0336

deesse

0337

**KENZO**MENSHOES

0338

mahanuala

0339

---

**0332.** Anne Kelly / Mattisimo   **0333.** Talene Reilly / Alfalfa   **0334.** Wassingue / Atelier Télescopique   **0335.** Sterne, Puma Inc. / Bionic Systems   **0336.** Nakara / SightTwo   **0337.** Deesse / SightTwo   **0338.** Kenzo Men Shoes / Atelier Télescopique   **0339.** Mahanuala, Puma Inc. / Base Design

0340

ROYAL LABEL

OSKLEN LIMITED EDITIONS

0341

0342

0343

0344

0345

De Beers

0346

0347

**0340–0343.** Osklen / Comparsas   **0344.** Austral, Osklen / Comparsas   **0345.** Entity International / Clark Studios   **0346.** De Beers / The Partners   **0347.** Intrigue Eyewear / Clark Studios

0348

0349

0350

0351

0352

0353

0354

0355

0356

0357

0358

0359

0360

0361

0362

0363

**0348.** Jenny Dyer London / Aloof Design   **0349.** Maria Filó / Ricardo Leme Lopes   **0350.** Pinpops / Tak! Design   **0351.** Nee Noon / Ben Loiz   **0352.** Onna Mitsu / Bruno Richter   **0353.** Mr. Ego / Coast Design   **0354.** Util Outdoors / Mar Design   **0355.** Jock Lock / SightTwo   **0356.** Xsampl / Transporter   **0357.** SGT Pervert / Resistro   **0358.** Jim Style Urban Wear / Weissraum   **0359.** Kult Industries / Magma   **0360.** Osklen / Comparsas   **0361.** Ka / Yomar Augusto   **0362.** Charlotte Weiss / Sille Bjarnhof   **0363.** Zoogami / Zanon Design

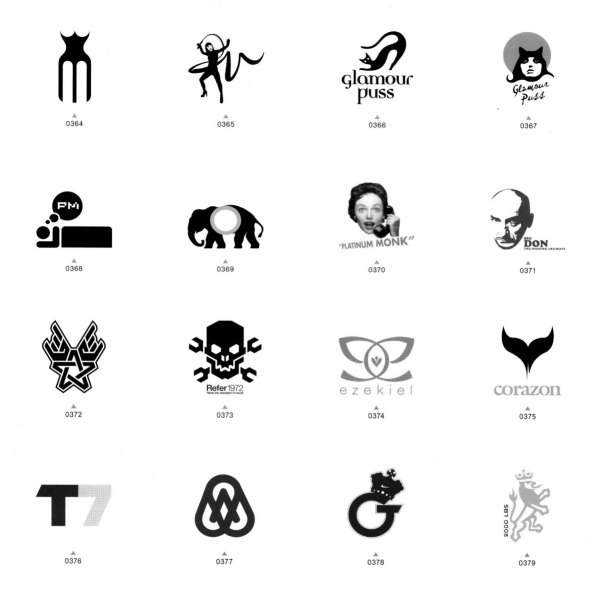

0364

0365

0366

0367

0368

0369

0370

0371

0372

0373

0374

0375

0376

0377

0378

0379

**0364.** Mistress / Soap Creative　**0365.** Mistress Wicked / Soap Creative　**0366.** Glamour Puss / Soap Creative　**0367.** Glamour Puss Evening / Soap Creative　**0368.** PM Clothing / Estudiotres　**0369.** Zoogami / Zanon Design　**0370.** Platinum Monk / Soap Creative　**0371.** Big Don *(self-promo)* / Clusta　**0372.** Refer / Power Graphixx　**0373.** Refer / Power Graphixx　**0374.** Ezekiel Clothing / Clark Studios　**0375.** Corazon / Attak　**0376.** Taré 7, Airwalk Int. / Bluelounge　**0377.** Flye / Mattisimo　**0378.** Geoff Hollister Athletic Club, Nike / Mattisimo　**0379.** 2000LBs / Ricardo Leme Lopes

0380

0381

0382

0383

0384

0385

0386

0387

0388

0389

0390

0391

---

**0380.** Casué / Simon & Goetz   **0381.** OMG Clothing / SkinnyCorp   **0382.** Chloé Laclau / Soter Design   **0383.** Yarell / Simon & Goetz
**0384.** KB Accessoires / Atalier   **0385.** Sykum Footwear / Viagrafik   **0386.** Casa das Meninas / Soter Design   **0387.** Dinomoda / Simon & Goetz   **0388.** Marangoni / Simon & Goetz   **0389.** Melt London / Agitprop   **0390.** Squirrel / Unreal   **0391.** Emory / Supperstudio

0392

0393

0394

0395

0396

0397

0398

0399

0400

0401

0402

0403

**0392.** 55dsl / Viagrafik  **0393.** Sykum Footwear / Viagrafik  **0394.** US Forty Clothing / Viagrafik  **0395–0397.** Sizzle Clothing / Clusta  **0398.** Offset / 3Deluxe  **0399.** Refer / Power Graphixx  **0400.** Gaitán / Atalier  **04001.** Etura, Airwalk International / Bluelounge  **04002.** Vollinsky / Zanon Design  **0403.** Reality Broken / BLK/MRKT

0404

0405

0406

0407

0408

0409

0410

0411

0412

0413

0414

0415

**0404.** Jim Style Urban Wear / Weissraum   **0405.** Taré 7, Airwalk Int. / Bluelounge   **0406.** Joop / Peter Schmidt Group   **0407.** Bgreen Apparel / SightTwo   **0408.** Urge Footwear / Soap Creative   **0409.** Sandpiper / Caótica   **0410–0412.** Dirty Dirts / DBXL   **0413.** Nuttygear USA / Mule Industry   **0414.** Khós / Oestudio   **0415.** Drop / Domani Studios

0416

0417

0418

0419

0420

0421

0422

0423

0424

0425

0426

0427

**0416.** NYLC / Amster Yard  **0417–0427.** NYLC, *studies* / Amster Yard

0428

**0428.** Jardim XS / Oestudio

0429

0430

0431

0432

---

**0429.** Jardim XS, *t-shirt application* / Oestudio  **0430.** Jardim XS, *fashion collection application* / Oestudio  **0431–0432.** Jardim XS / Oestudio

0433

0434

0435

0436

0437

0438

0439

0440

0441

0442

0443

0444

**0433.** Fresh / Marcos Leme  **0434.** Pro, Nike / Bepositive Design  **0435.** T-Shock / Formikula  **0436.** Fresh / Marcos Leme  **0437.** Pro, Nike / Bepositive Design  **0438.** T-Shock / Formikula  **0439–0441.** Threadless / SkinnyCorp  **0442.** Kenner, *main logo* / Oestudio **0443–0444.** Kenner, *variation* / Oestudio

0445

0445. Skull, Puma Inc. / Bionic Systems

# GEORGINAGOODMAN

△
0446

△
0447

△
0448

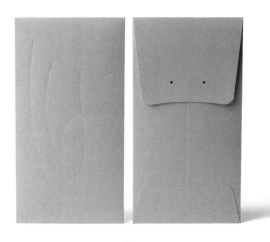

△
0449

---

**0446–0449.** Georgina Goodman / Aloof Design

0450

**0450.** Georgina Goodman / Aloof Design

0451

0452

0453

0454

**0451.** Jim Style Urban Wear / Weissraum   **0452.** MHT / Spill   **0453.** Hebrew School Girls / Ben Loiz   **0454.** Schoger / Mule Industry

0455

0456

0457

**0455.** Womens' Secret Underwear / Viagrafik   **0456.** Sha Sha Fine Shoes (Billy Lane) / 9Myles   **0457.** Sandpiper / Caótica

# INSTITUTIONS, GOVERNMENT & REGIONAL

ORGANIZATIONS, ASSOCIATIONS, UNIVERSITIES, COLLEGES, INSTITUTES, SCHOOLS, FOUNDATIONS, SPORT CLUBS, CITY AND STATE IDENTITY, COMMUNITIES, COUNTRIES

0458

0459

0460

0461

0462

0463

0464

0465

0466

0467

0468

0469

**0458.** Madeleines / Kontrapunkt   **0459–0469.** Madeleines, *variations* / Kontrapunkt

0470

0471

0472

0473

0474

0475

0476

0477

0478

0479

0480

0481

0482

0483

0484

0485

**0470.** Panamerican Olympic Village / PVDI Design   **0471.** McDonald's Children's Charities / Essex Two   **0472.** The Cardamom Project / 9Myles   **0473.** Carolina Tempest Soccer Team / Amster Yard   **0474.** CIZ – Centrum Indicatiestelling Zorg / TelDesign   **0475.** Pediatric Palliative Care Institute / Essex Two   **0476.** Chemistry student union / Yomar Augusto   **0477.** Storstrøm Hospital, *unpublished* / Made + Toke Nielsen   **0478.** Servite Houses / CDT Design   **0479.** U / Rural University, student union / Yomar Augusto   **0480.** Indiana Health for All / Essex Two   **0481.** Zone Defense / Essex Two   **0482.** Herbin Language Institute / Identy   **0483.** Maternal Health, Missouri Health Department / Blacktop Creative   **0484.** Non Profit / 9Myles   **0485.** Little Red Door Cancer Agency / Essex Two

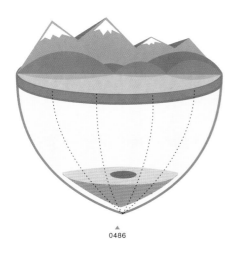

0486

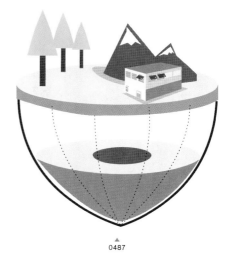

0487

0488

0489

---

**0486–0487.** The Great Park / Futurefarmers  **0488–0489.** Kulturarvsstyrelsen, Danish National Heritage Agency / Kontrapunkt

0490

**KINGS & QUEENS**
SOCCER CLUB

0491

0490–0491. Kings & Queens Soccer Club / Oestudio

0492

0493

0494

0495

0496

0497

0498

0499

0500

0501

0502

0503

0504

0505

---

**0492.** Negril United Footbal Club / Ricardo Leme Lopes  **0493.** Philadelphia Electrix Soccer Team / Amster Yard  **0494.** Washington Freedom Soccer Team / Amster Yard  **0495.** San Francisco Front Soccer Team / Amster Yard  **0496.** Borussia Dortmund / SoDesign  **0497.** AFC Ajax, Amsterdam / SoDesign  **0498.** FC Bayern München / SoDesign  **0499.** KNVB, Zeist (Royal Dutch Football Association) / SoDesign  **0500–0505.** Women's United Soccer Association / Amster Yard

0506

0507

Flowerfield Arts Centre

0508

0509

0510

0511

PREMIER ENVIRONMENTAL GROUP, LLC

0512

**Michel** Mein Michel

0513

THERAPNE

0514

BIBLIOTECA POPULAR LA QUEBRADA

0515

agir

0516

FIGHTING SCOTS
OF GORDON COLLEGE

0517

---

**0506.** oppTree / IE Design + Communications   **0507.** CARE - Center for Activity Research and Education / IE Design + Communications   **0508.** Flowerfield Arts Centre / Tandem Design & Front Design   **0509.** Criações Gastronômicas / Oestudio   **0510.** Yorkshire Forward, Centres of Industrial Collaboration / Brahm Design   **0511.** Caspian Energy Centre, Science Museum London/BP / Carter Wong Tomlin   **0512.** Premier Environmental Group / Archetype   **0513.** Michel Mein Michel Foundation / Peter Schmidt Group   **0514.** Therapne / PhormaStudio Design   **0515.** Biblioteca Popular La Quebrada / Damián Di Patrizio   **0516.** Agir / Amodesign   **0517.** Athletic Dept and sports teams of Gordon College / asmallpercent and Grant Hanna

*voedsel en groen*
*van internationale klasse*

*Groen ondernemen,*
*innovatieve kracht*

*Nieuwe paden,*
*vitale natuur*

*Veilig voedsel,*
*bewuste keus*

*Vertrouwd platteland,*
*verrassend perspectief*

0518

**0518.** Dutch Ministry of Agriculture, Nature and Food Quality / Studio Dumbar

0519

0520

0521

0522

0523

0524

0525

0526

0527

0528

0529

0530

**0519.** Museo di Fotografia Contemporanea / Damián Di Patrizio  **0520.** Sata / PVDI Design  **0521.** Pulsar, Intranet Hospitais S.A. / Amodesign  **0522.** Maserati Quattroporte owner's club, *proposal* / Luca Cighetti for Alvillage  **0523.** Pavilion / Brahm Design  **0524.** Milano 2006, *proposal* / Luca Cighetti for Alvillage  **0525.** Hamburg Police Dept / Peter Schmidt Group  **0526.** Ciesu / PVDI Design  **0527.** Fondation Lycée Jean Monnet / Sign*  **0528.** P.M.K. / transporter  **0529.** NVF (Netherlands Association of Film Distributors) / SoDesign  **0530.** Scale Safe Association / Twisted Interactive

0531

0532

0533

0534

0535

0536

0537

0538

0539

0540

---

**0531–0534.** The James Joyce Centre, *logo system* / Image Now   **0535–0540.** Masterdam, ROC ASA, *logo system* / Shamrock Int.

0541

0542

---

**0541.** Salto, Swiss Foundation for Health / Superbüro    **0542.** Stichting Altviool Testore / SoDesign

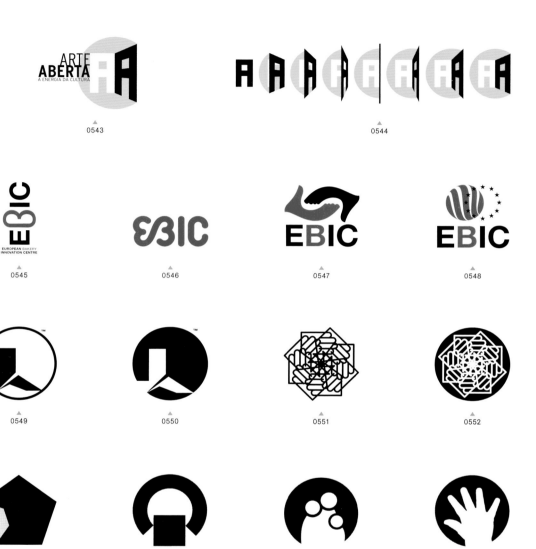

0543

0544

0545

0546

0547

0548

0549

0550

0551

0552

0553

0554

0555

0556

**0543.** Arte Aberta / Felipe Taborda   **0544.** Arte Aberta, *animation* / Felipe Taborda   **0545–0548.** EBIC - European Bakery Innovation Centre, *proposals* / DHM Graphic Design   **0549–0550.** Plan B Science and Entertainment / Tom Muller   **0551–0552.** Fifth Avenue Committee, *sketch* / Default   **0553.** Pentagon Memorial (9/11), Call for Entries Identity for Pentagon Memorial / 2x4 Inc.   **0554.** Design Museum / Essex Two **0555.** Family Communications / Essex Two   **0556.** Children's Memorial Hospital / Essex Two

d. institute

0557

act:onaid

0558

0559

MINNESOTA
DENTAL
ASSOCIATION

0560

0561

DaVita.

0562

0563

0564

Museumsinsel

0565

read·ing mat·ters

0566

---

**0557.** Stanford Design Institute / Department 3   **0558.** Actionaid / CDT Design   **0559.** LaagHolland, National Landscape Association / Eden Design & Communication   **0560.** Minnesota Dental Association / Franke+Fiorella   **0561.** PET - Danish Security Intelligence Service / Kontrapunkt   **0562.** DaVita, Kidney Dialysis Company / IE Design + Communications   **0563.** Bibliobus, City of Lille / Atelier Télescopique **0564.** Arttable, *study* / 2x4 Inc.   **0565.** Museumsinsel, Berlin / Baumann & Baumann   **0566.** Reading Matters / Brahm Design

0567

0568

0569

**0567.** Radboud University Nijmegen, *original logo*    **0568.** Radboud University Nijmegen, *redesign* / Nies & Partners    **0569.** Radboud University Nijmegen, *studies* / Nies & Partners

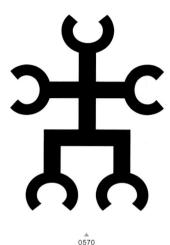

0570

0571

0572

0573

**0570—0573.** Centraal Museum, Utrecht, The Netherlands, *logo system* / Thonik   **Next page** Centraal Museum, Utrecht, The Netherlands, *posters* / Thonik

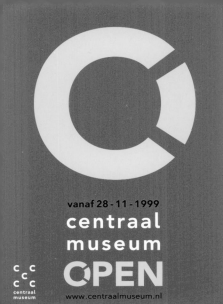

vanaf 28 - 11 - 1999
centraal
museum
OPEN

C C C
C C C
centraal
museum

www.centraalmuseum.nl

c - style
a b c d e f
g h i j k l m
n o p q r s
t u v w x y
z ?!

# centraal museum krant

| Open, open!! | Ingmar Heytze | Erich Wichman | C C GRATIS |
|---|---|---|---|
| Open, open, open open o-open, open! Open, open open! | Van dolhuis tot doofhof | 'k zou een omweg maken, om niet langs Utrecht te hoeven' | C centraal museum  Nr 3 najaar 99  Nicolaaskerkhof 10  3512 XC Utrecht |
| pagina 3, 5, 6, 7, 9 | pagina 6, 7 | pagina 8 | |

OPEN
OPEN
OPEN

Open, open open open open, open!

**Open, open, open! Open! Open Open!** Open open, open open Open. Open, open, open open-open Open! Open open! Open-pen open! Open o-pen open open, open open! Open open! Open Open Open, open. Open open! Open, open, open open.

Open Open! Open open, open open! Open Open! Open open, open open Open Open! Open open, open open! Open Open! Open open, open open O-Open! Open Open open, open open O-**Open! Open! Open!** Open open, open open! Open open, open open! Open open, open open open O-

pen! Open, open, open open! open, open open open open! Open, open-open open! open open open, open open! Open open! Open, open, open open O-**Open!** Open open, open, open open O-pen! Open, open, open, open open! open, open Open, open, open!

# centraal museum krant

| Open, open!! | Panorama 2000 | Ronald Giphart | C C GRATIS |
|---|---|---|---|
| Open, open, open open o-open, open! Open, open open! | 160.000 mensen beklommen de Domtoren | Column: Niet blk weg | C centraal museum  Nr 6 winter 01  Agnietenstraat 3  3512 XA Utrecht |
| pagina 5,6,7,8,9 | pagina 3 | pagina 11 | |

made in japan

ORANGE COUNTY MUSEUM OF ART

▲
0574

▲
0575

▲
0576

▲
0577

▲
0578

|| PARQUE BOTÂNICO ||
Vale do Rio Doce

▲
0579

|| PARQUE ZOOBOTÂNICO ||
de Carajás

▲
0580

|| PARQUE BOTÂNICO ||
de São Luís

▲
0581

**0574.** Orange County Museum of Art / Futurefarmers  **0575.** Fondation Mimi / Hoet & Hoet  **0576–0578.** DATA - Dublin Art and Technology Association / Futurefarmers  **0579–0581.** CVRD Parks / Dupla Design

# håndtryk til hjemløse

# - giv din hånd

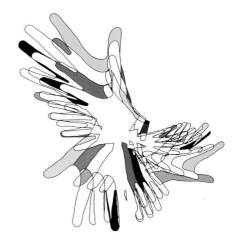

0582

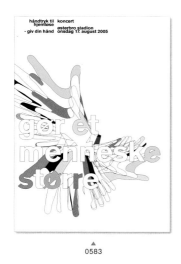

0583

0584

---

**0582.** The Homeless Project / Kontrapunkt  **0583–0584.** The Homeless Project, *posters* / Kontrapunkt

0585

0586

0587

0588

---

**0585.** Lake Forest School / Alberto Cerriteño   **0586.** Leven in Guatemala / Twisted Interactive   **0587.** United Nations ICT Task Force / Image Now   **0588.** Technovium, ROC Nijmegen / Nies & Partners

0589

0590

0591

0592

skytrack™

0593

0594

0595

Politie

0596

SOMERSET
CHRISTIAN
COLLEGE

0597

0598

0599

0600

0601

0602

0603

0604

---

**0589.** H20 Pals, Cooper-Hewitt Museum / Futurefarmers   **0590.** Volksschule Lochau (school) / Sagmeister   **0591.** Eco Logo, The Great Park / Futurefarmers   **0592.** Ferris University / Essex Two   **0593.** Skytrack / Twisted Interactive   **0594.** Incines Film School / IAAH   **0595.** Faultier Institute / Viagrafik   **0596.** Policy of Belgium / Hoet & Hoet   **0597.** Somerset Christian College / 3rd Edge Communications   **0598.** World Model Association / Simon & Goetz   **0599.** Die Econauten / Simon & Goetz   **0600.** Maison de la Photographie de Grenoble / Idsigner   **0601.** National Therapy Seminars / Fahrenheit Studio   **0602.** Born Learning / Essex Two   **0603.** Treetoperails / Twisted Interactive   **0604.** Upgrade Institute of English / Ricardo Leme Lopes

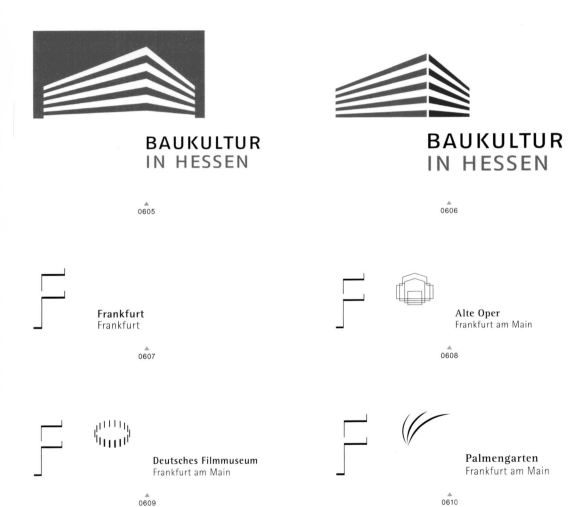

**BAUKULTUR**
IN HESSEN

0605

**BAUKULTUR**
IN HESSEN

0606

**Frankfurt**
Frankfurt

0607

**Alte Oper**
Frankfurt am Main

0608

**Deutsches Filmmuseum**
Frankfurt am Main

0609

**Palmengarten**
Frankfurt am Main

0610

---

**0605–0606.** Baukultur in Hessen - ANP, Imorde, Kassel / Machbar  **0607–0610.** City of Frankfurt, *logo system* / Baumann & Baumann

0611

0612

0613

LEIPZIG 2012

0614

**FALKLANDS FINEST**

0615

Burgen, Schlösser,
Altertümer
Rheinland-Pfalz

0616

0617

Bennett

0618

0619

0620

0621

0622

---

**0611–0613.** Valle d'Aosta, Italy / Sonar Media & Design   **0614.** Leipzig 2012, free-study / Zum Kuckuck   **0615.** Falklands Finest / The Partners   **0616.** State-owned Castles, Palaces and Monuments in the Rhineland-Palatinate / Adler & Schmidt Kommunikations-Design   **0617.** SBLO Sistema Bibliotecario Lario Ovest / Studio FM Milano   **0618.** Bennett / Mar Design   **0619.** Vivid / Clusta Design   **0620.** HERO for Africa's Children Project, United Nations Association for USA / de.MO   **0621.** KWF Kankerbestrijding, Fundraising-organisation for Cancer / Tel Design   **0622.** Skytrack / Twisted Interactive

0623

**0623.** City of Amsterdam, *logo system* / Eden Design & Communication & Thonik

0624

---

SETÚBAL
MUNICÍPIO PARTICIPADO

0625

Mercado
municipal de Palmela

0626

illuminate

0627

MIT RECHT.KARLSRUHE
KULTURHAUPTSTADT EUROPAS 2010

0628

it's
nature's
greenland

0629

The
Yorkshire
Dales

0630

British
Waterways

0631

NCCR CLIMATE
Swiss Climate Research

0632

---

**0625.** City of Setúbal, Market / Amodesign   **0626.** City of Palmela, Market / Amodesign   **0627.** Illuminate / Brahm Design   **0628.** City Of Karlsruhe, Application for the European Cultural Capital in 2010 / MAGMA [Büro für Gestaltung]   **0629.** Greenland Home Rule / Kontrapunkt   **0630.** The Yorkshire Dales / Brahm Design   **0631.** British Waterways / Design Bridge   **0632.** NCCR climate / Superbüro

**Paddington Walk**

0633

0633. Paddington Walk, Paddington Basin / Ico Design

0634

0635

0636

0637

0638

0639

0640

0641

0642

0643

0644

0645

**0634.** Local authority of the city of Uden / Nies & Partners   **0635–0645.** Local authority of the city of Uden, *studies* / Nies & Partners

0646

0647

0648

0649

0650

0651

**0646.** City of Ouro Preto, Brazil / PVDI Design    **0647–0651.** City of Ouro Preto, Brazil, *applications* / PVDI Design

# MEDIA

TV, RADIO, MAGAZINES,
NEWSPAPERS, FILMS, BOOKS,
WEB SITES, PORTALS,
PUBLISHERS, CAMPAIGNS

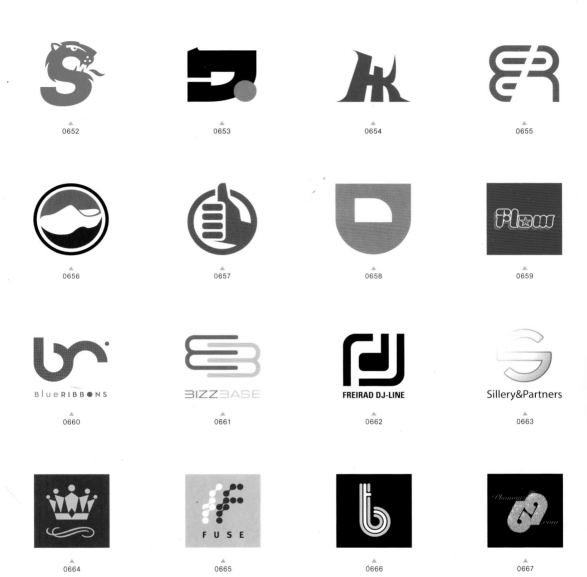

0652

0653

0654

0655

0656

0657

0658

0659

BlueRIBBONS
0660

BIZZBASE
0661

FREIRAD DJ-LINE
0662

Sillery&Partners
0663

0664

FUSE
0665

0666

0667

**0652.** Studio Sport / Shamrock Int.   **0653.** Yakuza Attack Dog / Marc Herold   **0654.** Yakuza Attack Dog / Marc Herold   **0655.** Embassy Row / Mattisimo   **0656.** Kanaal Klomp / DHM Graphic Design   **0657.** Cinema Bewertungs-Daumen / Formikula   **0658.** Blog / Mattisimo **0659.** Flow Magazine / Archetype   **0660.** Blueribbons, Nike & +81 Magazine / Artless   **0661.** Bizzbase / Simon & Goetz   **0662.** Freirad DJ Line / Marc Herold   **0663.** Sillery & Partners / Mirco Studio   **0664.** VIP Guestlist / Simon & Goetz   **0665.** Fuse / Archetype   **0666.** Be the Boss / Unreal   **0667.** Phamous 69 / Ten4 Design

0668

0669

0670

0671

StickerNation.Net
0672

Swallow
0673

ZWERFVUIL
BLIKSEMSNEL IN DE BAK!
0674

LORE
0675

0676

0677

0678

0679

0680

EDITION
52
0681

0682

0683

0668. B2 / Viagrafik  0669–0670. Shengna / Segura Inc.  0671. Yo / Slang  0672. Sticker Nation / Tak! Design  0673. Swallow, Ashley Wood, *proposal* / Tom Muller  0674. Zwerfvuil / Attak  0675. Lore, Ashley Wood / Tom Muller  0676. Yakuza Attack Dog / Marc Herold  0677. Yakuza Attack Dog / Marc Herold  0678. Sun Times Inc. / Essex Two  0679. Comic-Strich / Formikula  0680–0683. Edition 52 / Formikula

0684

items

0685

0686

0687

0688

0689

0690

M MENT

0691

0692

BOX

0693

0694

0695

**0684.** BUR / Mucca Design   **0685.** Items / Studio Dumbar   **0686.** Fugue / SightTwo   **0687.** Donemus / SoDesign   **0688.** Lightseeker / Area 3   **0689.** Filmfan / Bandage   **0690.** Katusch / The Bruhn Family   **0691.** Moment / Bandage   **0692.** Bridgeworks, Coca Cola / Blacktop Creative   **0693.** Hbox / Exopolis   **0694.** Blog do Tas, *www.blogdotas.com.br* / Rodrigo Silveira   **0695.** Lodown / Viagrafik

0696

0697

0698

0699

0700

0701

0702

0703

0704

asri

0705

**0696.** DC Comics / IAAH   **0697.** Trust / Viagrafik   **0698.** Wag Mag / Viagrafik   **0699.** Flesh / Viagrafik   **0700.** Minimal / Viagrafik
**0701.** Minimal / Viagrafik   **0702.** Glam / Yomar Augusto   **0703.** Extralife / PhormaStudio   **0704.** Wall of Sound / Amster Yard   **0705.** Griya
Asri / Bluelounge

0706

0707

0708

0709

0710

0711

0712

0713

0714

0715

0716

0717

**0706.** Mr. Bite / RDYA **0707.** Jetwin / Simon & Goetz **0708.** Mystreak / Fluidesign **0709.** Hbox / Mattisimo **0710.** Yakuza Attack Dog / Marc Herold **0711.** FRDM / Viagrafik **0712.** Terranova / DMC Group **0713.** Pilot TV / Also Design **0714.** BeTV / Base Design **0715.** Cd Art, Rotovision / Crush **0716.** Move up / Frontmedia **0717.** 3FM Serious Radio / 4vs5

0718

0719

0720

0721

0722

0723

0724

0725

0726

0727

0728

0729

**0718.** Gamepepper / Bjarne Melin   **0719.** Capitalism / Made   **0720.** Capitalism / Made   **0721.** Sensor / Kaliforniarepublik   **0722.** Favourite Website Awards / Dual   **0723.** Waves / Magma   **0724.** Aha! / Essex Two   **0725.** FAB / Milkxhake   **0726.** Ear / Matissimo   **0727.** Juice / Viagrafik   **0728.** Desaine / Cookie   **0729.** Balcony / 123Buero

0730

0731

0732

0733

0734

0735

0736

0737

0738

0739

0739

0740

0741

---

**0730.** Yahoo! Conexion / RDYA  **0731.** AMC / 4vs5  **0732.** Disney / IE Design + Communications  **0733.** Lokau / Ana Couto Branding & Design  **0734.** Qupu Qupu & Kepu Kepu / FuriFuri  **0735.** Siebenstein / Simon & Goetz  **0736.** Safety Thirst / Tom Leach  **0737.** Tivi, ZDF / Simon & Goetz  **0738.** Heute, ZDF / Simon & Goetz  **0739.** Travel Channel / Clark Studios Graphic Design  **0740.** Tivi, ZDF / Simon & Goetz  **0741.** Loser / Resistro

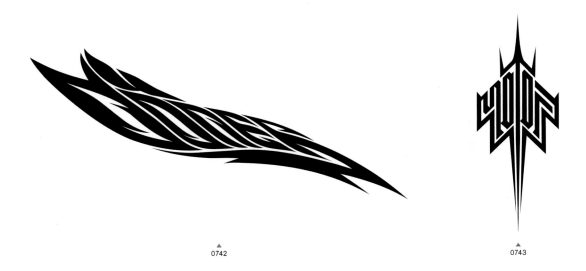

0742

0743

0744

---

**0742.** Döner Magazine / Bandage    **0743.** Filmfan / Bandage    **0744.** MTV Videogames / Bjarne Melin

0745

0746

0747

0748

---

**0745–0748.** MTV Videogames / Bjarne Melin

SHERRIF 13

0749

0750

0751

GRANDE FANTA

ASHLEY WOOD ARTWORK 2000-2004

0752

0753

**0749.** Sheriff 13, Ashley Wood / Tom Muller   **0750.** Afterwar Book / De.Mo   **0751.** Canal Animacion / The Cocoe Conspiracy   **0752.** Grande Fanta, Ashley Wood / Tom Muller   **0753.** Hector Umbra / Formikula

0754

0755

0756

0757

0758

0759

0760

0761

0762

0763

0764

0765

---

**0754.** Street Network, *characters* / BLK/MRKT   **0755.** Street Network / BLK/MRKT   **0756–0759.** Street Network, *studies* / BLK/MRKT
**0760.** Yamagishi World / Viagrafik   **0761.** Auto Spies / 9Myles   **0762.** Adventure Zone Network / Move Design   **0763.** Norsk Vodka Book /
Crush   **0764.** Blackbox Magazine / Bandage   **0765.** Faxine / Bjarne Melin

0766

0767

0768

0769

0770

0771

0772

0773

0774

0775

0776

0777

**0766–0771.** Abel & Baker website / Bjarne Melin   **0772–0777.** TNN, The National Network, *studies* / Segura Inc.

0778

0779

0780

0781

0778. Web TV Olho Vivo, Petrobrás / Oestudio   0779. Outdoor Life Network, *proposal* / Amster Yard   0780. AIDS Africa campaign / Amster Yard   0781. AIDS Africa campaign, *studies* / Amster Yard

0782

0783

0784

0785

0786

0787

0788

0789

**0782.** Perennial / Unreal   **0783.** Checkmyscores / Fluidesign   **0784.** Viazoo / Viagrafik   **0785.** Freerider / Comparsas   **0786.** Trust Leo / Viagrafik   **0787.** Unfold / Viagrafik   **0788.** Paperjam / Viagrafik   **0789.** Backspin / Viagrafik

0790

0791

0792

0793

0794

0795

0796

PORNHOUNDS

0797

---

0790. DeBretts / The Partners  0791. De Boeck / Sign*  0792. Mandrake / 2Pix  0793. Wegener / Eden Design  0794. Walkie Talkie / Tak!
Design  0795. Readymade / Department 3  0796. Charmed / SightTwo  0797. Pornhounds / Barfutura

0798

0799

0800

0801

**0798.** S!, Clarín Newspaper / RDYA   **0799.** Pop, S!, Clarín Newspaper / RDYA   **0800.** Rock, S!, Clarín Newspaper / RDYA   **0801.** Techno, S!, Clarín Newspaper / RDYA

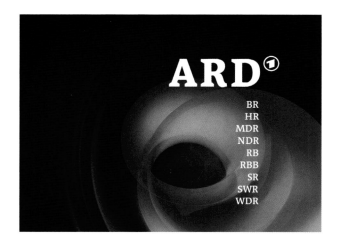

**0802.** ARD, TV Station / DMC Group  **0803.** RBB, TV Station / DMC Group

# MUSIC

BANDS, DJs, RECORD LABELS, RECORD STUDIOS, CDs, MUSIC WEB SITES, MUSIC PORTALS, CONCERTS, MUSIC FESTIVALS

0804

0805

0806

0807

0808

---

**0804–0808.** Black Eyed Peas, Elephunk, Interscope, A&M Records / BLK/MRKT

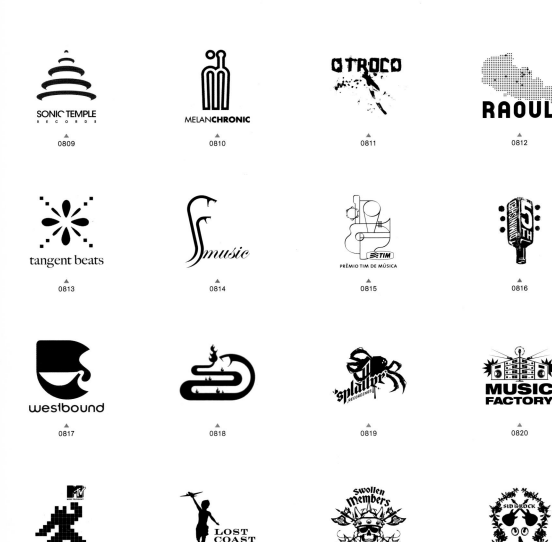

0809

0810

0811

0812

0813

0814

0815

0816

0817

0818

0819

0820

0821

0822

0823

0824

**0809.** Sonic Temple Records / Dual **0810.** Melanchronic Music / Department 3 **0811.** O Troco / Yomar Augusto **0812.** Raoul / Atelier Télescopique **0813.** Tangent Beats / Andreas Emenius **0814.** Fuck Music / Oestudio **0815.** TIM Music Awards / Tátil Design **0816.** Diminished Fifth Band / Blacktop Creative **0817.** Westbound Records / SightTwo **0818.** Fuck Music / Oestudio **0819.** Splatter Recordings / Bionic Systems **0820.** Music Factory / Mata Limited **0821.** Tangent Beats / Andreas Emenius **0822.** Lost Coast Records / Dual **0823.** Swollen Members, Battle Axe Records / BLK/MRKT **0824.** Sid LeRock / Weissraum

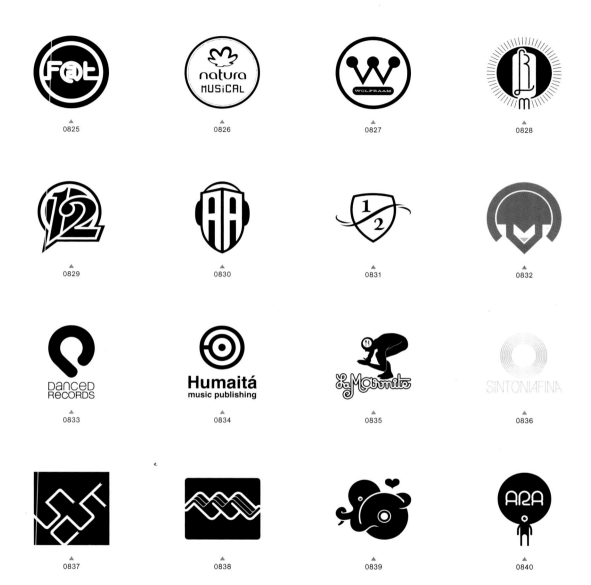

0825    0826    0827    0828

0829    0830    0831    0832

0833    0834    0835    0836

0837    0838    0839    0840

**0825.** Fat / Crush Design    **0826.** Natura Musical / Tátil Design    **0827.** Wolfraam / DBXL    **0828.** Lou Reed Music / Sagmeister    **0829.** 12 RPM / SightTwo    **0830.** Armin Audio / DBXL    **0831.** 1=2 Sound / Monderer Design    **0832.** DJ AJG / Clusta Design    **0833.** Dance Records / Weissraum    **0834.** Humaitá Music Publishing / 6D Estúdio    **0835.** La Marmite / Atelier Télescopique    **0836.** Sintonia Fina / 6D Estúdio    **0837.** Uncut Records / Ben Loiz    **0838.** Music / Bonsaimai    **0839.** Kraki / Bionic Systems    **0840.** Ara / Atelier Télescopique

0841

0842

0843

0844

0845

0846

DEEDS NOT WORDS

0847

0848

---

**0841.** Divine Recordings / Ben Loiz  **0842.** Now in Stereo / Farfar  **0843.** Switchfoot / Clark Studios Graphic Design  **0844.** Yakuza, United Records / DBXL  **0845.** Spoonliquor / DBXL  **0846.** Deportees / Yonderland  **0847.** Deeds Not Words / nssgraphica  **0848.** Faultline Productions / Clark Studios Graphic Design

0849

0850

0851

0852

0853

0854

0855

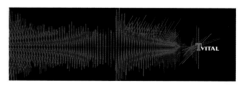

0856

---

**0849.** Allgorythm / Rumbero Design  **0850.** Pepperman Music / Joana Leal  **0851.** Typhoon Dance Project / Pure Communication
**0852.** Bossa Nova Lounge / 6D Estúdio  **0853.** Freidenker, Grönland Records / Viagrafik  **0854.** Martin Luther / SightTwo  **0855.** Monaco
Music Festival / Damián Di Patrizio / Sonar Media & Design  **0856.** Tennent's Vital, Music Festival / Design Bridge

0857

0858

0859

0860

0861

0862

0863

0864

0865

0866

0867

0868

**0857.** Plebe Rude, EMI Brazil / Caótica   **0858.** One Love CD Compilation / Crush Design   **0859.** Amulet, Sony Music / Made   **0860.** Ezra / Mule Industry   **0861.** Artists Without A Label / Polychrome   **0862.** Kid606 / Slang   **0863.** Furto / Oestudio   **0864.** Buddist Punk, Mattafix / Kleber Design   **0865.** Murder / Andreas Emenius   **0866.** Stylus Record Sleeve / Image Now   **0867.** Beatz / Listen Design   **0868.** Deluxe, Cd Compilation / Fluoro

0869

0870

0871

0872

0873

0874

0875

0876

0877

0878

0879

0880

**0869.** 1 Mile North / Domani Studios  **0870.** Punkrok / Clusta Design  **0871.** Miracle of 86, Defiance Records / Viagrafik  **0872.** Funk, Hot Shit Records / Viagrafik  **0873–0874.** Phonologic / IAAH  **0875.** Spitt Rap Battle / DBXL  **0876.** DJ Roog / DBXL  **0877.** Lamya, J Records / Popglory  **0878.** Gen Music / Area3 Barcelona  **0879.** Etid / Crush Design  **0880.** Peace, Olympic compilation CD, EMI Paris / BLK/MRKT

0881

0882

0883

0884

0885

0886

0887

0888

0889

0890

0891

0892

**0881.** The Ark / Zion Graphics   **0882.** Rise, Anti-racism Festival, Greater London Authority / Unreal   **0883.** Lizard, Combination Records / Bionic Systems   **0884.** Lamya, J Records / Popglory   **0885.** DJ Uve / The Cocoe Conspiracy   **0886.** Nero Recordings / Zion Graphics   **0887.** bebop / Tom Leach   **0888.** DJ HKN / Crush Design   **0889.** Tah Mac / Agent8 Design   **0890.** Da Lata / Crush Design   **0891.** Gabriel Magalha / Resistro   **0892.** The Donnas Spend The Night, Atlantic Records / Popglory

0893

0894

0895

0896

0897

0898

0899

0900

0901

0902

0903

0904

**0893.** Freebase Records / Bionic Systems  **0894.** Balloons / nssgraphica  **0895.** Benz & MD / Velocity Studio & Associates  **0896.** Vale Música / Dupla Design  **0897.** MusicFans / Department 3  **0898.** Lou Reed Music / Sagmeister  **0899.** Speechboyz / Milkxhake  **0900.** Silky Smooth / Simon & Goetz  **0901.** Freebase Records / Bionic Systems  **0902.** Gangsta Audio / DBXL  **0903.** Music Festival Weeks / Bonsaimai  **0904.** Tennent's Vital, Music Festival / Design Bridge

0905

0906

0907

0908

0909

0910

0911

0912

---

**0905.** Speed of Sounds, Combination Records / Bionic Systems   **0906.** Spend the Night, Combination Records / Bionic Systems
**0907.** Shibuya, Combination Records / Bionic Systems   **0908.** Transatlantic Records / Crush Design   **0909.** Dance Records / Weissraum
**0910.** Minimal Soul / Listen Design   **0911.** Ladytron / Polychrome   **0912.** The Hilt / IAAH

0913

0914

0915

0916

0917

0918

0919

0920

**0913.** Mulekes, EMI Brasil / Yomar Augusto   **0914.** Remote, New State Entertainment / Zip Design   **0915.** Phonologic / IAAH
**0916.** Vinylized / DBXL   **0917.** Festival de Sablé / Atelier Télescopique   **0918.** Ana Carolina, BMG Brasil / Yomar Augusto   **0919.** DJ Sleep / Caótica   **0920.** Agf/Delay / Slang

0921

0922

0923

0924

0925

0926

0927

0928

**0921.** Robert Johnson / Crush Design   **0922.** Dj Cubixx / Superieur Graphique   **0923.** Nokia Trends / Tátil Design   **0924.** Aurium Recordings / Velocity Studio & Associates   **0925.** Whar / Sign*   **0926.** Marina Lima, Unplugged MTV, EMI Brasil / Yomar Augusto   **0927.** Siesta Music / SightTwo   **0928.** Beyond / SightTwo

0929

0930

0931

0932

0933

0934

0935

0936

0937

0938

0939

0940

**0929.** Save The Music / Buck  **0930.** Epitaph Records / BLK/MRKT  **0931.** Combi / Weissraum  **0932.** Les Mauvaises Langues, Verone Music / Atelier Télescopique  **0933.** 15 Megs of Fame / SkinnyCorp  **0934.** Headphone Heroes / TAK! Design  **0935.** Dualism Music / Weissraum  **0936.** J Rae Productions / Polychrome  **0937.** Gal Costa, Acústico MTV / Caótica  **0938.** Afrodizzyscratch / Clusta Design  **0939.** Music Monkeys / Polychrome  **0940.** Titãs / Christiano Calvet, Gualter Pupo, Toni Vanzolini

0941

0942

0943

0944

0945

0946

0947

0948

0949

0950

0951

0952

**0941.** Open Air St. Gallen / Atalier   **0942–0952.** Open Air St. Gallen, *studies* / Atalier

0953

0954

0955

**0953.** Bodies Without Organs / Zion Graphics   **0954.** The Mish / Base Two   **0955.** Blue Saphir Recordings / Bionic Systems

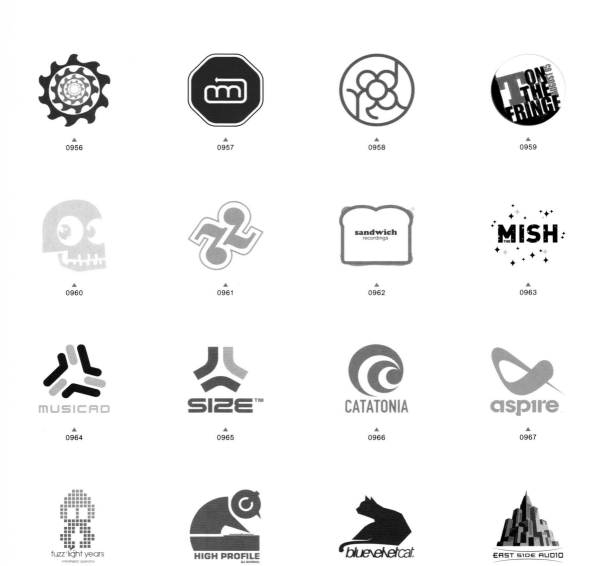

0956

0957

0958

0959

0960

0961

0962

0963

0964

0965

0966

0967

0968

0969

0970

0971

**0956.** Solar / Marcos Leme   **0957.** Mulekes, EMI Brasil / Yomar Augusto   **0958.** Gabriel Magalha / Nú-Dës   **0959.** Tennent's T-on-the-Fringe, Music Festival / Design Bridge   **0960.** Spika in Snüzz / Formikula   **0961.** 12 RPM / SightTwo   **0962.** Sandwich Recordings / Mattisimo   **0963.** The Mish / Base Two   **0964.** Musicad Limited / Archetype   **0965.** Size Recordings / Zion Graphics   **0966.** Catatonia / Crush Design   **0967.** Aspire / SightTwo   **0968.** Fuzz Light Years / Crush Design   **0969.** High Profile / Atalier   **0970.** Blue Velvet Cat / SightTwo   **0971.** East Side Audio / Ricardo Leme lopes, The Abelson Co.

0972

0973

0974

0975

0976

0977

0978

0979

0980

0981

0982

0983

---

**0972.** Caspian / Attak   **0973.** Rebel Soul Records / SightTwo   **0974.** Blue Rabbit Recordings / Soap Creative   **0975.** Wave Music / Archetype
**0976.** Boogie Nights / Crush Design   **0977.** Floodlight Records / Dual   **0978–0983.** Cosmic Music Network, *logo system* / Move Design

0984

0985

0986

0987

0984. Mooie Noten / DBXL   0985. Broken Beatz Mainz / Bionic Systems   0986. Broken Beatz Mainz / Bionic Systems   0987. Wolfraam / DBXL

0988

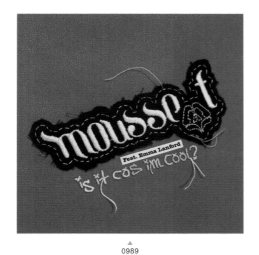

0989

0990

**0988.** Groove Armada, Jive / Zip Design   **0989–0990.** Mousse T, Free2air Records / Zip Design

▲
0991

▲
0992

---

**0991.** The Dalles / 3Deluxe   **0992.** The Dalles, *application* / 3Deluxe

0993

**0993.** The Dalles, *application* / 3Deluxe

0994

**0994.** TIM Music Festival / Tátil Design

0995

**0995.** TIM Music Festival, *application* / Tátil Design

0996

**0996.** Sondre Lerche, Virgin Records, Norway / BLK/MRKT

0997

0998

0999

1000

1001

1002

1003

---

**0997.** Get Alive, MTV Germany / Viagrafik  **0998–1001.** School's Out, MTV England / Viagrafik  **1002.** MTV / Zion Graphics
**1003.** School's Out, MTV England / Viagrafik

# RETAILERS & FOOD OUTLETS

## STORES, MARKETS, SUPERMARKETS, DEPT. STORES, ONLINE-STORES, RESTAURANTS, BARS

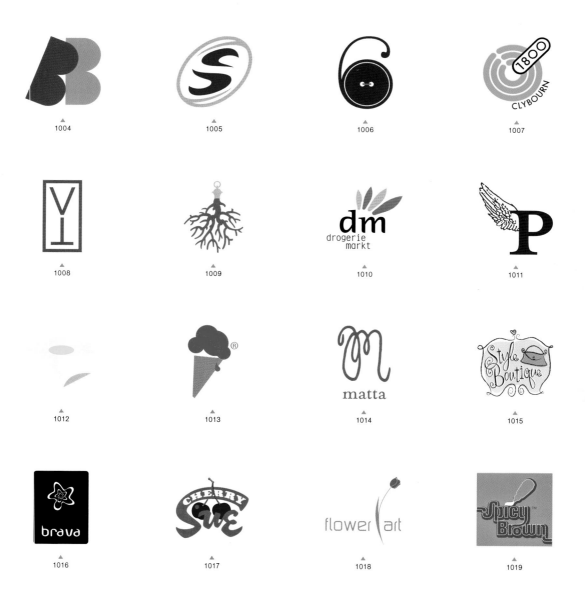

1004    1005    1006    1007

1008    1009    1010    1011

1012    1013    1014    1015

1016    1017    1018    1019

**1004.** Busy-Being Online Shop / Ben Loiz    **1005.** Surf Station / 9Myles    **1006.** Six Stitch / Mattisimo    **1007.** Clybourn1800 / Essex Two    **1008.** Vino Trade / DHM Graphic Design    **1009.** Red Coral Antiques / de.MO    **1010.** DM / HardCase Design    **1011.** The Pantry / Kaliforniarepublik    **1012.** Felton Floral / Matissimo    **1013.** Cold One / Matissimo    **1014.** Matta Boutique / Mucca Design    **1015.** Style Boutique / Blacktop Creative    **1016.** Brava Beachwear Store / Soter Design    **1017.** Cherry Sue / Shamrock Int.    **1018.** Flower Art / Superieur Graphique    **1019.** Spicy Brown / Bluelounge Design

1020

1021

1022

1023

1024

1025

1026

1027

1028

threequarters™

1029

1030

1031

---

**1020–1022.** world360 / Tom Leach   **1023–1025.** Pizza.de / Formikula   **1026.** Threequarters - Creative Design Outlet / Agent8 Design
**1027–1028.** Donut Pub, *sketch* / 2x4 Inc.   **1029.** Threequarters - Creative Design Outlet / Agent8 Design   **1030–1031.** MTBX Online Store / Machinas

eureka

1032

1033

PROBOX™

1034

**Relic**
~ SURF & SPORT ~

1035

1036

forme
beats.eats.treats

1037

THE
STUDIO
By ProWolfMaster

1038

LE BONHEUR_
EPICERIE
AUDIO
VISUELLE

1039

erotica
BOUTIQUE
BIZARRE

1040

ESTETIK
SILVER JEWELRY

1041

KappAhl®

1042

1043

---

**1032.** Eureka / Aloof Design   **1033.** Honey for the Bear / Ben Loiz   **1034.** Probox / Lumen Design   **1035.** Relic Surf & Sport / Clark Studios Graphic Design   **1036.** Smoke Lounge Bar & Cigar / Bruno Richter   **1037.** Forme / Clusta Design   **1038.** The Studio / Milkxhake   **1039.** Le Bonheur / Coast Design   **1040.** Boutique Bizzarre / DMC Group Hamburg   **1041.** Estetik Silver Jewelry / Heavyform   **1042.** KappAhl / Stockholm Design Lab + TEArk (Thomas Eriksson Arkitekter)   **1043.** Twisters Frozen Custard / Blacktop Creative

1044

1045

1046

1047

1048

1049

1050

1051

1052

1053

1054

1055

**1044.** pillowpillow / DHM Graphic Design   **1045.** Ascendor online shop / Synopsismedia   **1046.** Åhléns / Stockholm Design Lab   **1047.** Xuny, Online urbanwear retailer / Move Design   **1048.** Eziba / Ricardo Leme Lopes, Benjamin Bailey (Eziba)   **1049.** Obtain / Power Graphixx **1050.** Smula / Machinas   **1051.** Mäser Austria Sportswear / Simon & Goetz   **1052.** Nuance / Soter Design   **1053.** Amulet / Contentfree Rockets   **1054.** Beautiful Crime online gallery and shop / Tak! Design   **1055.** The Pantry / Kaliforniarepublik

1056

1057

1058

1059

MERCADO

1060

---

**1056.** Harvey Nichols Department Store / Zip Design   **1057.** l'obsidienne / Atelier Télescopique   **1058.** 't Voorhuis Antique Furniture / Attak
**1059.** Apparat HiFi Store / 802   **1060.** Mercado / Yomar Augusto

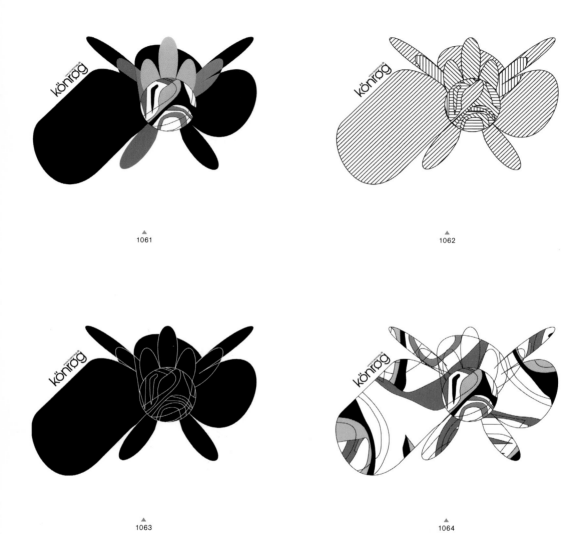

1061

1062

1063

1064

**1061.** Könrog Fashion Store / Andreas Emenius   **1062–1064.** Könrog Fashion Store, *variations* / Andreas Emenius

1065

1065. Pearl / IE Design + Communications

mdrp

1066

gonuts
by GÓRTZ

1067

1068

GOLDSMITHS
— SINCE 1778 —

1069

GÓRTZ SHOES

1070

REDCORP

1071

1072

GÓRTZ
one

1073

1074

1075

1076

Winzz

1077

---

**1066.** Mare Fashion Store / Twisted Interactive   **1067.** Görtz Shoes Store / Peter Schmidt Group   **1068.** Onenak - Bakeries, Bread and Cakes / Supperstudio   **1069.** Goldsmiths / The Partners   **1070.** Görtz Shoes Store / Peter Schmidt Group   **1071.** Redcorp / Sign   **1072.** Jet Set Fashion Store / Twisted Interactive   **1073.** Görtz Shoes Store / Peter Schmidt Group   **1074.** Spicy Brown / Bluelounge Design   **1075–1077.** Winzz / Bepositive Design

1078

1079

1080

1081

1082

1083

1084

1085

1086

1087

1088

1089

**1078–1083.** Eziba, *studies* / Ricardo Leme Lopes, Benjamin Bailey (Eziba)    **1084.** 3G mobile, Sigma Wireless / Image Now    **1085–1089.** 3G mobile, Sigma Wireless, *studies* / Image Now

1090

1091

1092

1093

1094

1095

1096

1097

1098

1099

1100

1101

---

**1090.** Drink & Fun / Simon & Goetz   **1091.** Fusion Cuisine / Oestudio   **1092.** Papio Wines / Department 3   **1093.** Lam Asian Bistro / Oestudio   **1094.** Franzz / Formikula   **1095.** Brown Tiki lounge / Seven   **1096.** Bar Times / Sonar Media & Design   **1097.** Fou de - Restaurant / Atelier Télescopique   **1098.** Mezzo Restaurant / Twisted Interactive   **1099.** Angel Bar, Dewar's / Amster Yard   **1100.** An Tonio / Oestudio **1101.** Point Guiba / Refinaria Design

1102

1103

1104

1105

1106

1107

1108

1109

1110

1111

1112

1113

**1102.** El Perla Negra Sea Food & Grill / Alberto Cerriteño  **1103.** Salt & Chopp Bar and Restaurant / Ricardo Leme Lopes  **1104.** Zazá Bistrô Tropical / Marcos Leme  **1105.** JFK Bar / Damián Di Patrizio  **1106.** Aprazivel Restaurant / PVDI Design  **1107.** Malt Cross Café Bar / Newpollution  **1108.** Poppy Red / Clusta Design  **1109.** .IT, XYZ Reply / studio FM milano  **1110.** Pitzock / Transporter  **1111.** Code Café / Archetype  **1112.** Felix Restaurant / Peter Schmidt Group  **1113.** Cyprus Café / Archetype

1114

1115

1116

1117

1118

1119

1120

1121

1122

1123

1124

1125

---

**1114.** CocoonClub / 3Deluxe   **1115.** Silk Restaurant / 3Deluxe   **1116.** Micro Restaurant / 3Deluxe   **1117.** Serafina Bar / Damián Di Patrizio
**1118.** Jin Ju Restaurant / Estudiotres   **1119.** Rosso Café / 802   **1120.** Zuka Restaurant / Marcos Leme   **1121.** Ici Restaurant / Base Design
**1122.** Pulp / Coast Design   **1123.** Défilé / Lumen Design   **1124.** Omnia Retaurant & Bar / Atelier Télescopique   **1125.** Raw Sushi & Grill / 802

1126

1127

ZAFFERANO

1128

1129

1130

1131

1132

1133

**1126–1127.** Peko Peko Restaurant, *proposal* / 3Deluxe  **1128.** Zafferano Restaurant / Viagrafik  **1129.** For Coffee / Clusta Design  **1130.** Poppy Red / Clusta Design  **1131.** Minima Galery & Restaurant / Oestudio  **1132–1133.** Smoking Lounge / Caótica

1134

1135

1136

1137

1138

1139

1140

1141

1142

1143

1144

1145

**1134–1136.** Lam Asian Bistro / Oestudio  **1137–1139.** Intro / Buck  **1140–1145.** Country Restaurant, *multiple logo system* / Mucca Design

1146

**1146.** Fusion Cuisine / Oestudio

1147.

1148.

1149.

1150.

1151.

1152.

1153.

1154.

1155.

1156.

1157.

1158.

1159.

**1147.** Real Mex Restaurants / IAAH   **1148–1159.** Real Mex Restaurants, *studies* / IAAH

JUCHHEIM
DIE MEISTER

1160

LA FLEUR DE SEL
RESTAURANT

1161

THORNTON'S
RESTAURANT

1162

1163

Factory

1164

1165

metroclub

1166

PIAZZETTA
Buitoni

1167

1168

bernstein

1169

1170

THE PEACOCK

1171

---

**1160.** Juchheim / Peter Schmidt Group  **1161.** La Fleur de Sel Restaurant / Image Now  **1162.** Thorntons Restaurant / Image Now  **1163.** Beach / Mirco Studio  **1164.** Factory / Clusta Design  **1165.** Rouge Bar / Seven  **1166.** Metro Club / Estudiotres  **1167.** Piazzetta Buitoni, Nestlé France / Atelier Télescopique  **1168.** Bikini / Transporter  **1169.** Bernstein Bar / Weissraum  **1170.** Fusion Cuisine / Oestudio  **1171.** Peacock Bar and Restaurant / Zip Design

1172

**1172.** Peacock Bar and Restaurant / Zip Design

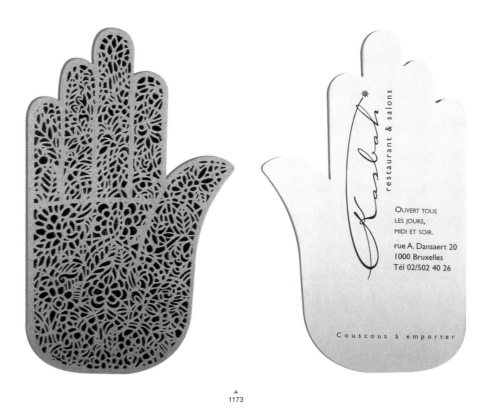

1173

**1173.** Kasbah / Sign*

1174

1175

**1174.** Presidio Social Club Restaurant / Mucca Design   **1175.** Sant Ambroeus Restaurant / Mucca Design

1176

1177

---

**1176.** Schiller's Liquor Bar / Mucca Design   **1177.** EN Japanese Brasserie / Mucca Design

# SERVICE BUSINESS

## LOGISTICS, INSURANCE, BANKING, TELECOMMUNICATION, OTHER SERVICES

1178

1179

1180

1181

1182

1183

1184

1185

1186

1187

---

**1178**. Camp Buffalo / Essex Two   **1179.** Victory Management Inc. / Essex Two   **1180.** Elenxis / Simon & Goetz   **1181.** Wicked Roots, *study* / BLK/MRKT   **1182.** Wicked Roots, *study* / BLK/MRKT   **1183.** Weaving Workshop, Inc. / Essex Two   **1184.** Aquatic Solutions / Essex Two **1185**. Freedom Home Care / Essex Two   **1186.** Woweffect / Tom Leach   **1187.** Corporate Ink / Tom Leach

1188

1189

1190

1191

1192

1193

1194

1195

1196

1197

1198

1199

1200

1201

1202

1203

**1188.** Garantia DTVM / Oestudio   **1189.** Gabriela Vieira Dentist / Marcos Leme   **1190.** Heidemann / Formikula   **1191.** Burack & Company / Essex Two   **1192.** Bevan Brittan / CDT Design   **1193.** Normandy Ventures / Huge   **1194.** 4D Cultural Production / Marcos Leme **1195.** QualityPress / Contentfree   **1196.** Arcantis / Identy   **1197.** Bosom Buddies / Design Bridge   **1198.** Easy Chair / IAAH   **1199.** Ecopolo / Comparsas   **1200.** SAS, Scandinavian Airlines / Stockholm Design Lab + TEArk (Thomas Eriksson Arkitekter)   **1201.** Grow / Simon & Goetz **1202.** DLA / CDT Design   **1203.** Beyond Bookings / DBXL

1204

1205

1206

1207

1208

1209

1210

1211

1212

1213

1214

1215

1216

1217

1218

1219

**1204.** Radar Works / Contentfree  **1205.** Domono / Synopsismedia  **1206.** Hetrick Communications, Inc. / Essex Two  **1207.** Neverous Construction, Inc. / Essex Two  **1208.** Oba!Web / Bruno Richter  **1209.** Ocean A / Weissraum  **1210.** Sport Factory / Dupla Design  **1211.** Guyom Corp. / Identy  **1212.** Ferential Systems / 3rd Edge Communications  **1213.** InterPark / Essex Two  **1214.** Paternoster Square / CDT Design  **1215.** NTSI Communications / Estudiotres  **1216.** Portima / Hoet & Hoet  **1217.** 32 Montorgueil / Identy  **1218.** SpotLight Projects / Essex Two  **1219.** Weidinge / Kashi Design

FLORISBELA

1220

jazz cut

1221

MOLECUTEX™

1222

CordVida

1223

MULTISTRATA
Inteligência em Soluções Logísticas

1224

SUN WIN
Logistics Limited

1225

connected

1226

[ V³ PERSONAL SOLUTIONS ]

1227

kpn

1228

RED WOLF
HIGH LEVEL SECURITY

1229

K.LARSEN
GARANTI

1230

NETCHEMISTRY

1231

JOHN NOLLET
PARIS

1232

AUTOUR
DE LA
FEUILLE

1233

rotweiss
FAST DELIVERY
ANYWHERE ANYONE ANYTIME

1234

superVIA

1235

---

**1220.** Florisbela / Ouro Sobre Azul   **1221.** Jazz Cut Salon / Archetype   **1222.** Molecutex Biotech Lab / Oestudio   **1223.** Cordvida / Ana Couto Branding & Design   **1224.** Multistrata / Ana Couto Branding & Design   **1225.** Sun Win Logistics Limited / Archetype   **1226.** Connected / Lumen Design   **1227.** V³ Personal Solutions / Mar Design   **1228.** KPN / Studio Dumbar   **1229.** Red Wolf / Base Two   **1230.** K. Larsen / Tom Leach   **1231.** Netchemistry / 9Myles   **1232.** John Nollet Paris / Identy   **1233.** Autour de la feuille / Idsigner   **1234.** Rotweiss / Bionic Systems   **1235.** Supervia / Ana Couto Branding & Design

1236

1237

1238

1239

1240

1241

1242

1243

1244

1245

1246

1247

1248

1249

1250

1251

**1236.** Beat Booking / Weissraum  **1237.** Proteus / TelDesign  **1238.** PocketCard / Segura Inc.  **1239.** Herbert Richards / Felipe Taborda  **1240.** VIVA Mobile / Bionic Systems  **1241.** Cryptek / 9Myles  **1242.** Dragon Sour / Weissraum  **1243.** USB Pet, Disloc / Bionic Systems  **1244.** VIVA Ringtone Charts / Bionic Systems  **1245.** Lincolnshire Broadband / Newpollution Design  **1246.** Mountains & Peaks Travel / Listen Design  **1247.** General Buildings Project / PhormaStudio Design  **1248.** M3S2 Investiments / Oestudio  **1249.** Vaciclin / Marcos Leme  **1250.** Orcangola / PVDI Design  **1251.** Carré 92 / Sign*

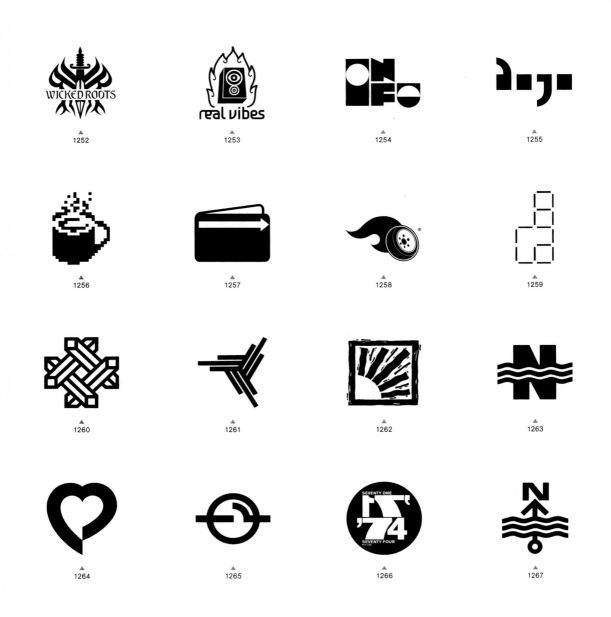

1252

1253

1254

1255

1256

1257

1258

1259

1260

1261

1262

1263

1264

1265

1266

1267

**1252.** Wicked Roots, *study* / BLK/MRKT   **1253.** Real Vibes / Ricardo Leme Lopes, Marcos Leme Lopes   **1254.** Info / Essex Two   **1255.** Dojo / Default   **1256.** Cyberia Internet Cafe / Default   **1257.** Pocketcard, *study* / Default   **1258.** Rio Pneus / Oestudio   **1259.** Dojo / Default   **1260.** Ben A.Borenstein & Company / Essex Two   **1261.** United African Companies / Essex Two   **1262.** P&G/Spanish / Essex Two   **1263.** River North Association / Essex Two   **1264.** FirstHealth / Essex Two   **1265.** InterCultura, Inc. / Essex Two   **1266.** Ashley Wood / Tom Muller   **1267.** River North Association / Essex Two

 LATOURES
VASTGOED ONTWIKKELING

1268

 urbis
D E V E L O P M E N T

1269

 **Doran**
CONSULTING
DELIVERING ENGINEERING EXCELLENCE

1270

corporateink

1271

1272

 cicle

1273

evolutionary
MEDIA GROUP

1274

**ProChem**
TECHNOLOGIES

1275

 VÉSPER

1276

FINANCES

1277

 el nido

1278

MARKS|MARKUS inc.

1279

---

**1268.** Latoures / Twisted Interactive  **1269.** Urbis / Hoet & Hoet  **1270.** Doran Consulting / Tandem Design + Front  **1271.** Corporate Ink / Tom Leach  **1272.** Spectrum Works / Bionic Systems  **1273.** Cicle / Ana Couto Branding & Design  **1274.** Evolutionary Media Group / Exopolis  **1275.** ProChem Technologies / Essex Two  **1276.** Vésper / Ana Couto Branding & Design  **1277.** CH Finances / Identy  **1278.** El Nido / Contentfree  **1279.** Markus + Markus, Inc. / Segura Inc.

1280

1281

1282

1283

1284

1285

1286

1287

1288

1289

1290

1291

---

**1280.** Tnext / Ana Couto Branding & Design   **1281.** PrintXtra / Nerv Media   **1282.** Provox Marketing / Heavyform   **1283.** Star One / Ana Couto Branding & Design   **1284.** Delta Gás / Amodesign   **1285.** Ampla / Ana Couto Branding & Design   **1286.** Micronic Traceable Sampling Solutions / SoDesign   **1287.** Connected / Newpollution Design   **1288.** Bridge / Move Design   **1289.** Kuhlmann Beauty / Simon & Goetz **1290.** IllFX / DBXL   **1291.** VIVA Mobile / Bionic Systems

1292

1293

1294

1295

1296

1297

1298

1299

1300

1301

1302

1303

---

**1292.** Egotel Communications / PhormaStudio Design   **1293.** Travelplace / Bruno Richter   **1294.** JobRun / Dadeo   **1295.** Cairn / Sign*
**1296.** People Plus / Tandem Design + Front   **1297.** Vivium Insurance / Sign*   **1298.** PocketCard / Segura Inc.   **1299.** Lachmann / Ana Couto Branding & Design   **1300.** Peregrine / The Jones Group   **1301.** NatWest / The Partners   **1302.** Imperial Laundry / Unreal   **1303.** The Oven / Unreal

1304

Clockwise

1305

1306

1307

 cognio

1308

1309

1310

1311

DOCUNET™

1312

ToolSyndicate

1313

Mediacode

1314

1315

---

**1304.** Urban Leading Logistics / Peter Schmidt Group   **1305.** Clockwise / Pure Communication   **1306.** Netkeepers / Velocity Studio & Associates   **1307.** Ecopolo / Comparsas   **1308.** Cognio Inc. / Monderer Design   **1309.** Tornado Communications / Lumen Design   **1310.** Trivialbiz / Amodesign   **1311.** Ballin Entertainment / SightTwo   **1312.** Docunet / ColoPlay   **1313.** Tool Syndicate / Department 3   **1314.** Mediacode / Department 3   **1315.** Kalypsys, Mediacode / Department 3

1316

1317

1318

1319

1320

Tenon

1321

Zahnarztpraxis

1322

1323

1324

Alltrade Pharma

1325

1326

1327

**1316.** Informations Manufaktur / Weissraum   **1317.** Magen Boys Entertainment / Velocity Studio & Associates   **1318.** Xoomsys Technologies / Yeeda Design   **1319.** Contax Contact Center / Ana Couto Branding & Design   **1320.** Rio Offices / Bruno Richter   **1321.** Tenon / Tayburn   **1322.** Dr. Nordlund (Dentist) / Zum Kuckuck   **1323.** Ipanema 2000 / 6D Estúdio   **1324.** Zenetti / SightTwo   **1325.** Alltrade Pharma / Cookie   **1326.** Geneva Technology / Simon & Goetz   **1327.** Ultralink Media / Nerv Media

1328

323 AGENCY

1329

1330

digital

1331

Amherst
Information
Group

1332

&PARTNERS

1333

AFRICA OCIDENTAL
INVESTIMENTOS S.A.

1334

My Jamaica Escapes

1335

culinair adviseur

1336

corusant
CONSULTING GROUP

1337

wannaplay
TENNIS

1338

computerlowcost

1339

---

**1328.** Tiaxa / Segura Inc.   **1329.** 323 Agency / Exopolis   **1330.** Waterproef / SoDesign   **1331.** Cinc Digital / Fabiana Prado   **1332.** AIG Amherst Information Group / Fabiana Prado   **1333.** RCM2 & Partners / Hoet & Hoet   **1334.** Africa Ocidental Investiments S.A. / Oestudio **1335.** My Jamaica Escapes / Ricardo Leme Lopes (Generousitas)   **1336.** Martin van de Kimmenade / Attak   **1337.** Corusant Consulting Group / Velocity Studio & Associates   **1338.** Wannaplay / Unreal   **1339.** CLC computer low cost / Bikini

wannaplay TENNIS

1340

CYMBIS

1341

magnet

1342

woweffect

1343

betanix

1344

TOUR & TAXIS

1345

thelounge

1346

RKMnet

1347

npower

1348

airBaltic

1349

SCORE.

1350

ZEST.

1351

**1340.** Wannaplay / Unreal   **1341.** Cymbis Finance / Seven   **1342.** Magnet / Fluoro   **1343.** Woweffect / Tom Leach   **1344.** Betanix / Bluelounge Design   **1345.** Tour & Taxis / Sign*   **1346.** The Loungue / Frontmedia   **1347.** RKMnet. Regional Knowledge Management / Supperstudio   **1348.** RWE npower / WPA Pinfold   **1349.** Air Baltic / Stockholm Design Lab + TEArk (Thomas Eriksson Arkitekter)   **1350.** Score / SightTwo   **1351.** Zest / Tom Leach

1352

1353

1354

1355

1356

boomBang

1357

1358

1359

blah!

1360

1361

Woosh

1362

blend

1363

---

**1352.** Panus Inc. / SightTwo   **1353.** Haus / Seven   **1354.** Americap Mortgage, Inc / Mirco Studio   **1355.** Lightbridge / Monderer Design   **1356.** DeFacto Technologies / Yeeda Design   **1357.** Boombang / Move Design   **1358.** eApennd / Unreal   **1359.** Oba!Web / Bruno Richter   **1360.** Blah! / Ana Couto Branding & Design   **1361.** Funky Solutions / Kashi Design   **1362.** Woosh Wireless Limited / Seven   **1363.** Blend / Clusta

facial plastic surgery

1364

premioss
THE IP VALUE PRODUCT SUITE

1365

SYNDICATE
COMPUTER SYSTEMS

1366

COAST GROUP

1367

KIMOTION

1368

ComponentScience

1369

test matters

1370

stadlmeyer

1371

---

**1364.** Rocky Mountain Facial Plastic Surgery / IE Design + Communications **1365.** Premioss by IP Value / Simon & Goetz **1366.** Syndicate Computers / Velocity Studio & Associates **1367.** Coast Group / Superieur Graphique **1368.** Kimotion Technologies / Yeeda Design **1369.** Component Science / Estudiotres **1370.** Test Matters / Grand Creative **1371.** Stadlmeyer / Transporter

▲
1372

▲
1373

▲
1374

---

**1372.** Greyhound / Hoet & Hoet   **1373.** F. Preisig AG, Bauingenieure und Planer / Superbüro   **1374.** Woods of Bradford / Blacktop Creative

1375

1376

1377

1378

1379

1380

Twynstra Gudde

1381

1382

---

**1375.** Telemais / Soter Design   **1376.** Cruzeiro do Sul / Soter Design   **1377.** Snowflake / Stockholm Design Lab   **1378.** Varig Log Trading / PVDI Design   **1379.** Lessings Finance & Insurances/ Simon & Goetz   **1380.** Apriori Business Solutions / Simon & Goetz   **1381.** Twynstra Gudde / Eden Design & Communication   **1382.** Elenxis / Simon & Goetz

Center for Male Reproductive Medicine

1383

1384

1385

1386

1387

---

**1383.** Center for Male Reproductive Medicine / SightTwo  **1384.** Dresdner Bank / Claus Koch  **1385.** Unibanco / Ana Couto Branding & Design  **1386.** QualityPress / Contentfree  **1387.** Elandau / Ana Couto Branding & Design

1388

1389

1390

1391

1392

**1388.** Olitoria Humanist Investment / Sign* **1389.** Air Madagascar / Peter Schmidt Group **1390.** Wired Sussex / Crush **1391.** V.O.F. Gert Baartmans / Attak **1392.** Sterling Hager / Monderer Design

1393

1394

1395

1396

1397

1398

**1393.** The Rebel Organization / BLK/MRKT  **1394.** Heimanns & Eljabi Wappen, GCS Catering / Bionic Systems  **1395.** Phamous Hair & Makeup / Ten4 Design  **1396.** Thomas Eidefors / 802  **1397.** The Unusual Staff / Ten4 Design  **1398.** Stripes / Sign*

1399

1400

1401

1402

KØKKEN UDEN GRÆNSER

1403

**1399.** De Badkuipenkoning.nl / Shamrock Int.   **1400.** Graphic Response / The Jones Group   **1401.** The Pedal Wrench / Listen Design
**1402.** Applocker / Heavyform   **1403.** Køkken Uden Grænser / Gul Stue

1404

1405

1406

**1404.** Ice Discotec / Amodesign   **1405.** Club Rock / Zip Design   **1406.** Chiba / Yonderland

1407

1408

1409

1410

1411

1412

**1407–1412.** The Echo Club, *studies* / Buck

# FreeSpirit
## MASSAGE & BODY THERAPIES
▲
1413

# BIKRAM YOGA
## COLLEGE OF INDIA · SANDY
▲
1414

ZIRMERHOF
SÜDTIROL
▲
1415

WHITE LOTUS HOTELS.
▲
1416

SÜLLBERG
KARLHEINZ HAUSER
▲
1417

club tracks
▲
1418

unique
garden
▲
1419

JAKE'S
▲
1420

---

**1413.** Free Spirit / Listen Design  **1414.** Bikram Yoga Sandy / Listen Design  **1415.** Zirmerhof Hotel / Simon & Goetz  **1416.** White Lotus Hotels / SightTwo  **1417.** Süllberg / Peter Schmidt Group  **1418.** Club Tracks / Soap Creative  **1419.** Unique Garden / Ricardo Gertrudes  **1420.** Jake's Beach Resort / Ricardo Leme Lopes (Generousitas)

1421

1422

1423

1424

1425

1426

1427

1428

---

**1421.** Nirvana Spa / Tandem Design + Front   **1422.** Famous Night-Club / DBXL   **1423.** Lenora Ellen Spa / Blacktop Creative
**1424.** Bodymechanics / Formikula   **1425.** Cha Cha Cha Motel / Oestudio   **1426.** Sap Lounge / Hoet & Hoet   **1427.** Golf Room /
Formikula   **1428.** Espaço Interno / Soter Design

1429

**1429.** Clandestino / Zip Design

**alignment in motion**

1430

Kairos®

1431

sparsha
espaço holístico

1432

1433

**1430.** Alignment in Motion / 9Myles  **1431.** Kairos / Oestudio  **1432.** Sparsha Espaço Holístico / PVDI Design  **1433.** Ocho Rios Bathing Club / Ricardo Leme Lopes

# MISCELLANEOUS

TRANSPORT, FOOD, BEVERAGE, SPORT, ELECTRONICS, HOTELS, SPAS, TRAVEL AGENCIES, YOGA INSTITUTES, NIGHT-CLUBS

1450. EachDay.com / Contentfree  **1451.** *self-promo* / Dadeo  **1452.** *self-promo* / Essex Two  **1453.** Herdade das Palmas / Oestudio  **1454.** Enviro-logo / Futurefarmers  **1455.** Eco-marc II / Futurefarmers  **1456.** Stingray / Ricardo Leme Lopes  **1457.** Coastal / Mattisimo  **1458.** NetLive / Contentfree  **1459.** Trevo / Renata de Castro  **1460.** *self-promo* / Essex Two  **1461.** Sonneveld / DHM Graphic Design  **1462.** *self-promo* / Dadeo  **1463.** Sonneveld / DHM Graphic Design  **1464.** *self-promo* / Dadeo  **1465.** Pranner Hof / Formikula

1466 1467 1468 1469

1470 1471 1472 1473

1474 1475 1476 1477

FLY CLIP    mutoid    DEAD MAN'S PIPES    DOMESTIKA
1478 1479 1480 1481

**1466.** Domestika.org / The Cocoe Conspiracy  **1467.** Octopus / Truly Design  **1468.** Utopoly / Resistro  **1469.** Pohuta / Umeric Rockets
**1470.** Moai / Truly Design  **1471.** Srirama / Default  **1472.** Rockwell Arotec / Essex Two  **1473.** Samui Winery / Default  **1474.** Girls Power
Manifesto / Furi Furi  **1475.** Snakeshop / Farfar  **1476.** Temavento / Zanon Design  **1477.** N-Gage Academy, *Nokia* / Farfar  **1478.** Fly Clip /
Estudiotres  **1479.** Mutoid / Dadeo  **1480.** Dead Man's Pipes / Dual  **1481.** Domestika.org / The Cocoe Conspiracy

1482

1483

1484

1485

1486

1487

1488

1489

1490

1491

1492

1493

1494

1495

1496

1497

---

1482. Vaja / RDYA   1483. Corpuspax / Amodesign   1484. Hype Asia / Archetype   1485. Giro Post / Damián Di Patrizio / Sonar   1486. Dri-Balance / Polychrome   1487. Ringster / 4vs5   1488. TV People / Mattisimo   1489. Mixin / DBXL   1490. Almog / Attak   1491. Ringster / 4vs5 1492. Nest / Asmallpercent   1493. Vibrasan / Damián Di Patrizio / Sonar   1494. El Juncal / Damián Di Patrizio   1495. Girl Touch / Damián Di Patrizio / Sonar   1496. Gradiente / Ana Couto Branding & Design   1497. Massana Group / Medusa

Plantema Beheer

▲
1498

ROTWILD
BY ADP ENGINEERING

▲
1499

geisha

▲
1500

iris

▲
1501

Goaliath
KICKER

▲
1502

GIRLSCOUT
KALIFORNIAREPUBLIK

▲
1503

urban solutions

▲
1504

DIGIMAX

▲
1505

ΠΕΤΕΣ

▲
1506

projector

▲
1507

STATUTO

▲
1508

california

▲
1509

Plungees

▲
1510

BiTmaP

▲
1511

SOUL

▲
1512

eidetics

▲
1513

---

**1498.** Plantema Beheer / Dadeo   **1499.** Rotwild by ADP Engineering / Simon & Goetz   **1500.** Geisha / The Cocoe Conspiracy   **1501.** Iris / Estudiotres   **1502.** Goaliath Kicker / Machbar   **1503.** Girl-Scout / Kaliforniarepublik   **1504.** Urban solutions / Simon & Goetz   **1505.** Digimax / heavyform   **1506.** Netec / Synopsismedia   **1507.** Projector / Artless   **1508.** Statuto / Mirco Studio   **1509.** California / Estudiotres   **1510.** Plungees / Segura Inc.   **1511.** BiTmaP / Estudiotres   **1512.** Soul / RDYA   **1513.** Eidetics / SightTwo

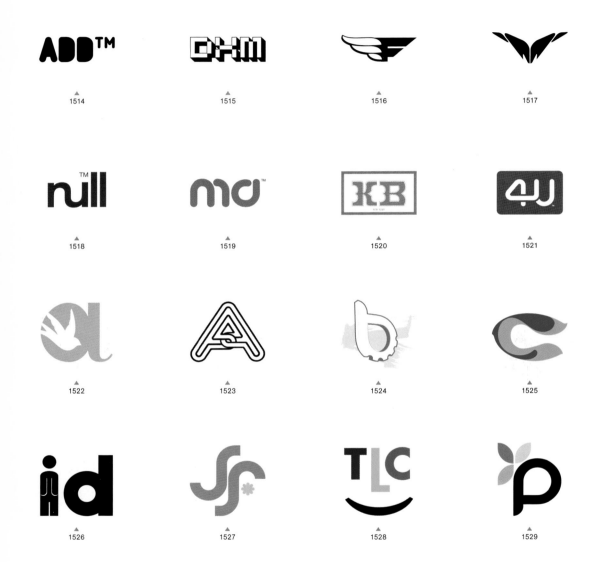

1514. ADD / 123 Buero   1515. DXM / Machinas   1516. Fresh Freddy / Dhm Graphic Design   1517. Stroessel / Yonderland   1518. Null / Artless   1519. Md / Medusa   1520. Kwigy-Bo / Also Design   1521. 4U / Fluoro   1522. Wedding Emblem / Mucca   1523. Ace ChainLink Fence / Essex Two   1524. Braking / Adrenalab   1525. Beach Football School / Marcos Leme   1526. ID. / Default   1527. Stonefarm / Frontmedia   1528. TLC / Essex Two   1529. Bikini / Transporter

1530

1531

1532

1533

1534

1535

1536

1537

1538

1539

1540

1541

1542

1543

1544

1545

---

**1530.** *self-promo* / Dadeo   **1531.** *self-promo* / Dadeo   **1532.** Tsunami / The Cocoe Conspiracy   **1533.** Sonneveld / DHM Graphic Design
**1534.** Chicken / Truly Design   **1535.** Boxer / Truly Design   **1536.** Mermaid / Truly Design   **1537.** Cat / Truly Design   **1538.** Grossmen Plastic
Tubing / Essex Two   **1539.** Finca Epona / Barfutura   **1540.** LJ 64-95 / Airside   **1541.** Icon / Umeric   **1542.** Lawson Fenning / SightTwo   **1543.**
CSR NZ Limited / Seven   **1544.** Pranner Hof / Formikula   **1545.** Waterways Corporation / NervMedia

1546

1547

1548

---

**1546.** BSA Boxes / Essex Two   **1547.** Fire / Yomar Augusto   **1548.** Bruxa 7 / Oestudio

REFLECTIONS

1549

1550

JAGUAR

1551

1552

1553

1554

1555

1556

1557

1558

1559

1560

---

**1549.** Reflections / Superieur Graphique   **1550.** Ford Motor Company / The Partners   **1551.** Jaguar / The Partners   **1552.** Green Horn / Atalier **1553.** Bash9 / Furi Furi   **1554.** Palm Beach / Zion Graphics   **1555.** On-John / Yonderland   **1556.** Free Soil / Futurefarmers   **1557.** Revolution / Kaliforniarepublik   **1558.** Erotic Foxtrott / Atalier   **1559.** Monkey Rise / Furi Furi   **1560.** Valentinoise / Simon & Goetz

1561

1562

1563

1564

1565

1566

1567

1568

1569

1570

**1561–1562.** Venice is not sinking / Fake I.D. **1563–1564.** Curvy / Umeric **1565–1566.** a & m / idsigner **1567–1568.** Traksy, Yamaha / Bionic Systems **1569–1570.** Arte 21 / Ouro Sobre Azul

literati group

1571

TROFFTOP

1572

Kimmie kakes

1573

INLIMINE

1574

zone av

1575

creapure

1576

FLUID™

1577

URSa
Grupo Uralita

1578

ivantica

1579

GMUND

1580

FREEBORD

1581

LEUTSCHER

1582

---

**1571.** Literati Group / Estudiotres  **1572.** TroffTop NZ / NervMedia  **1573.** Kimmie Kakes Uniforms / Mucca  **1574.** Inlimine / Estudiotres  **1575.** ZoneAV / D.Workz  **1576.** Creapure / 4vs5  **1577.** Fluid Skincare / Department 3  **1578.** Ursa / Peter Schmidt Group  **1579.** Ivantica / NervMedia  **1580.** Gmund / Simon & Goetz  **1581.** Freebord Manufacturing / Department 3  **1582.** Leutscher / Dadeo

1583

1584

1585

1586

1587

1588

1589

1590

1591

1592

---

**1583.** Sarotti / Peter Schmidt Group   **1584.** Nygårda / Zion Graphics   **1585.** Grolsch / DHM Graphic Design   **1586.** Sopa Light / Amodesign
**1587.** The Brand Distillery / Aloof Design   **1588.** The Brand Distillery / Aloof Design   **1589.** Smoove Energy Drink / Ricardo Leme Lopes /
Generousitas   **1590.** Taste of Asia / Formul 8   **1591.** Miss Sally / Twisted Interactive   **1592.** U'luvka Vodka / Aloof Design

COOPER GROVES

1593

1594

*loriers*
traiteur

1595

1596

1597

1598

1599

1600

1601

1602

1603

1604

---

**1593.** Cooper Groves / Domani Studios **1594.** Frury Tropical / Supperstudio **1595.** Loriers Traiteur / Hoet & Hoet **1596.** Khush / Crush Design **1597.** Bhang / Crush Design **1598.** Kullu / Crush Design **1599.** Beer to Dine For, Greene King / Design Bridge **1600.** Oja / Carter Wong Tomlin **1601.** Ativa / Komatsu Design **1602.** HP Sauce / Unreal **1603.** Carb Up / Komatsu Design **1604.** Sakura / Komatsu Design

 CUEL

1605

 CUBE

1606

 iris

1607

 Frog

1608

 INDUSTRIAL SHEETMETALS

1609

HERDADE® DAS PALMAS

1610

 verek

1611

 vaja™

1612

 eachday

1613

 spectrum systems

1614

 netlive
Meeting. Better.

1615

 NORDMETALL
Verband der Metall- und Elektro-Industrie e.V.

1616

---

**1605.** Cuel / Machinas  **1606.** Cube / Mata Limited  **1607.** Iris / Fluidesign  **1608.** Frog / Transporter  **1609.** Industrial Sheetmetals / NervMedia  **1610.** Herdade das Palmas / Oestudio  **1611.** Verek / Zion Graphics  **1612.** Vaja / RDYA  **1613.** EachDay.com / Contentfree  **1614.** Spectrum Systems / Also Design  **1615.** NetLive / Contentfree  **1616.** Nordmetal / Peter Schmidt Group

1617

1618

1619

1620

1621

1622

1623

1624

1625

1626

1627

1628

---

**1617.** SmartTalk Global / NervMedia   **1618.** Jetpack / NervMedia   **1619.** Mosaic / Franke+Fiorella   **1620.** Boomerang / MircoStudio   **1621.** E-sense / Image Now   **1622.** Ambion / Machbar   **1623.** Antipodean Group Limited / Mata Limited   **1624.** Soul / RDYA   **1625.** X-Ray Solutions / Machbar **1626.** Play Safe / Kaliforniarepublik   **1627.** Monowise / Grand Creative   **1628.** Lexicality / Fabiana Prado

1629

1630

1631

1632

1633

1634

schüco

1635

oppo.

1636

stage

1637

SOCKET

1638

VeRGe

1639

1640

---

**1629.** SDL / Medusa   **1630.** Awa / Supperstudio   **1631.** Vak / Medusa   **1632.** Linde / Peter Schmidt Group   **1633.** Cocoe-Cola / The Cocoe Conspiracy   **1634.** Cocoe / The Cocoe Conspiracy   **1635.** Schüco / Peter Schmidt Group   **1636.** Oppo / Studio Dumbar   **1637.** Stage / Magma   **1638.** Socket / Unreal   **1639.** Verge / Polychrome   **1640.** Beyond / newpollution

1641

1642

1643

1644

1645

1646

1647

1648

1649

1650

1651

1652

**1641.** Hobby / Zion Graphics **1642.** Hurt / The Cocoe Conspiracy **1643.** Iboff / The Cocoe Conspiracy **1644.** Bazook / Fluoro **1645.** Slamm / Shamrock **1646.** Union / Periphery **1647.** Proxy / Dual **1648.** Helvetica / Attak **1649.** Refinery29 / Also Design **1650.** Input Output / Umeric **1651.** Guerilla Utopia / Magma **1652.** Tawaya / Komatsu Design

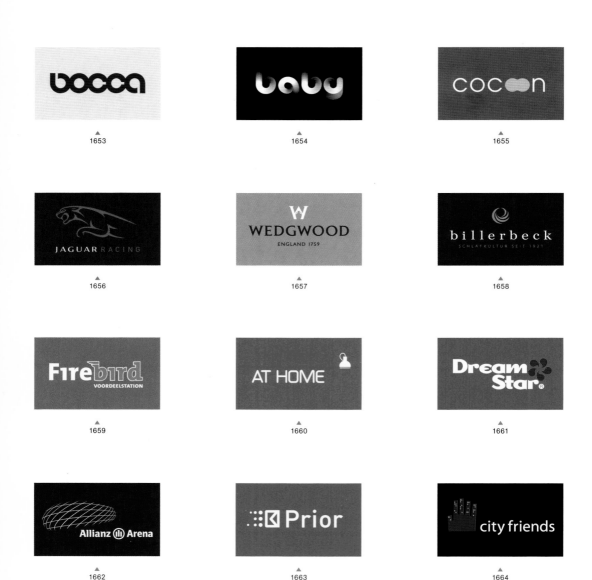

1665

1666

1667

1668

1669

1670

1671

1672

1673

1674

**1665.** C'est le ton... / Bonsaimai   **1666.** Homework / Archetype   **1667.** Viakonsum / Viagrafik   **1668.** Aquaflex Osklen Boarding / Comparsas
**1669.** Eternal Power / Archetype   **1670.** Refinery29 / Also Design   **1671.** Sachs Power Chain / Simon & Goetz   **1672.** Mitsuri / The Cocoe
Conspiracy   **1673.** Pixelatopia / Synopsismedia   **1674.** Vision Ex / IAAH

1675

1676

1677

1678

1679

1680

1681

1682

---

**1675.** Lawson Fenning / SightTwo  **1676.** Gebrüder Schaffrath / Simon & Goetz  **1677.** Nova Amafrutas, Amafrutas / Dupla Design  **1678.** Escola Densa, Amafrutas / Dupla Design  **1679.** Aquasprite Systems / Frontmedia  **1680.** Clearwave, Inc. / The Jones Group  **1681.** Soles Genus / Simon & Goetz  **1682.** HS Genion / Simon & Goetz

eurofiber

1683

ergotango*

1684

1685

SOUVENIR

1686

ONEgas 11

1687

ROCHDÄLE

1688

1689

1690

---

**1683.** Eurofiber / Studio Dumbar   **1684.** Ergotango / Supperstudio   **1685.** Silk Road / Image Now   **1686.** Souvenir / Mata Limited   **1687.** Onegas (Shell) / SoDesign   **1688.** Rochdale / SoDesign   **1689.** Royal Ahrend / Eden   **1690.** Kirkhoff / Sille Bjarnhof

1691

1692

1693

1694

1695

1696

1697

1698

**1691.** Delacado / Domani Studios   **1692.** Herdade das Palmas / Oestudio   **1693.** BührmannUbbens / TelDesign   **1694.** KSV International / Momkai   **1695.** Waterways Corporation / NervMedia   **1696.** Inturio, Inc. / Bluelounge Design   **1697.** Inox Tubos / Ana Couto Branding & Design   **1698.** MouseWorks / Domani Studios

1699

1700

1701

1702

1703

1704

1705

1706

**1699.** Auto Herbst / Machbar  **1700.** The Levitation Project / Listen Design  **1701.** crosscan / Grand Creative  **1702.** M foundry / Kaliforniarepublik  **1703.** Fapa / de.MO  **1704.** Hostmaster / NervMedia  **1705.** CSR NZ Limited / Seven  **1706.** GWG / Machbar

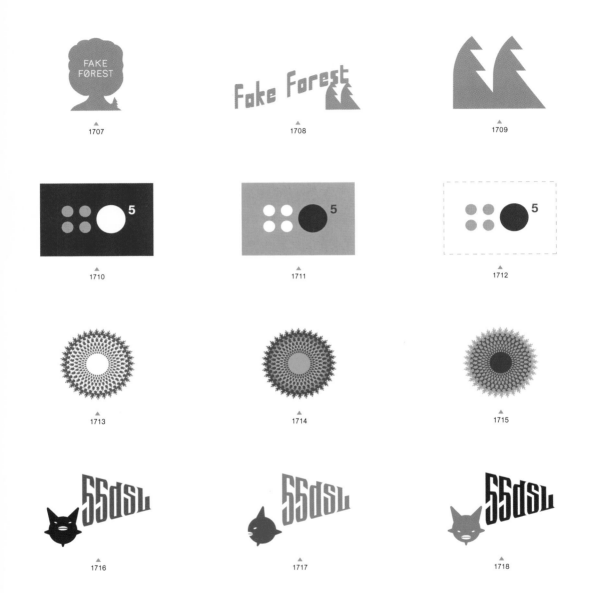

1707

1708

1709

1710

1711

1712

1713

1714

1715

1716

1717

1718

**1707–1709.** Fake Forest / Fake I.D.   **1710–1712.** Nike 5 years / Artless   **1713–1715.** Dormente / Marcos Leme   **1716–1718.** 55 DSL / Milkxhake

1719.

1720.

1721.

1722.

1723.

1724.

1725.

1726.

1727.

1728.

1729.

1730.

**1719.** Oh! My Cat / The Cocoe Conspiracy   **1720.** Brandon Shelton / Mattisimo   **1721.** Ellince / The Cocoe Conspiracy   **1722.** Robots Cry Too / The Cocoe Conspiracy   **1723.** Konijntje / Momkai   **1724.** Bad Robota / The Cocoe Conspiracy   **1725.** Freshandfonky / Momkai   **1726.** Angry Dog / The Cocoe Conspiracy   **1727.** Japan Lover / The Cocoe Conspiracy   **1728.** Pollon / The Cocoe Conspiracy   **1729.** Microbians / The Cocoe Conspiracy   **1730.** Atomic Bomb / The Cocoe Conspiracy

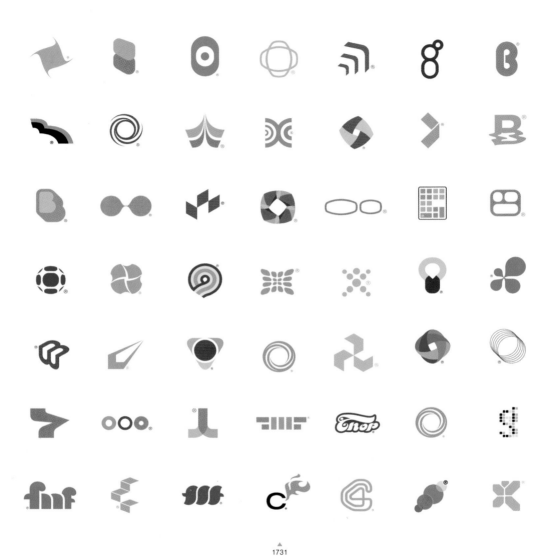

1731

1731. *self-promo* / Bepositive Design

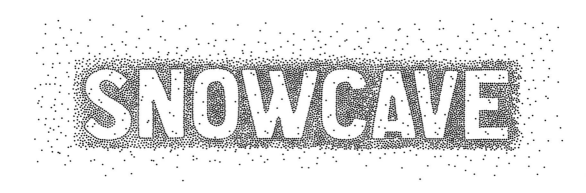

1732

1733

1734

1735

1736

1737

1738

---

**1732.** Snowcave / Periphery  **1733.** Bastard / Magma  **1734.** Vibe / Design MW  **1735.** Absolut Threetracks / Farfar  **1736.** Softish / Yonderland  **1737.** Guerilla Utopia / Magma  **1738.** Summertour N-Gage Nokia / Farfar

1739

1740

1741

1742

1743

1744

1745

1746

1747

1748

1749

1750

**1739–1744.** Manitou / Magma   **1745–1750.** Bergwerk / Magma

1751

1752

1753

1754

1755

1756

1757

1758

1759

1760

1761

---

**1751–1752.** Brand Igloo / character design: Maiko Gubler, Bonsaimai / logo design: Daniel Goddemeyer   **1753–1755.** Spin Balon / Buck
**1756–1758.** One Industries MX / Bionic Systems   **1759–1761.** 21 Grams Snowboards / Truly Design

THE CUDDLY TOYS
Pee&Poo™

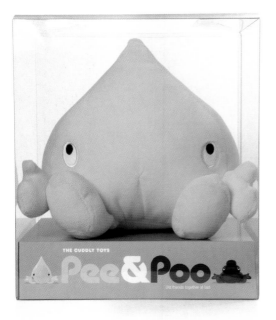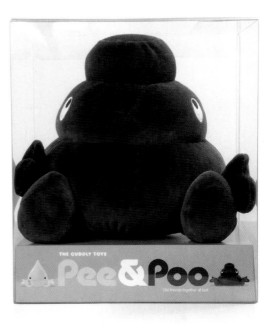

1762

**1762.** Pee & Poo / Zion Graphics

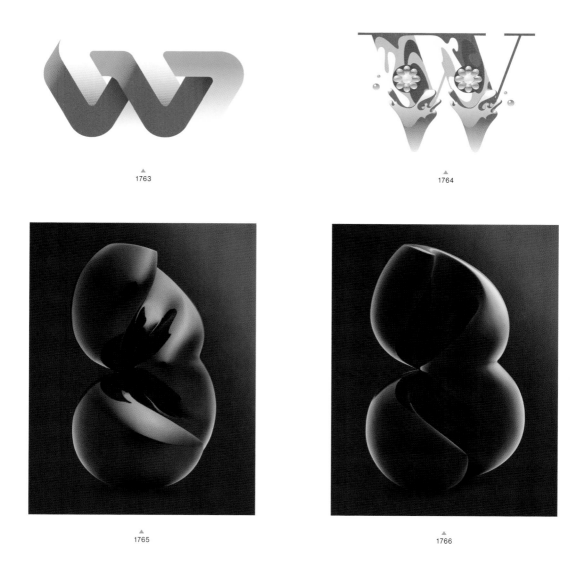

1763

1764

1765

1766

1763. Logo development for Interbrand / Miles Newlyn   1764. Logo development for Interbrand / Miles Newlyn
1765–1766. B Communications / Miles Newlyn & Ali Coleman

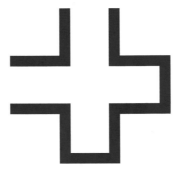

1767

1768

**1767.** Hästens / Stockholm Design Lab & TEArk (Thomas Eriksson Arkitekter)   **1768.** Vårdförbundet / Stockholm Design Lab

1769

**1769.** Snowtours N-Gage Nokia / Farfar

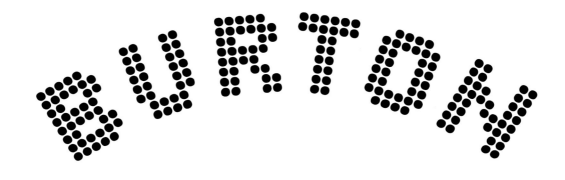

▲
1770

▲
1771

▲
1772

▲
1773

▲
1774

▲
1775

▲
1776

**1770–1776.** Burton Snowboards / Kinsey & George Trumbull, BLK/MRKT

1777

1778

1779

1780

1781

1782

1783

1784

1785

**1777.** Fanatic Snowboards / 3Deluxe   **1778.** Fanatic Snowboards / 3Deluxe   **1779–1785.** Fanatic Snowboards, *studies* / 3Deluxe

1786

1787

---

**1786.** Fanatic Snowboards, *snowboards collection* / 3Deluxe   **1787.** Fanatic Snowboards, *catalogue* / 3Deluxe

1788–1791. Fanatic Snowboards, *snowboards model series* / 3Deluxe

1792

1793

1794

1795

**1792**–**1795.** Fanatic Snowboards, *snowboards model series* / 3Deluxe

1796

1797

---

**1796–1797.** Mitea / Segura Inc.

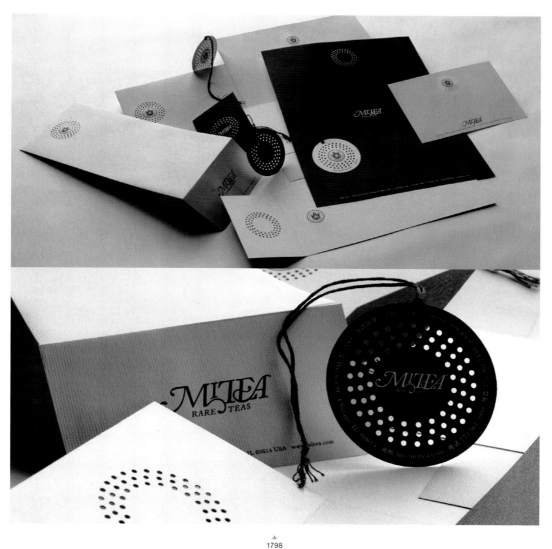

1798

**1798.** Mitea / Segura Inc.

1799

**1799.** Hook Norton Brewery Co. Ltd / WPA Pinfold

1800

---

**1800.** T&R Theakston Ltd / WPA Pinfold

# INDEX

# THANKS

To produce a book like this, it is nearly impossible without the help and hard work of a lot of people - people I was glad to have around me. Just to start with some figures, we collaborated with over 200 design offices worldwide, from New Zealand to Stockholm, from Buenos Aires to Hong Kong. We had to go through more than 6000 different logos and judge carefully which ones would give our readers the most joy and knowledge. Not the easiest of tasks. Undoubtedly, my right hand man in all this has been Daniel Siciliano Brêtas, he is the first person I need to thank, for his hard work, commitment, knowledge and excellent organizational skills. Without him this book would not have been possible.

With Daniel also working in the office, we both had the support of people from across 30 countries that would send us materials and revise texts, write cases and coordinate material delivery, send recommendations and research information. From among all these people I would like to start by thanking our contributors to the case studies, because their work will definitely give designers and all other professionals an insight into how things work in the world of branding. They are Jörg Zintzmeyer, Rafael Esquer, Peter Arnell, Dmitri Lavrov, Hernán Berdichevsky, Gustavo Ariel Stecher, Interbrand, Peter Knapp, Metadesign, Brent Oppenheimer, David Hillman, Neville Brody, Marco Giusti, Carlos Segura, Pia Kemper and Lee Comber. Along with them I would also like to thank the many other interfaces that helped to make it happen including Annette Michael, Astrid Range, Steven Bateman, John Kwo, Catherine Larkin, Jeff Knowles, Jenny Lee, Leah Speakman, Tara Grote, and all the others who contributed to the cases.

My next big thanks goes to all the design offices that submitted work and spent their time on enriching the publication. They are the ones in charge of creating the visual revolution we have been going through. We communicated via thousands of emails, and many of them we now know personally, nevertheless you can be sure that we value every single bit of effort you have put into this.

Once more, Stefan Klatte has been our right hand man on the production front, always making things easier for us and finding solutions to make the book more beautiful. The aim of this book was to really try and give it an overwhelming precision (with his help), and with fewer corrections, we were able speed up the process. Moreover, Andy Disl has given us his unwavering support with enhancing the design he created. I hope you will find this book not just inspiring, but also a useful guide to go through once in a while.

Julius Wiedemann

# IMPRINT

To stay informed about upcoming TASCHEN titles, please request our magazine at **www.taschen.com/magazine** or write to TASCHEN, Hohenzollernring 53, D-50672 Cologne, Germany, **contact@taschen.com**, Fax: +49-221-254919. We will be happy to send you a free copy of our magazine which is filled with information about all of our books.

**Design:** Sense/Net, Andy Disl and Birgit Reber, Cologne & Daniel Siciliano Brêtas
**Layout:** Daniel Siciliano Brêtas & Julius Wiedemann
**Production:** Stefan Klatte

**Editor:** Julius Wiedemann
**Editorial Coordination:** Daniel Siciliano Brêtas

**French Translation:** Claire Allesse, Aurélie Daniel
**German Translation:** Claudia Dzallas, Daniela Thoma
**Spanish Translation:** Agnès Felis, Mar Portillo
**Italian Translation:** Marco Barberi
**Portuguese Translation:** Alcides Murtinheira

Printed in China
ISBN: 978-3-8228-4622-3